Company's Coming ®

Celebrating the
Harvest
RECIPES FOR FALL & WINTER GATHERINGS

JEAN PARÉ

SPECIAL OCCASION SERIES

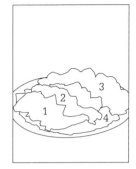

Front cover:
1. Spiced Roast Turkey, page 76
2. Brandy Apple Cranberry Sauce, page 160
3. Roasted Harvest "Ratatouille," page 101
4. Herb and Fruit Stuffing, page 103

Back cover:
Autumn Vegetable Purée, page 35

First Printing September 2011

Library and Archives Canada Cataloguing in Publication

Paré, Jean, date
Celebrating the Harvest : recipes for fall & winter gatherings / Jean Paré.
(Special occasion series)
Includes indexes.
ISBN 978-1-897477-44-1
   1. Cookery. I. Title. II. Series: Special occasion series.
TX714.P3517 2010   641.5'64   C2009-906536-3

Published by
Company's Coming Publishing Limited
2311 – 96 Street
Edmonton, Alberta, Canada T6N 1G3
Tel: 780-450-6223 Fax: 780-450-1857
www.companyscoming.com

Company's Coming is a registered trademark owned by Company's Coming Publishing Limited

We acknowledge the financial support of the Government of Canada through the Canada Book Fund for our publishing activities.

Printed in Malaysia

Celebrating the Harvest: Recipes for Fall and Winter Gatherings
was created thanks to the dedicated
efforts of the people and organizations listed below.

Company's Coming Publishing Limited

Author	Jean Paré	Contributors	Andre Bodnar
President	Grant Lovig		Miriam Boody
Research & Development Manager	Jill Corbett		Sheryll Meade-Clift
Editorial Director	Tabea Berg		Patricia Meili-Bullock
Creative Director	Heather Markham	Copy Editor/Proofreader	Laurie Penner
Editors	Sandra Bit	Editorial Assistant/Writer	Brett Bailey
	Janet Fowler	Senior Tester	James Bullock
Managing Food Editor	Eleana Yun	Testers	Allison Dosman
Senior Food Editor	Lynda Elsenheimer		Audrey Smetaniuk
Food Editors	Mary Anne Korn	Photographer	Stephe Tate Photo
	Stephanie Moore	Photography Coordinator/Image Editor	Heather Latimer
Researcher	Frieda Lovig	Food Stylist	Ashley Billey
Recipe Editor	Michael Macklon	Prop Stylist	Tiffany Day
Nutritionist	Vera Mazurak, Ph.D.	Prep Assistant	Linda Dobos
		Designer	Titania Lam
		Production Designers	Gregory Brown
			Michael Cooke

We gratefully acknowledge the following suppliers for their generous support of our Test and Photography Kitchens:

Broil King Barbecues
Corelle®
Hamilton Beach® Canada
Lagostina®
Proctor Silex® Canada
Tupperware®

Our special thanks to the following businesses for providing props for photography:

Peachwood Custom Cabinets Ltd.
Stokes
Tin Box

Whole-Wheat Seed Bread, page 110

TABLE OF CONTENTS

When the leaves turn colour and there's a nip in the air, you want to pull out those cosy sweaters and dig into heartwarming comfort food. Long evenings spent sharing the bounties of the season with friends and family are the hallmark of autumn.

Although we are saying goodbye to summer, we're saying hello to new school friends, welcoming back old customs and traditions and getting an opportunity to give thanks for all we have. Let's not forget that it's also a great time to entertain. Labour Day, Thanksgiving, Halloween—even an ordinary cold winter's day—are all ideal occasions for parties.

FOREWORD

Fall and the approaching winter are the seasons when our thoughts turn from enjoying the lightness and fun of summer to getting back into the routines of life. Kids go back to school, summer holidays are over, there's a chill in the air, twilight comes sooner. While some may feel saddened by these changes, we think the fun is just beginning.

This is the time of year to enjoy all the wonderful things about the season—the beautiful fall colours, the abundant fresh produce, the rich holiday and sporting traditions, the bustling farmers' markets, the delicious foods and the warmth of family and friends as we celebrate all of these things with them. Although we are saying goodbye to summer, we're also saying hello to new school friends, welcoming back old customs and traditions and getting an opportunity to give thanks for all we have. Let's not forget that it's also a great time to entertain. Labour Day, Thanksgiving, Halloween—even an ordinary cold winter's day—are ideal occasions for parties, and we've got just the book to make your gatherings affairs to remember.

In *Celebrating the Harvest*, we've put together an outstanding collection of original recipes and harvest trivia to satisfy both your inquiring mind and your appetite. Naturally we've included classic favourites, such as Beef Stew and Dumplings, Apple Herb-Glazed Ham and Spiced Roast Turkey with Garlic

Mashed Potatoes and Brandy Apple Cranberry Sauce. For a decidedly less-than-traditional take on this time of year, try a Tropical Fish Curry, Polenta Spinach Triangles or a warm bowl of Fennel Chowder. Delicious! To help you entertain with ease, we've included several delicious slow-cooker recipes as well as a variety of fall and winter menus (page 166) to highlight dishes that perfectly complement each other.

An entire section is devoted to breads, because there's nothing quite as appetizing on a cool fall evening or wintery day as baked bread, fresh from the oven. We also have a section on condiments and preserves to take advantage of the fruits and vegetables so plentiful at this time of year. Make a few jars of Cranberry Plum Freezer Jam or Pear and Almond Butter to spread on a slice of Sweet Harvest Loaf or Pumpkin Wheat Bread and recapture summer in the middle of winter! Don't forget to make enough to give to a special someone in your life. A steaming mug of Butterscotch Hot Chocolate or a healthful Tropical Carrot Smoothie makes the perfect accompaniment.

Your family and friends will not soon forget the fabulous meals you'll put together using *Celebrating the Harvest*. It will give everyone even more reason to be thankful and celebrate the season!

Jean Paré

NUTRITION INFORMATION GUIDELINES

Each recipe is analyzed using the most current version of the Canadian Nutrient File from Health Canada, which is based on the United States Department of Agriculture (USDA) Nutrient Database.

- If more than one ingredient is listed (such as "butter or hard margarine"), or if a range is given (1 – 2 tsp., 5 – 10 mL), only the first ingredient or first amount is analyzed.
- For meat, poultry and fish, the serving size per person is based on the recommended 4 oz. (113 g) uncooked weight (without bone), which is 2 – 3 oz. (57 – 85 g) cooked weight (without bone)—approximately the size of a deck of playing cards.

- Milk used is 1% M.F. (milk fat), unless otherwise stated.
- Cooking oil used is canola oil, unless otherwise stated.
- Ingredients indicating "sprinkle," "optional," or "for garnish" are not included in the nutrition information.
- The fat in recipes and combination foods can vary greatly depending on the sources and types of fats used in each specific ingredient. For these reasons, the amount of saturated, monounsaturated and polyunsaturated fats may not add up to the total fat content.

Vera C. Mazurak, Ph.D., Nutritionist

The harvest season is bursting with unique customs, symbols and sights. The often long winter that follows is spent enjoying the fruits—literally—of the labour-intensive harvest. Even if you aren't personally reaping crops from the fields, you can celebrate many of the rich traditions associated with harvest time and the sometimes long winter that follows.

HARVEST MOON

The unusually large moon that appears at the end of harvest season is a farmer's friend throughout the time of reaping. In the northern hemisphere, around late September, the moon's angle of orbit becomes minimal compared to Earth's horizon, causing the moon to appear much sooner than usual. During this lunar phenomenon, farmers are able to work later, labouring under the light provided by the bright moon. As well as being a night light for farmers, the harvest moon also provides inspiration; artists in many media have referenced it in their creations.

PILGRIMS AND THE ORIGINS OF THANKSGIVING

Most people associate the origins of Thanksgiving dinner with Puritan settlers. We picture the scene of Puritan people in stovepipe hats, putting aside their differences with Native Americans and sharing the rewards of their harvests with each other. While this makes for cheerful folklore, this account of the earliest Thanksgiving is controversial. There is no record that Puritans ever wore such hats, and it is argued that any selfless gestures to the Native Americans may have been political strategy. Canada lays a loose claim to the first Thanksgiving, pointing to European settler Martin Frobisher's landing in Newfoundland in 1578. Frobisher is said to have served a meal for his crew at which he said a prayer of thanks for their safe arrival in the New World. American historians argue that the meal was not the result of a harvest (they ate salted fish), so it was not a true harvest celebration.

THE CORNUCOPIA

Also known as the "horn of plenty," this ancient Greek icon signifies abundance. The symbol originated as a curved goat's horn overflowing with fruits and grains. It represents the horn carried by Zeus's nurse, the nymph Amalthaea, which could be filled with whatever the owner wished. You can purchase a wicker basket shaped like a goat's horn from a craft store and fill it to make your own decorative cornucopia. Legumes and grains are common fillers, but other ornamental items such as flowers and grasses can also be used.

CORN DOLLIES

The tradition of crafting corn dollies from sheaves of corn goes back thousands of years to Pagan culture. Traditionally, the dollies were made at harvest time from the last sheaves of corn cut from the field. It was believed that the Spirit of the Corn would live in the dollies and stay there until the next growing season. The Spirit would then bless the new crop of corn, ensuring another successful harvest in the fall. Often, the dollies would be displayed prominently at the dinner table. Today, the tradition of making corn dollies lives on as a popular craft project for the harvest season.

Continued on page 10

FOOTBALL

For many North American families, fall's biggest seasonal celebration, Thanksgiving Day, is made up of some long-standing traditions—the family gathered around the table, battles over parts of the turkey and football fanatics glued to the television. The Canadian Football League has a tradition of televising two games on Thanksgiving Monday—one of only two Mondays in the year when CFL games are played. For truly rabid football fans, the United States offers up many football games from the professional and collegiate ranks. And when weather permits, fields across the continent become home to friendly pick-up games of football, billed as "Turkey Bowls."

WINTER SOLSTICE

In the Northern Hemisphere, the winter solstice occurs when the Earth is tilting at the furthest angle away from the sun, making it the time of year with the shortest amount of daylight and the longest amount of darkness. Although no one is quite sure when humans began celebrating this time of the year, many customs date back thousands of years. Why celebrate? Because it is so dark and cold at this time of year, people in wintery climes can get lethargic and depressed, so a boost to their spirits is just what they need. This is likely why so many winter celebrations revolve around lights and fire. Ancient cultures, which didn't have the benefit of modern astronomy, might have believed that the sun would die out completely and never return if they didn't intervene with vigils, fertility rites and other festivities in an effort to draw the sun back to the Earth. There is also an amazing variety of tombs, temples, cairns and observatories that were built by ancient peoples specifically to align with both equinoxes and solstices, one of the most famous being Stonehenge in England—a sure sign of just how important it was to humans to mark these times of the year.

CANNING AND PRESERVING

The custom of processing food to keep for long periods came as a result of the enormous quantity of fruits, vegetables and grains that are reaped at harvest. All this fresh food needed to be stored in a way that would prevent spoiling, ensuring plenty of rations to nourish people through the lean winter months. One popular preserving method was (and still is) canning goods in sealed Mason jars, but many other traditional methods are still used today. Drying, freezing, pickling, smoking, salting and curing are all great ways to preserve, and in some instances, add flavour to food. Even if you don't have your own garden to harvest, you can reap items from your local farmers' market, preserve them and enjoy farm-fresh food throughout the winter. Start preserving today and try Freezer Southwest Salsa, on page 164, or Bread and Butter Pickles, on page 159.

City dwellers may not operate combines and threshers at harvest time, but they can still be part of the harvest tradition. Backyard gardens can provide fresh produce and a taste of what it's like to live off the land, even if there's only room for a single row at the side of the house or a window-box herb garden. These micro-crops offer the simple satisfaction of eating food that you've grown yourself, as well as the comfort of knowing exactly where your food came from.

Winter Festivals

Winter in the northern hemisphere is known for its short daylight hours and sometimes menacing climate. However, that doesn't mean you have to let the dark and cold make you a shut-in. To break the winter blues, there are many events to draw you out from the home and into the action. One such event is the Celtic tradition of the Winter Solstice Festival, which is held in the northern hemisphere in late December. This day marks the point at which the short days begin to lengthen and there are more hours of daylight to delight in. Many communities stage concerts, banquets, dances, bonfires—any excuse to come together and celebrate the return to life in the light. Currently, the largest winter festival in the world is the Quebec Winter Carnival, which attracts nearly one million people each year. For 17 days in January, participants can enjoy a variety of activities including horse sleigh races, ice skating, snow slides and ice fishing.

FEATURED HARVEST INGREDIENTS

The recipes in this book highlight fruits and vegetables and other "products of the land" that are typically harvested in large quantities throughout North America. Here are just a few of the many fruits and vegetables associated with a plentiful harvest

POTATOES

The ancient Incas were the first recorded civilization to harvest this tuber. Thousands of years later, the potato has become a staple in kitchens around the world. Potatoes offer a range of textures and flavours and are great for any cooking method. High in starch and low in moisture, russet potatoes are perfect for baking or frying. Tender potatoes, such as Yukon Gold, are high in moisture, making them a popular choice for boiling and mashing. Baby or new potatoes are simply potatoes picked before they fully develop their size and starch content. This makes for a waxy potato with a thin skin that is perfect for roasting and boiling. Go for potatoes that are firm, well shaped and free of blemishes. Store them in a cool, dry place. All varieties will keep for approximately two weeks, with the exception of baby potatoes, which are best enjoyed within three days of purchase.

RHUBARB

The thick stalks of rhubarb may look like celery, but they taste very different. Known for its extremely tart flavour, rhubarb is popular in many sweet desserts, or simply enjoyed raw with a sprinkle of sugar. It is typically at its peak from April to June, but hothouse rhubarb (grown in heated greenhouses) is available year round. Pick rhubarb that has crisp stalks and fresh-looking, blemish-free leaves. Fresh rhubarb expires quickly, so wrap it tightly in plastic and store in the refrigerator for no more than three days, or chop and freeze it in freezer bags for later use. Be sure to remove the leaves when you wash and trim your rhubarb, as they contain a natural acid that can be toxic.

SQUASH

Squash has been harvested in the western hemisphere for over 5,000 years, and its many varieties are divided into two main categories: summer and winter squash. Summer squash, such as zucchini and pattypan, have a thin skin, mild flavour and high water content that makes them easy to cook. Winter squash, such as butternut and acorn, have hard, thick skins with a firm flesh that requires longer cooking. Both types are available year round, but winter squash are best from early fall through the winter. Choose summer squash that are on the small side and free of spots and bruises. When choosing winter squash, go for those that are heavy for their size, with a hard, densely coloured rind that is free of blemishes. Wrap summer squash in plastic and store in the refrigerator for no more than five days. Winter squash will keep well in a dry, cool place throughout the winter.

TOMATOES

As a member of the nightshade family, the tomato had trouble gaining renown outside of its native South and Central America. People were once skeptical of any member of the nightshade family (eggplant and potatoes are also members), claiming they were poison. With this myth fortunately debunked, the tomato plant has now spread across the world and into dozens of varieties. Though often referred to as a vegetable, tomatoes are properly classified as a type of fruit. Tomatoes are enjoyed both raw and cooked and are the base for many popular sauces, most notably those found in Mediterranean cooking. The best flavour and texture are found in vine-ripened tomatoes; however, they are very perishable and aren't always available. While most varieties of tomatoes are available year round, the peak season is from June through September. Choose those that are firm, well shaped, heavy for their size and free of blemishes. Store ripe tomatoes at room temperature for about three days.

APPLES

Apples have been harvested for nearly 3,000 years and have increased to over 1,000 varieties. Great for baked goods, preserving or enjoying raw, apples are best picked from September to November, when they are at their freshest. Choose apples that are firm and fresh-smelling, with a smooth, unblemished skin. Apples are best stored in cool, dark places—preferably the refrigerator.

CABBAGE

Cabbage crops originated in the Mediterranean and Western Europe about 2,000 years ago. The leaves range in colour from red to green to white, although the flavour remains largely the same regardless of the colour. Choose cabbage heads that are heavy for their size and have crisp, unblemished and tightly packed leaves. Store cabbage, tightly wrapped, in the refrigerator for up to one week.

BEETS

Beets exist in several varieties, but the one most common to North American soil is the "garden" beet. The beet itself is firm, round and has a rich red colour. The leafy tops of beets are also edible and are quite nutritious. Choose beets that are firm and have a smooth skin. Keep them in a plastic bag in the refrigerator for up to three weeks.

SWEET PEPPERS

Sweet peppers are native to the western hemisphere and found fame in Spanish cuisine after Christopher Columbus brought them back from the New World. Bell peppers, aptly named for their shape, are the most popular variety of sweet pepper. While available in many colours, most bell peppers start as bright green and change colour as they ripen. Store them in a plastic bag in the refrigerator for up to a week.

CARROTS

Part of the parsley family, carrots are nutritious and versatile, whether cooked or raw. Baby, or young, carrots are popular for their tender texture; however, they aren't as flavourful as their "grownup" counterparts. Trim the stems from carrots as soon as they are purchased or picked, as they detract moisture from the root, causing early spoiling. To store, wrap tightly in plastic and keep in the crisper of your refrigerator.

CORN

Corn's versatility was first discovered by Mexican and aboriginal cultures, but it is now grown throughout the world. Once picked, corn's natural sugars begin to turn to starch, reducing its sweetness. Choose ears with bright green, tightly fitting husks and plump kernels that run the full length of the cob. Fresh corn is best the day it is purchased, but you can keep it in the refrigerator for a day.

TURNIPS

The turnip is a hearty root vegetable that has been a part of British harvests for centuries. With the exception of their purple-tinged tops, turnips are white throughout. This variety is different from the yellow turnip, often known as a rutabaga. The taste of a turnip varies with its size. Smaller turnips have a slightly sweet flavour, while larger, older ones develop a stronger flavour and have a coarser flesh. Turnips are available year round, but peak season is from October to February. Choose turnips that are smaller and heavy for their size, as they tend to have better taste and texture. Turnips can be refrigerated for up to two weeks; however, they keep better in a cool, well ventilated space, such as a root cellar.

CRANBERRIES

Tart and crimson, cranberries grow wild in northern Europe and the northern United States. Farmed in vast sandy bogs, cranberries peak in October, and fresh ones are widely available until December. Due to their extreme tartness, cranberries are often paired with sweeter fruits such as apples and apricots. Store them in the refrigerator, tightly wrapped, for up to two months, or freeze them for up to a year.

Cranberry Mint Punch, page 16

BEVERAGES

Cool-weather beverages have a friendly quality about them that creates instant comfort—a hot mug is like a hug when you come in from the cold, and a festive cocktail will make guests feel at home. Flavourful and aromatic, our selection of drinks will have you covered at both ends of the entertaining spectrum—from brewing an afternoon warmer for a few friends to mixing a pitcher of spiced cocktails to spread cheer at a more formal gathering.

CHAI TEA

Brew a harvest of warm spices into this creamy "anytime" treat. This is the perfect recipe for when a handful of guests drop by—simply double the recipe to ensure everyone gets their fill. The amount of sugar can be adjusted to suit your preference.

Water	2 1/2 cups	625 mL
Orange pekoe tea bags	4	4
Fennel seed	1 1/2 tsp.	7 mL
Cinnamon stick (4 inches, 10 cm), broken up	1	1
Piece of ginger root (1 inch, 2.5 cm, length), thinly sliced	1	1
Whole black peppercorns	1/2 tsp.	2 mL
Whole cloves	8	8
Whole green cardamom, bruised (see Tip, below)	6	6
Milk	2 cups	500 mL
Brown sugar, packed	2 tbsp.	30 mL

Combine first 8 ingredients in medium saucepan. Bring to a boil. Reduce heat to medium-low. Simmer, uncovered, for about 20 minutes until fragrant. Strain through sieve into large bowl. Discard solids. Return to same pot.

Add milk and sugar. Stir. Heat on medium until bubbles form around edge of saucepan. Makes about 4 cups (1 L).

1 cup (250 mL): 78 Calories; 1.3 g Total Fat (0.5 g Mono, 0 g Poly, 0.8 g Sat); 8 mg Cholesterol; 13 g Carbohydrate; 1 g Fibre; 5 g Protein; 65 mg Sodium

Pictured below.

CANDY APPLE COCKTAIL

A fun drink for a grown-up Halloween party! Add a cute garnish with an apple slice—cut crosswise for a pretty star effect—or a butterscotch candy stick. This recipe is part of a suggested menu on page 166.

Amber (golden) rum (1 oz., 30 mL)	2 tbsp.	30 mL
Butterscotch schnapps (1 oz., 30 mL)	2 tbsp.	30 mL
Lemon juice	1 tbsp.	15 mL
Grenadine syrup	1 tsp.	5 mL
Ice cubes	4	4
Sparkling dry apple cider (with alcohol), chilled	1/2 cup	125 mL

Combine first 4 ingredients in cocktail shaker.

Add ice. Replace lid. Hold firmly and shake vigorously until cold. Strain though sieve into cocktail glass.

Add apple cider. Stir. Makes about 1 cup (250 mL).

1 cup (250 mL): 252 Calories; 0.1 g Total Fat (trace Mono, trace Poly, trace Sat); 0 mg Cholesterol; 34 g Carbohydrate; trace Fibre; trace Protein; 17 mg Sodium

Pictured below.

Left: Chai Tea, above; Right: Candy Apple Cocktail, above

TIP

To bruise cardamom, pound pods with mallet or press with flat side of wide knife to "bruise," or crack them open slightly.

BUTTERSCOTCH HOT CHOCOLATE

A not-too-sweet treat—thick, rich hot chocolate with butterscotch toffee undertones. This recipe is part of a suggested menu on page 166.

Milk	8 cups	2 L
Cocoa, sifted if lumpy	3/4 cup	175 mL
Box of instant butterscotch pudding powder (4-serving size)	1	1
Whipped cream (or whipped topping)	1 cup	250 mL
Crushed hard caramel candies (such as Werther's), see Tip, page 17	2 tbsp.	30 mL

Whisk first 3 ingredients in 3 1/2 to 4 quart (3.5 to 4 L) slow cooker until pudding powder is dissolved. Cook, covered, on Low for 4 to 5 hours or on High for 2 to 2 1/2 hours until heated through. Whisk until combined. Makes about 8 cups (2 L). Pour into 8 mugs.

Spoon whipped cream over top. Sprinkle with candy. Serves 8.

1 serving: 295 Calories; 15.0 g Total Fat (4.6 g Mono, 0.6 g Poly, 9.1 g Sat); 56 mg Cholesterol; 33 g Carbohydrate; 3 g Fibre; 12 g Protein; 217 mg Sodium

Pictured below.

CRANBERRY MINT PUNCH

Refreshing mint and tart cranberry combine to make this beautifully vibrant crimson punch memorable. Garnish with sprigs of fresh mint and whole cranberries.

Fresh (or frozen) cranberries	4 cups	1 L
Water	4 cups	1 L
Granulated sugar	1 1/2 cups	375 mL
Fresh mint leaves, lightly packed	1/2 cup	125 mL
Ginger ale, chilled	4 cups	1 L
Club soda, chilled	2 cups	500 mL

Combine first 3 ingredients in large saucepan. Bring to a boil. Reduce heat to medium-low. Simmer, covered, for about 7 minutes until cranberries are softened.

Add mint. Stir. Cool. Strain cranberry mixture through cheesecloth-lined sieve, pressing solids, into large pitcher. Discard solids. Chill.

Add ginger ale and club soda. Stir. Makes about 10 cups (2.5 L).

1 cup (250 mL): 129 Calories; trace Total Fat (0 g Mono, trace Poly, 0 g Sat); 0 mg Cholesterol; 36 g Carbohydrate; 2 g Fibre; trace Protein; 10 mg Sodium

Pictured on page 14 and below.

Left: Cranberry Mint Punch, above; Right: Butterscotch Hot Chocolate, above

Spiced Apple Cider, below

SPICED APPLE CIDER

This hot beverage is perfect for the kids or for large family gatherings. Lemon and pepper add refreshing depth—this is one cider that's not too sweet! This recipe is part of a suggested menu on page 166. Garnish with lemon wedges and cinnamon sticks.

Cinnamon stick		
(4 inches, 10 cm)	1	1
Whole black peppercorns	1 tsp.	5 mL
Whole cloves	3	3
Apple juice	4 cups	1 L
Brown sugar, packed	2 tbsp.	30 mL
Lemon juice	2 tbsp.	30 mL
Grated lemon zest	1/2 tsp.	2 mL
(see Tip, page 160)		

Put first 3 ingredients in medium saucepan. Heat and stir on medium for about 4 minutes until fragrant.

Add apple juice and brown sugar. Stir. Bring to a boil, stirring occasionally. Strain through sieve into small heatproof pitcher. Discard solids.

Add lemon juice and zest. Stir. Makes about 4 cups (1 L).

1 cup (250 mL): 135 Calories; 0 g Total Fat (0 g Mono, 0 g Poly, 0 g Sat); 0 mg Cholesterol; 36 g Carbohydrate; trace Fibre; trace Protein; 10 mg Sodium

Pictured above.

TIP

To crush hard candy, place in large resealable freezer bag. Seal bag. Gently hit with flat side of meat mallet or with rolling pin.

JACK FROST

Who is Jack Frost and why is he nipping at your nose, ears and toes? According to various legends, he is of English, Scandinavian, Russian or German origins. Most commonly he is depicted as an elf-like personification of frost and wintery weather, and he could be considered a sprightlier version of Old Man Winter. Part of the myth surrounding Jack Frost is that he leaves patterns of frost on window panes on cold winter mornings.

Left: Vanilla Honey Sipper, below; Right: Tropical Carrot Smoothie, right

VANILLA HONEY SIPPER

When the first cool fall evening settles in, you'll want to be sipping this smooth, frothy beverage. Light, sweet and comforting with a hint of cinnamon. This recipe is part of a suggested menu on page 166.

Skim milk (see Note)	5 cups	1.25 L
Liquid honey	1/4 cup	60 mL
Vanilla extract	1 tbsp.	15 mL
Ground cinnamon, sprinkle (optional)		

Combine milk and honey in large saucepan. Heat and stir on medium for about 10 minutes until hot, but not boiling. Remove from heat.

Add vanilla. Beat on high for about 4 minutes until frothy. Makes about 5 cups (1.25 L) Pour into 4 mugs, using large spoon to hold back froth. Spoon froth over top.

Sprinkle with cinnamon. Serves 4.

1 serving: 190 Calories; 0 g Total Fat (0 g Mono, 0 g Poly, 0 g Sat); 4 mg Cholesterol; 34 g Carbohydrate; 0 g Fibre; 11 g Protein; 163 mg Sodium

Pictured above.

NOTE: Whole or 2% milk may be used if you prefer more richness, but skim milk makes the most froth to spoon over top.

MULLED PORT WINE MIXER

Festive and comforting, with mild spiciness balanced with sweetness. The addition of port makes a smoother, more rounded spiced wine.

Water	1/2 cup	125 mL
Orange juice	1/4 cup	60 mL
Brown sugar, packed	2 tbsp.	30 mL
Cinnamon stick (4 inches, 10 cm)	1	1
Whole cloves	6	6
Whole allspice	4	4
Bottle of dry red wine	26 oz.	750 mL
Port wine	1/2 cup	125 mL

Combine first 6 ingredients in medium saucepan. Bring to a boil. Reduce heat to medium-low. Simmer, uncovered, for about 10 minutes, stirring occasionally, until fragrant.

Add red and port wine. Heat and stir until hot, but not boiling. Strain through sieve into small heatproof pitcher. Discard solids. Makes about 3 3/4 cups (925 mL).

1 cup (250 mL): 249 Calories; trace Total Fat (trace Mono, trace Poly, 0 g Sat); 0 mg Cholesterol; 18 g Carbohydrate; trace Fibre; trace Protein; 11 mg Sodium

Pictured at left.

TROPICAL CARROT SMOOTHIE

Sometimes dreary fall or winter mornings require an extra boost to get you going. Carrots, tropical fruit and fresh ginger combine in a tasty, colourful drink to kick-start your day.

Water	2 cups	500 mL
Chopped carrot	1 cup	250 mL
Ice water		
Frozen chopped fresh pineapple (see Note)	1 cup	250 mL
Frozen mango pieces	1 cup	250 mL
Frozen medium banana, chopped (see Note)	1	1
Finely grated ginger root (or 1/4 tsp., 1 mL, ground ginger)	1 tsp.	5 mL

Combine water and carrot in small saucepan. Bring to a boil. Reduce heat to medium. Boil gently, covered, for about 10 minutes until tender. Drain, reserving 1 1/3 cups (325 mL) cooking water.

Plunge carrot into ice water in medium bowl. Let stand for 10 minutes until cold. Drain. Transfer to blender or food processor.

Add remaining 4 ingredients and reserved cooking water. Process until smooth. Makes about 3 1/3 cups (825 mL).

1 cup (250 mL): 102 Calories; 0.4 g Total Fat (0.1 g Mono, 0.1 g Poly, 0.1 g Sat); 0 mg Cholesterol; 26 g Carbohydrate; 4 g Fibre; 1 g Protein; 28 mg Sodium

Pictured at left.

NOTE: Cut pineapple, mango and banana into 2 inch (5 cm) chunks and freeze on a baking sheet. Once frozen, transfer to freezer bag for use in blended beverages. You can also look for these frozen fruits at the grocery store.

Mulled Port Wine Mixer, left

Creamy Cheese Tomato Tarts, page 28

APPETIZERS

Get the fun started with these appealing dips and nibbles, perfect for drawing guests in and putting them at ease. Assorted appetizers featuring simple harvest ingredients are especially welcoming, and can be served as a tasty prelude to a meal or as small bites to keep the party going. Whether your group is crowded around the TV for a football game or gathering at the dining room table, offer a selection of savoury delights that celebrate the season.

AUTUMN VEGETABLE SAMOSAS

These familiar samosa turnovers hold a mélange of autumn vegetables spiced with traditional Indian seasonings. This recipe is part of a suggested menu on page 166. Great served with mango chutney on the side.

Diced butternut squash (1/4 inch, 6 mm, pieces)	1 cup	250 mL
Diced waxy potato (1/4 inch, 6 mm, pieces)	3/4 cup	175 mL
Salt	1/4 tsp.	1 mL
Cooking oil	1 tbsp.	15 mL
Chopped onion	2/3 cup	150 mL
Frozen kernel corn	1/2 cup	125 mL
Hot curry paste	2 tsp.	10 mL
Garam masala	1 tsp.	5 mL
Frozen tiny peas	1/3 cup	75 mL
Finely grated ginger root (or 1/2 tsp., 2 mL, ground ginger)	2 tsp.	10 mL
Garlic cloves, minced (or 1/2 tsp., 2 mL, powder)	2	2
Brown sugar, packed	1/2 tsp.	2 mL
Butter (or hard margarine), melted	1/3 cup	75 mL
Garam masala	1/4 tsp.	1 mL
Phyllo pastry sheets, thawed according to package directions	6	6
Butter (or hard margarine), melted	2 tbsp.	30 mL

Pour water into small saucepan until about 1 inch (2.5 cm) deep. Add first 3 ingredients. Bring to a boil. Reduce heat to medium. Boil gently, covered, for about 8 minutes until tender. Drain.

Heat cooking oil in medium frying pan on medium. Add next 4 ingredients. Cook for about 8 minutes, stirring often, until onion is softened.

Add next 4 ingredients and squash mixture. Heat and stir for about 3 minutes until fragrant and heated through.

Combine butter and second amount of garam masala in small cup.

Place 1 pastry sheet on work surface. Cover remaining sheets with damp towel to prevent drying. Brush sheet with butter mixture. Cut lengthwise into 4 strips. Spoon about 1 tbsp. (15 mL) squash mixture onto bottom of strip. Fold 1 corner diagonally towards straight edge to form triangle. Continue folding back and forth, enclosing filling (see diagram). Repeat with remaining pastry sheets, butter mixture and squash mixture. Arrange on greased baking sheets with sides (see Note).

Brush with second amount of butter. Bake in 375°F (190°C) oven for about 14 minutes until golden. Makes 24 samosas.

1 samosa: 66 Calories; 4.5 g Total Fat (1.4 g Mono, 0.4 g Poly, 2.3 g Sat); 9 mg Cholesterol; 6 g Carbohydrate; 1 g Fibre; 1 g Protein; 75 mg Sodium

Pictured below.

NOTE: Samosas can be frozen unbaked at this point. To serve, brush frozen samosas with 2 tbsp. (30 mL) melted butter. Bake in 375°F (190°C) oven for about 17 minutes until golden and heated through.

Autumn Vegetable Samosas, above

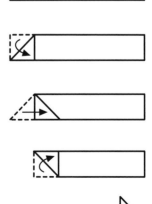

POTATO SALAD BITES

Appealing appearance meets classic flavour. Creamy potato salad is transformed into a neat handheld starter with these loveable bites.

Spreadable cream cheese	1/2 cup	125 mL
Finely chopped red pepper	2 tbsp.	30 mL
Grated medium Cheddar cheese	2 tbsp.	30 mL
Grated Parmesan cheese	2 tbsp.	30 mL
Mayonnaise	2 tbsp.	30 mL
Thinly sliced green onion	2 tbsp.	30 mL
Garlic powder	1/4 tsp.	1 mL
Paprika	1/8 tsp.	0.5 mL
Pepper	1/8 tsp.	0.5 mL
Baby potatoes, halved (about 1 1/2 lbs., 680 g)	20	20
Salt	1 tsp.	5 mL

Fresh parsley leaves, for garnish

Combine first 9 ingredients in small bowl. Chill.

Pour water into large saucepan until about 1 inch (2.5 cm) deep. Add potatoes and salt. Bring to a boil. Reduce heat to medium. Boil gently, covered, for 12 to 15 minutes until tender. Drain. Rinse with cold water. Drain well. Trim bottom of each potato half to make flat. Arrange potatoes, trimmed-side down, on platter. Spoon about 1 tsp. (5 mL) cream cheese mixture onto each potato half.

Garnish with parsley leaves. Makes 40 bites.

1 Potato Salad Bite: 32 Calories; 1.8 g Total Fat (0.3 g Mono, trace Poly, 0.8 g Sat); 4 mg Cholesterol; 3 g Carbohydrate; trace Fibre; 0.9 g Protein; 22 mg Sodium

Pictured below.

ROASTED CORN SALSA

Fresh and colourful with a lively hint of cilantro. Serve this beautiful salsa with your favourite chips, crackers or bread—it also makes a lovely accompaniment to fish or chicken.

Cooking oil	1 tbsp.	15 mL
Frozen kernel corn, thawed	3 cups	750 mL
Diced tomato	2 cups	500 mL
Diced red onion	1/2 cup	125 mL
Chopped fresh cilantro	2 tbsp.	30 mL
Lime juice	2 tbsp.	30 mL
Chopped fresh parsley	1 tbsp.	15 mL
Finely chopped fresh jalapeño pepper (see Tip, page 27)	1 tsp.	5 mL
Garlic clove, minced (or 1/4 tsp., 1 mL, powder)	1	1
Salt	1/4 tsp.	1 mL
Pepper	1/4 tsp.	1 mL

Heat cooking oil in large frying pan on medium. Add corn. Cook for about 10 minutes, stirring occasionally, until golden. Transfer to medium bowl. Cool.

Add remaining 9 ingredients. Stir. Makes about 4 cups (1 L).

1/2 cup (125 mL): 75 Calories; 2.2 g Total Fat (1.1 g Mono, 0.6 g Poly, 0.2 g Sat); 0 mg Cholesterol; 13 g Carbohydrate; 2 g Fibre; 2 g Protein; 79 mg Sodium

Pictured at right.

Potato Salad Bites, above

Left: Roasted Corn Salsa, left; Right: Pumpkin Pizza Wedges, below

PUMPKIN PIZZA WEDGES

The jack-o'-lantern jumps into the pizza pan for these cheesy wedges! These could serve as a fabulously grown-up Halloween appetizer, their fall flavours of fresh sage and pumpkin pairing well with a full-bodied red wine. This recipe is part of a suggested menu on page 166.

Butter (or hard margarine)	1 tbsp.	15 mL
Cooking oil	1 tbsp.	15 mL
Thinly sliced onion	2 cups	500 mL
Salt	1/4 tsp.	1 mL
Pepper	1/8 tsp.	0.5 mL
Canned pure pumpkin (no spices), see Tip, right	1 cup	250 mL
Chopped fresh sage (or 3/4 tsp., 4 mL, dried)	1 tbsp.	15 mL
Prebaked pizza crust (12 inch, 30 cm, diameter)	1	1
Grated Asiago cheese	1 1/2 cups	375 mL
Finely chopped green onion	2 tbsp.	30 mL

TIP

Store any leftover pumpkin in an airtight container in the refrigerator for 3 to 5 days or in the freezer for up to 12 months.

Heat butter and cooking oil in large frying pan on medium-low until butter is melted. Add next 3 ingredients. Cook for about 25 minutes, stirring occasionally, until onion is caramelized.

Combine pumpkin and sage in small bowl. Spread over pizza crust, almost to edge. Scatter onion mixture over pumpkin mixture.

Sprinkle with cheese. Cook in 450°F (230°C) oven for about 15 minutes until crust is golden and cheese is melted.

Sprinkle with green onion. Cuts into 16 wedges.

1 wedge: 76 Calories; 5.2 g Total Fat (0.7 g Mono, 0.3 g Poly, 2.4 g Sat); 11 mg Cholesterol; 5 g Carbohydrate; 1 g Fibre; 3 g Protein; 161 mg Sodium

Pictured above.

Cranberry Bison Meatballs, below

CRANBERRY BISON MEATBALLS

A cranberry glaze gives wonderful flavour to these lean bison meatballs—perfect to snack on in front of the big game. A great way to use up leftover cranberry sauce! This recipe is part of a suggested menu on page 166.

Large egg, fork-beaten	1	1
Cranberry cocktail	1/2 cup	125 mL
Fine dry bread crumbs	1/2 cup	125 mL
Ground allspice	1/2 tsp.	2 mL
Salt	1/2 tsp.	2 mL
Pepper	1/8 tsp.	0.5 mL
Ground bison	1 lb.	454 g
Canned whole cranberry sauce	1 cup	250 mL
Barbecue sauce	1/4 cup	60 mL
White vinegar	1 tsp.	5 mL
Pepper	1/8 tsp.	0.5 mL

Combine first 6 ingredients in large bowl.

Add bison. Mix well. Roll into 3/4 inch (2 cm) balls. Arrange in single layer on greased baking sheet with sides. Cook in 375°F (190°C) oven for about 15 minutes until no longer pink inside. Makes about 64 meatballs.

Combine remaining 4 ingredients in medium frying pan. Heat and stir on medium until boiling. Add meatballs. Heat and stir for about 1 minute until glazed. Makes about 4 cups (1 L).

1/2 cup (125 mL): 226 Calories; 10.1 g Total Fat (3.8 g Mono, 0.5 g Poly, 4.1 g Sat); 66 mg Cholesterol; 21 g Carbohydrate; 1 g Fibre; 12 g Protein; 337 mg Sodium

Pictured above.

CRANBERRY BEEF MEATBALLS: Replace ground bison with lean ground beef and reduce cranberry cocktail to 1/4 cup (60 mL).

BUTTERNUT MINI-QUICHES

Cute little quiches featuring sweet, tender bites of a favourite autumn ingredient. These mild and creamy tarts also have an infusion of fresh rosemary, which would also make a lovely garnish.

Butter (or hard margarine)	2 tsp.	10 mL
Diced butternut squash	1 cup	250 mL
Diced onion	1/4 cup	60 mL
Unsweetened tart shells	12	12
Grated Parmesan cheese	1/4 cup	60 mL
Large eggs	2	2
Half-and-half cream	1/2 cup	125 mL
Finely chopped fresh rosemary (or 1/8 tsp., 0.5 mL, dried, crushed)	1/2 tsp.	2 mL
Pepper	1/8 tsp.	0.5 mL

Melt butter in medium frying pan on medium. Add squash and onion. Cook for about 8 minutes, stirring often, until vegetables are softened and starting to brown. Cool.

Arrange tart shells on baking sheet with sides. Sprinkle cheese into shells. Spoon squash mixture over top.

Whisk remaining 4 ingredients in small bowl. Pour over squash mixture. Bake on bottom rack in 375°F (190°C) oven for about 18 minutes until pastry is golden and knife inserted in centre of quiche comes out clean. Let stand for 5 minutes. Makes 12 mini-quiches.

1 mini-quiche: 136 Calories; 8.2 g Total Fat (0.8 g Mono, 0.2 g Poly, 3.8 g Sat); 46 mg Cholesterol; 12 g Carbohydrate; trace Fibre; 3 g Protein; 133 mg Sodium

Pictured at right.

GREEK BRUSCHETTA

Dig into this warmly coloured tomato mix with delicious Greek-inspired seasonings. Serve with whole-wheat pita chips, toasted whole-grain baguette slices or tortilla chips.

Diced seeded tomato	1 1/3 cups	325 mL
Crumbled feta cheese	1/3 cup	75 mL
Diced yellow pepper	1/3 cup	75 mL
Chopped pitted kalamata olives	1/4 cup	60 mL
Chopped fresh basil	2 tbsp.	30 mL
Finely chopped red onion	2 tbsp.	30 mL
Chopped fresh oregano	1 tbsp.	15 mL
Olive (or cooking) oil	1 tbsp.	15 mL
Lemon juice	1 tbsp.	15 mL
Garlic clove, minced (or 1/4 tsp., 1 mL, powder)	1	1
Grated lemon zest (see Tip, page 160)	1/2 tsp.	2 mL
Liquid honey	1/2 tsp.	2 mL
Salt	1/2 tsp.	2 mL
Coarsely ground pepper	1/4 tsp.	1 mL

Combine all 14 ingredients in medium bowl. Let stand, covered, at room temperature for 2 hours to blend flavours. Makes about 2 1/4 cups (550 mL).

1/2 cup (125 mL): 86 Calories; 6.5 g Total Fat (3.0 g Mono, 1.1 g Poly, 2.0 g Sat); 10 mg Cholesterol; 6 g Carbohydrate; 1 g Fibre; 2 g Protein; 451 mg Sodium

Pictured below.

THESMOSPHORIA

Ancient Greeks were among the first peoples to celebrate the harvest, and they did so by paying homage to Demeter, their goddess of corn and other grains. Each autumn, a three-day festival called Thesmosphoria was held to honour her. On the first day, married women, considered the most fertile, built lean-to-like shelters for Demeter to take refuge in and furnished them with various comforts, such as seating made of greenery and offerings of food. On the second day, the women fasted in order to purify themselves for the feast ahead. On the third day, the fun really began, with a grand feast that featured fruits of the season, cakes and roasted pork, as well as gifts of seed corn to ensure Demeter's benevolence in granting a good harvest.

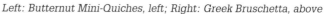

Left: Butternut Mini-Quiches, left; Right: Greek Bruschetta, above

Crispy Turnip Rolls, right

CRISPY TURNIP ROLLS

Humble roasted turnips become party fare when tossed with balsamic vinegar and wrapped in buttery phyllo. Other autumn veggies like parsnip and carrot can be rolled into these tasty bundles too!

Olive (or cooking) oil	2 tbsp.	30 mL
Balsamic vinegar	1 tbsp.	15 mL
Salt	1/2 tsp.	2 mL
Coarsely ground pepper	1/2 tsp.	2 mL
Yellow turnip (rutabaga) sticks (1/2 x 4 inch, 1.2 x 10 cm, pieces)	36	36
Butter (or hard margarine), melted	1/2 cup	125 mL
Dried basil	1 tsp.	5 mL
Phyllo pastry sheets, thawed according to package directions	6	6
Grated Asiago cheese	6 tbsp.	100 mL

Combine first 4 ingredients in large bowl. Add turnip. Toss until coated. Arrange in single layer on greased baking sheet with sides. Bake in 400°F (205°C) oven for about 12 minutes until tender-crisp. Cool.

Combine butter and basil in small cup.

Place 1 pastry sheet on work surface. Cover remaining sheets with damp towel to prevent drying. Brush sheet with butter mixture. Sprinkle with 2 tbsp. (30 mL) cheese. Place second pastry sheet over top. Brush with butter mixture. Cut lengthwise into 3 strips. Cut each strip into 4 rectangles. Place 1 turnip piece across long edge of 1 rectangle. Roll up from bottom to enclose filling. Arrange, seam-side down, on separate greased baking sheets with sides. Repeat with remaining ingredients. Bake in 400°F (205°C) oven for about 15 minutes until pastry is golden and turnip is tender. Makes 36 rolls.

1 roll: 48 Calories; 3.9 g Total Fat (1.2 g Mono, 0.4 g Poly, 1.9 g Sat); 8 mg Cholesterol; 3 g Carbohydrate; trace Fibre; 1 g Protein; 88 mg Sodium

Pictured at left.

Nacho Potato Skins, right

NACHO POTATO SKINS

For your next casual gathering, serve these soft and spicy potato boats with small bowls of your favourite nacho condiments such as salsa, sour cream and guacamole. This recipe is part of a suggested menu on page 166.

Medium unpeeled baking potatoes	3	3
Cooking oil	2 tbsp.	30 mL
Chili powder	1 tsp.	5 mL
Ground cumin	1/2 tsp.	2 mL
Salt	1/4 tsp.	1 mL
Pepper	1/4 tsp.	1 mL
Grated jalapeño Monterey Jack cheese	1 cup	250 mL
Chopped red pepper	1/4 cup	60 mL
Frozen kernel corn, thawed	1/4 cup	60 mL
Sliced black olives	1/4 cup	60 mL
Pickled jalapeño pepper slices	12	12

Place each potato on sheet of greased heavy-duty (or double layer of regular) foil. Fold edges of foil together over potatoes to enclose. Bake directly on centre rack of 425°F (220°C) oven for about 1 hour until tender. Transfer to cutting board. Carefully remove foil. Let stand until cool enough to handle. Cut potatoes lengthwise into quarters. Scoop out pulp, leaving 1/4 inch (6 mm) shell. Reserve pulp for another use.

Combine next 5 ingredients in small bowl. Brush over both sides of shells. Arrange shells, skin-side-up, on ungreased baking sheet with sides. Bake for about 10 minutes until starting to brown. Turn.

Sprinkle next 4 ingredients over shells, in order given. Top each potato skin with jalapeño pepper slice. Bake for about 5 minutes until cheese is melted. Makes 12 potato skins.

1 potato skin: 70 Calories; 5.7 g Total Fat (1.6 g Mono, 0.7 g Poly, 1.9 g Sat); 8 mg Cholesterol; 4 g Carbohydrate; 1 g Fibre; 2 g Protein; 148 mg Sodium

Pictured at left.

TIP

Hot peppers contain capsaicin in the seeds and ribs. Removing the seeds and ribs will reduce the heat. Wear rubber gloves when handling hot peppers and avoid touching your eyes. Wash your hands well afterwards.

Jalapeño Cheese Fondue, below

JALAPEÑO CHEESE FONDUE

Serve this cheesy, spicy fondue with toasted whole-grain bread cubes, bell pepper pieces or tortilla chips, and be sure to keep it warm in a dip warmer or fondue pot. This recipe is part of a suggested menu on page 166.

Grated jalapeño Monterey Jack cheese	2 cups	500 mL
Grated sharp Cheddar cheese	2 cups	500 mL
All-purpose flour	3 tbsp.	50 mL
Chili powder	1 tsp.	5 mL
Dry mustard	1/4 tsp.	1 mL
Garlic powder	1/4 tsp.	1 mL
Beer	1 cup	250 mL
Finely chopped fresh jalapeño pepper (see Tip, left)	2 tsp.	30 mL

Toss first 6 ingredients in large bowl until coated.

Combine beer and jalapeño pepper in medium saucepan on medium. Cook for about 2 minutes until hot, but not boiling. Add cheese mixture, 1 cup (250 mL) at a time, whisking after each addition until melted and smooth. Carefully pour into fondue pot. Keep warm over low flame. Makes about 2 1/2 cups (625 mL).

1/2 cup (125 mL): 379 Calories; 29.4 g Total Fat (4.3 g Mono, 0.4 g Poly, 17.5 g Sat); 87 mg Cholesterol; 7 g Carbohydrate; trace Fibre; 22 g Protein; 597 mg Sodium

Pictured above.

CREAMY CHEESE TOMATO TARTS

"Wow" flavours abound in an unassuming cheese tart. The filling is rich and creamy with the earthy flavour of smoky bacon—once guests get a taste of these, the tray will clear off fast. This recipe is part of a suggested menu on page 166.

Unsweetened tart shells	15	15
Chopped onion	1/2 cup	125 mL
Bacon slices, chopped	2	2
Garlic clove, minced	1	1
(or 1/4 tsp., 1 mL, powder)		
Block cream cheese, softened	4 oz.	125 g
Sour cream	1/2 cup	125 mL
All-purpose flour	1 tbsp.	15 mL
Large egg	1	1
Crumbled blue cheese	1/4 cup	60 mL
Cherry tomato slices	45	45

Arrange tart shells on ungreased baking sheet with sides. Bake on bottom rack in 350°F (175°C) oven for about 10 minutes until edges are just golden. Cool.

Combine next 3 ingredients in small frying pan on medium. Cook for about 5 minutes, stirring often, until onion is softened. Transfer to medium bowl.

Add next 3 ingredients to bacon mixture. Beat until combined.

Add egg and blue cheese. Beat well. Spread in tart shells. Bake for about 15 minutes until set. Let stand in pan on wire racks until cool.

Arrange 3 tomato slices over each tart. Makes 12 tarts.

1 tart: 179 Calories; 12.9 g Total Fat (2.1 g Mono, 0.4 g Poly, 6.6 g Sat); 43 mg Cholesterol; 12 g Carbohydrate; trace Fibre; 4 g Protein; 179 mg Sodium

Pictured on page 20 and at right.

EGGPLANT

Eggplant is a very moist vegetable. To counter this moisture, many cooks like to sprinkle salt on the eggplant slices to draw out the excess liquid. This step allows the eggplant to keep its consistency throughout the cooking process.

EGGPLANT ANTIPASTO ROLLS

A sophisticated yet easy-to-prepare appetizer with just the right amount of chili heat. The tuna is subtle but adds a delicious dimension to these intriguing-looking rolls. This recipe is part of a suggested menu on page 166.

Medium eggplants (with peel)	3	3
Salt, sprinkle		
Olive (or cooking) oil	1/3 cup	75 mL
Garlic clove, minced	1	1
(or 1/4 tsp., 1 mL, powder)		
Salt	1/8 tsp.	0.5 mL
Coarsely ground pepper	1/8 tsp.	0.5 mL
Dried crushed chilies	1/8 tsp.	0.5 mL
Can of flaked light tuna in water, drained	6 oz.	170 g
Mild salsa	1/2 cup	125 mL
Sliced green olives, chopped	1/4 cup	60 mL
Sun-dried tomato pesto	2 tbsp.	30 mL
Grated lemon zest	1/2 tsp.	2 mL
Emmenthal cheese sticks, (1/4 x 2 1/2 inch, 0.6 x 6.4 cm, pieces)	24	24

Cut eggplants lengthwise into ten 1/4 inch (6 mm) slices each. Discard outside slices. Sprinkle both sides of slices with salt. Transfer to large plate. Let stand for 1 hour. Rinse. Blot dry.

Combine next 5 ingredients in small cup. Brush over both sides of eggplant slices. Arrange in single layer on greased baking sheets with sides. Broil on centre rack in oven for about 8 minutes per side until tender and starting to brown. Cool.

Combine next 5 ingredients in small bowl. Spread over eggplant slices.

Place 1 cheese stick across end of 1 eggplant slice. Roll up tightly to enclose filling. Secure with wooden pick. Repeat with remaining eggplant slices and cheese. Makes 24 rolls.

1 roll: 142 Calories; 9.7 g Total Fat (4.3 g Mono, 0.7 g Poly, 4.3 g Sat); 22 mg Cholesterol; 6 g Carbohydrate; 3 g Fibre; 8 g Protein; 189 mg Sodium

Pictured at right.

Top: Eggplant Antipasto Rolls, above;
Bottom: Creamy Cheese Tomato Tarts, above

Fruity Wild Rice Salad, page 43

SOUPS & SALADS

There is no better way to create a masterpiece from your bountiful garden than with rich, hearty soups or colourful salads chock full of fresh produce. Serve up comforting bowls of filling soup for a casual gathering, or tempt guests with a delectably textured salad. Some of the smoother soups could even be served as starters for elegant autumn or winter dinner parties. Offer something you'd love to come home to, and your guests will feel truly welcomed.

EASY MINESTRONE

A quick, healthy and warming meal for your family.

Olive (or cooking) oil	1 tbsp.	15 mL
Chopped cabbage	1 cup	250 mL
Finely chopped celery	1/2 cup	125 mL
Finely chopped onion	1/2 cup	125 mL
Sliced carrot	1/2 cup	125 mL
Diced red pepper	1/3 cup	75 mL
Garlic clove, minced	1	1
(or 1/4 tsp., 1 mL, powder)		
Prepared vegetable	6 cups	1.5 L
(or chicken) broth		
Can of mixed beans,	19 oz.	540 mL
rinsed and drained		
Can of stewed tomatoes, cut up	14 oz.	398 mL
Tomato paste (see Tip,	2 tbsp.	30 mL
page 82)		
Parsley flakes	1 tbsp.	15 mL
Dried basil	1/2 tsp.	2 mL
Dried oregano	1/2 tsp.	2 mL
Ditali pasta (or elbow macaroni)	1/3 cup	75 mL
Salt	1/4 tsp.	1 mL
Grated Parmesan cheese	**2 tbsp.**	**30 mL**

Heat olive oil in large saucepan on medium-high. Add next 6 ingredients. Cook for about 5 minutes, stirring often, until vegetables start to soften and brown.

Add next 7 ingredients. Stir. Bring to a boil. Reduce heat to medium. Boil gently, partially covered, for about 15 minutes until vegetables are tender.

Add pasta and salt. Stir. Boil gently, uncovered, for about 12 minutes, stirring occasionally, until pasta is tender.

Sprinkle individual servings with Parmesan cheese. Makes about 9 cups (2.25 L).

1 cup (250 mL): 129 Calories; 2.7 g Total Fat (1.2 g Mono, 0.2 g Poly, 0.5 g Sat); 1 mg Cholesterol; 21 g Carbohydrate; 4 g Fibre; 6 g Protein; 583 mg Sodium

Pictured below.

Easy Minestrone, above

SPICED SQUASH AND APPLE SOUP

The sweetness of squash and apple blends well with warm spices in this smooth, velvety soup, with a crisp apple garnish providing contrasting texture.

Cooking oil	1 tbsp.	15 mL
Chopped butternut squash	3 cups	750 mL
Chopped peeled cooking apple (such as McIntosh)	2 cups	500 mL
Chopped onion	1 cup	250 mL
Ground allspice	1/2 tsp.	2 mL
Prepared vegetable broth	3 cups	750 mL
Unpeeled red apple slices, for garnish		

Heat cooking oil in large saucepan on medium. Add next 4 ingredients. Heat and stir for 1 minute. Reduce heat to medium-low. Cook, covered, for about 20 minutes, stirring occasionally, until squash is softened.

Add broth. Bring to a boil. Let stand for 5 minutes. Carefully process in blender or food processor until smooth (see Safety Tip, below).

Garnish individual servings with apple slices. Makes about 4 cups (1 L).

1 cup (250 mL): 187 Calories; 4.2 g Total Fat (2.1 g Mono, 1.2 g Poly, 0.3 g Sat); 0 mg Cholesterol; 38 g Carbohydrate; 7 g Fibre; 3 g Protein; 354 mg Sodium

Pictured below.

SAFETY TIP: Follow manufacturer's instructions for processing hot liquids.

Spiced Squash and Apple Soup, above

ROASTED CHICKEN SOUP

Roast chicken can be stretched into more than one meal when you boil the bones for soup! This homemade chicken and vegetable soup is subtly flavoured with ginger, garlic and lemon.

Precooked whole roasted chicken	3 lbs.	1.4 kg
Water	8 cups	2 L
Celery ribs, with leaves, quartered	2	2
Medium onion, quartered	1	1
Piece of ginger root (1 inch, 2.5 cm, length), sliced	1	1
Garlic cloves	2	2
Whole black peppercorns	6	6
Bay leaf	1	1
Diced red pepper	1/2 cup	125 mL
Frozen peas	1/2 cup	125 mL
Grated carrot	1/2 cup	125 mL
Salt	1 1/2 tsp.	7 mL
Grated lemon zest	1/2 tsp.	2 mL

Remove chicken from bones. Dice chicken to make 1 cup (250 mL). Chill. Reserve remaining chicken for another use. Place chicken bones in large saucepan.

Add next 7 ingredients. Bring to a boil. Reduce heat to medium-low. Simmer, partially covered, for 1 1/2 hours. Strain through sieve into large bowl. Discard solids. Return to same pot.

Add next 3 ingredients and chicken. Bring to a boil. Reduce heat to medium. Boil gently, uncovered, for about 10 minutes, stirring occasionally, until red peppers are tender-crisp.

Add salt and lemon zest. Stir. Makes about 7 cups (1.75 L).

1 cup (250 mL): 54 Calories; 1.6 g Total Fat (0.5 g Mono, 0.4 g Poly, 0.4 g Sat); 18 mg Cholesterol; 3 g Carbohydrate; 1 g Fibre; 7 g Protein; 539 mg Sodium

Pictured at right.

Left: Roasted Chicken Soup, left; Right: Homestyle Pea Soup, below

HOMESTYLE PEA SOUP

A thick, smooth pea soup infused with flavourful ham. Try making it with the ham bone from Apple Herb-Glazed Ham, page 62.

Cooking oil	1 tsp.	5 mL
Chopped onion	1 1/2 cups	375 mL
Chopped carrot	1 cup	250 mL
Chopped celery	1/2 cup	125 mL
Garlic clove, minced	1	1
(or 1/4 tsp., 1 mL, powder)		
Water	10 cups	2.5 L
Green split peas, rinsed	2 cups	500 mL
and drained		
Meaty ham bone	1 lb.	454 g
(or smoked pork hock)		
Parsley flakes	1 tbsp.	15 mL
Worcestershire sauce	1 tbsp.	15 mL
Bay leaves	2	2
Salt	1 tsp.	5 mL
Pepper	1/4 tsp.	1 mL

Heat cooking oil in Dutch oven or large pot on medium. Add next 4 ingredients. Cook for about 8 minutes, stirring often, until onion is softened.

Add remaining 8 ingredients. Bring to a boil. Reduce heat to medium-low. Simmer, covered, for about 2 hours until split peas are very soft and ham starts to fall off bone. Remove from heat. Remove and discard bay leaves. Carefully transfer ham bone to cutting board using tongs. Let stand until cool enough to handle. Remove ham from bone. Chop ham finely. Discard bone. Carefully process split pea mixture with hand blender or in blender in batches until smooth (see Safety Tip, below). Return to pot. Add ham. Stir. Makes about 10 cups (2.5 L).

1 cup (250 mL): 183 Calories; 1.2 g Total Fat (0.6 g Mono, 0.3 g Poly, 0.3 g Sat); 7 mg Cholesterol; 30 g Carbohydrate; 1 g Fibre; 14 g Protein; 435 mg Sodium

Pictured above.

SAFETY TIP: Follow manufacturer's instructions for processing hot liquids.

MEATBALL VEGGIE SOUP

*A soup to use up those bushels of garden zucchini!
Tender herbed chicken meatballs taste wonderful with
zucchini, peas and mushrooms in a flavourful broth. This
recipe is part of a suggested menu on page 166.*

Large egg, fork-beaten	1	1
Fine dry bread crumbs	1/2 cup	125 mL
Grated Parmesan cheese	1/3 cup	75 mL
Chopped fresh parsley	2 tbsp.	30 mL
(or 1 1/2 tsp., 7 mL, flakes)		
Dried oregano	1 1/2 tsp.	7 mL
Garlic clove, minced	1	1
(or 1/4 tsp., 1 mL, dried)		
Salt	1/2 tsp.	2 mL
Pepper	1/4 tsp.	1 mL
Lean ground chicken (or turkey)	3/4 lb.	340 g
Cooking oil	1 tbsp.	15 mL
Sliced fresh white mushrooms	2 cups	500 mL
Chopped zucchini (with peel)	1 1/2 cups	375 mL
Chopped onion	1 cup	250 mL
Salt	1/2 tsp.	2 mL
Pepper	1/4 tsp.	1 mL
Prepared chicken broth	7 cups	1.75 L
Frozen peas	1 cup	250 mL

Combine first 8 ingredients in medium bowl.

Add chicken. Mix well. Roll into 3/4 inch (2 cm) balls. Makes
about 44 meatballs.

Heat cooking oil in large saucepan on medium-high. Add
mushrooms. Cook for about 5 minutes, stirring occasionally,
until mushrooms are browned and liquid is evaporated.

Add next 4 ingredients. Stir. Cook for about 5 minutes, stirring
often, until onion starts to soften.

Add broth. Bring to a boil. Add meatballs. Stir. Bring to a boil.
Reduce heat to medium-low. Simmer, covered, for about
15 minutes until meatballs are no longer pink inside.

Add peas. Stir. Cook, covered, for about 4 minutes until peas
are heated through. Makes about 10 cups (2.5 L).

*1 cup (250 mL): 159 Calories; 7.1 g Total Fat (1.4 g Mono, 0.7 g Poly,
1.8 g Sat); 46 mg Cholesterol; 10 g Carbohydrate; 2 g Fibre; 14 g Protein;
940 mg Sodium*

Pictured below.

PESTO MEATBALL SOUP: Stir 1/3 cup (75 mL) of basil
pesto into soup when adding peas.

Meatball Veggie Soup, above

Autumn Vegetable Purée

A silky-textured, filling soup with a gorgeously orange colour and lovely flavours—perfect as a starter for a dinner party. Accompany with crusty, whole-grain bread to make it a light meal.

Butter (or hard margarine)	1 tbsp.	15 mL
Chopped onion	1 1/2 cups	375 mL
Ground ginger	1 tsp.	5 mL
Prepared vegetable broth	4 cups	1 L
Chopped carrot	2 cups	500 mL
Chopped peeled orange-fleshed sweet potato	1 cup	250 mL
Chopped peeled potato	1 cup	250 mL
Milk	1 cup	250 mL
Salt	1/4 tsp.	1 mL
Pepper	1/8 tsp.	0.5 mL
Orange juice	1/4 cup	60 mL
Grated orange zest (see Tip, page 160)	1/2 tsp.	2 mL

Melt butter in large saucepan on medium. Add onion and ginger. Cook for about 5 minutes, stirring often, until onion starts to soften.

Add next 4 ingredients. Stir. Bring to a boil. Reduce heat to medium. Boil gently, uncovered, for about 12 minutes until vegetables are tender. Remove from heat.

Add next 3 ingredients. Stir. Carefully process with hand blender or in blender in batches until smooth (see Safety Tip, below).

Add orange juice and zest. Stir. Makes about 6 1/2 cups (1.6 L).

1 cup (250 mL): 125 Calories; 2.7 g Total Fat (0.6 g Mono, 0.2 g Poly, 1.4 g Sat); 7 mg Cholesterol; 22 g Carbohydrate; 3 g Fibre; 4 g Protein; 500 mg Sodium

Pictured at right and on back cover.

SAFETY TIP: Follow manufacturer's instructions for processing hot liquids.

Preserving Our Plant Heritage

If you're a gardener, and even if you're not, you may have heard about heritage or heirloom plants. These are varieties of agricultural plants, including many kinds of fruits and vegetables, that are endangered because they are not widely grown anymore. Heritage seed organizations, such as Seeds of Diversity, have information on many different kinds of heirloom plants and where you can find seeds. Farmer's markets will sometimes sell heirloom plants such as tomatoes that you can transplant into your garden. Heirloom plants are often unique in both appearance and taste, and are well worth investigating if you like the idea of growing produce that is a little off the beaten path.

Autumn Vegetable Purée, left

ROASTED TOMATO SOUP

Tomato soup and grilled cheese sandwiches—together at last! Try serving it with a garnish of green onions and slices of Italian Cornbread Loaf, page 116.

Medium tomatoes, halved and seeded	12	12
Medium onions, cut into 8 wedges each	2	2
Cooking oil	2 tbsp.	30 mL
Garlic cloves, halved	3	3
Dried thyme	1 tsp.	5 mL
Pepper	1/2 tsp.	2 mL
Can of diced tomatoes (with juice)	28 oz.	796 mL
Prepared chicken broth	3 cups	750 mL
Water	1 cup	250 mL
Granulated sugar	2 tsp.	10 mL
Vermouth (optional)	1/4 cup	60 mL
GRILLED CHEESE CROUTONS		
Butter (or hard margarine), softened	3 tbsp.	50 mL
Whole-wheat bread slices	6	6
Grated jalapeño Monterey Jack cheese	3/4 cup	175 mL

Put first 6 ingredients into large bowl. Toss until coated. Arrange in single layer on greased baking sheet with sides. Cook in 400°F (205°C) oven for about 45 minutes until tomato starts to brown on edges. Transfer to Dutch oven.

Add next 4 ingredients. Stir. Bring to a boil. Reduce heat to medium. Boil gently, partially covered, for 20 minutes to blend flavours. Carefully process with hand blender or in blender in batches until smooth (see Safety Tip, below).

Add vermouth. Stir. Makes about 8 cups (2 L).

Grilled Cheese Croutons: Spread butter on each bread slice. Sprinkle 1/4 cup (60 mL) cheese on unbuttered side of 3 slices. Top with remaining bread slices, butter side up. Heat large frying pan on medium. Add sandwiches. Cook for 2 to 3 minutes per side until bread is golden and cheese is melted. Transfer to cutting board. Let stand for 5 minutes. Cut into 1/2 inch (12 mm) squares. Makes about 4 cups (1 L). Scatter over individual servings of soup. Serves 4.

1 serving: 498 Calories; 26.1 g Total Fat (7.7 g Mono, 3.6 g Poly, 10.5 g Sat); 41 mg Cholesterol; 53 g Carbohydrate; 11 g Fibre; 19 g Protein; 1495 mg Sodium

Pictured below.

SAFETY TIP: Follow manufacturer's instructions for processing hot liquids.

1. Barley and Lamb Soup, right
2. Kale, Bean and Bacon Soup, right
3. Roasted Tomato Soup, above

Kale, Bean and Bacon Soup

Serve up a rustic pot of this delicious bean and bacon soup, the classic flavour combination updated with plenty of root vegetables and nutritious kale. Make it ahead and store in an airtight container in the freezer for up to three months.

Bacon slices, chopped	4	4
Sliced leek (white part only)	2 cups	500 mL
Diced carrot	1 1/2 cups	375 mL
Diced celery root	1 cup	250 mL
Garlic cloves, minced (or 1/2 tsp., 2 mL, powder)	2	2
Caraway seed	1 tsp.	5 mL
Pepper	1/2 tsp.	2 mL
Bay leaf	1	1
Prepared chicken broth	6 cups	1.5 L
Chopped kale leaves, lightly packed (see Tip, below)	3 cups	750 mL
Water	2 cups	500 mL
Can of white kidney beans, rinsed and drained	19 oz.	540 mL

Cook bacon in large frying pan on medium until crisp. Transfer with slotted spoon to paper-towel lined plate to drain. Set aside. Drain and discard all but 1 tbsp. (15 mL) drippings.

Add next 7 ingredients to same frying pan. Cook for about 10 minutes, stirring often, until carrot and celery root are softened. Transfer to 5 to 7 quart (5 to 7 L) slow cooker.

Add next 3 ingredients. Stir. Cook, covered, on Low for 8 to 10 hours or on High for 4 to 5 hours.

Mash 2/3 cup (150 mL) beans with fork. Add to slow cooker. Add remaining beans and bacon. Stir. Cook, covered, on High for about 30 minutes until heated through. Remove and discard bay leaf. Makes about 10 1/2 cups (2.6 L).

1 cup (250 mL): 120 Calories; 3.3 g Total Fat (1.4 g Mono, 0.5 g Poly, 1.1 g Sat); 4 mg Cholesterol; 15 g Carbohydrate; 4 g Fibre; 8 g Protein; 592 mg Sodium

Pictured at left.

Tip

To remove the centre rib from lettuce or kale, fold the leaf in half along the rib and then cut along the length of the rib. To store, place leaves in large freezer bag. Once frozen, crumble in bag.

Barley and Lamb Soup

There's plenty of garden goodness in a rich lamb and barley soup, with a double dose of flavour from beer and pearl barley! This tasty soup can be stored in an airtight container in the freezer for up to three months.

Cooking oil	2 tsp.	10 mL
Lean ground lamb	1/2 lb.	225 g
Chopped onion	1 cup	250 mL
Sliced leek (white part only)	1 cup	250 mL
Diced celery	1/2 cup	125 mL
Dark beer (such as honey brown)	1 1/2 cups	375 mL
Prepared beef broth	6 cups	1.5 L
Water	2 cups	500 mL
Diced carrot	1 cup	250 mL
Diced parsnip	1 cup	250 mL
Diced yellow turnip (rutabaga)	1 cup	250 mL
Pearl barley	1/2 cup	125 mL
Tomato paste (see Tip, page 82)	1 tbsp.	15 mL
Dried rosemary, crushed	1/2 tsp.	2 mL
Dried thyme	1/2 tsp.	2 mL
Salt	3/4 tsp.	4 mL
Pepper	1/2 tsp.	2 mL
Bay leaf	1	1
Diced zucchini (with peel)	1 cup	250 mL

Heat cooking oil in Dutch oven on medium-high. Add next 4 ingredients. Scramble-fry for about 5 minutes until lamb is no longer pink.

Add beer. Heat and stir, scraping any brown bits from bottom of pan, until boiling.

Add next 12 ingredients. Stir. Bring to a boil. Reduce heat to medium-low. Simmer, covered, for about 45 minutes until barley is tender.

Add zucchini. Stir. Simmer, covered, for about 10 minutes until zucchini is tender. Skim and discard fat. Remove and discard bay leaf. Makes about 12 1/2 cups (3.1 L).

1 cup (250 mL): 113 Calories; 3.5 g Total Fat (1.5 g Mono, 0.4 g Poly, 1.1 g Sat); 12 mg Cholesterol; 14 g Carbohydrate; 3 g Fibre; 5 g Protein; 730 mg Sodium

Pictured at left.

Borscht, below

Add next 9 ingredients. Stir. Bring to a boil. Reduce heat to medium-low. Simmer, partially covered, for 20 minutes.

Add next 3 ingredients. Stir well. Simmer, partially covered, for about 25 minutes until vegetables are tender. Remove and discard bay leaf.

Add lemon juice. Stir. Makes about 9 1/2 cups (2.4 L).

1 cup (250 mL): 85 Calories; 1.9 g Total Fat (0.9 g Mono, 0.5 g Poly, 0.2 g Sat); 0 mg Cholesterol; 15 g Carbohydrate; 3 g Fibre; 3 g Protein; 312 mg Sodium

Pictured at left.

FENNEL CHOWDER

The anise overtones of fresh fennel and fennel seed add unique flavour to this thick, warming chowder—an exciting change from your run-of-the-mill soups. Enjoy the pleasant, lingering spice from Italian sausage. Try serving with a garnish of chopped McIntosh apples.

Cooking oil	1 tsp.	5 mL
Hot Italian sausage, casing removed, chopped	3/4 lb.	340 g
Chopped fennel bulb (white part only)	4 cups	1 L
Chopped onion	1 cup	250 mL
Chopped peeled potato	3 cups	750 mL
Prepared chicken broth	2 cups	500 mL
Water	2 cups	500 mL
Chopped peeled cooking apple (such as McIntosh)	1 cup	250 mL
Fennel seed	1/2 tsp.	2 mL
Salt	1/4 tsp.	1 mL
Pepper	1/4 tsp.	1 mL

Heat cooking oil in large saucepan on medium. Add sausage. Scramble-fry for about 10 minutes until browned.

Add fennel and onion. Stir. Cook, covered, for about 10 minutes, stirring often, until vegetables are softened.

Add remaining 7 ingredients. Bring to a boil. Reduce heat to medium-low. Simmer, covered, for about 20 minutes until potato is tender. Transfer 2 cups (500 mL) to blender. Carefully process until almost smooth (see Safety Tip, below). Return to same pot. Stir. Makes about 8 1/2 cups (2.1 L).

1 cup (250 mL): 203 Calories; 9.5 g Total Fat (0.5 g Mono, 0.2 g Poly, 3.1 g Sat); 22 mg Cholesterol; 23 g Carbohydrate; 4 g Fibre; 4 g Protein; 659 mg Sodium

Pictured at right.

SAFETY TIP: Follow manufacturer's instructions for processing hot liquids.

BORSCHT

With its classic combination of earthy beets, potatoes and cabbage, this soup is soothing in the cold winter months. For a traditional presentation, dish it up in white bowls to set off the lovely colour and top each with a dollop of sour cream and a sprinkle of fresh dill.

Cooking oil	1 tbsp.	15 mL
Chopped onion	1 cup	250 mL
Water	8 cups	2 L
Diced fresh peeled beets (see Tip, page 154)	3 cups	750 mL
Chopped carrot	1/4 cup	60 mL
Chopped celery	1/4 cup	60 mL
Envelope of vegetable soup mix	1 1/4 oz.	40 g
Dried dillweed	1/2 tsp.	2 mL
Salt	1/8 tsp.	0.5 mL
Pepper	1/4 tsp.	1 mL
Bay leaf	1	1
Diced peeled potato	1 cup	250 mL
Shredded green cabbage, lightly packed	1 cup	250 mL
Can of tomato paste	5 1/2 oz.	156 mL
Lemon juice	2 tsp.	10 mL

Heat cooking oil in Dutch oven on medium. Add onion. Cook for about 5 minutes, stirring often, until softened.

Hearty Goulash Soup

Traditional goulash is enhanced with smoked sweet paprika and harvest vegetables. Served with fresh bread and red wine, it makes a satisfying fall dinner.

Bacon slices, diced	8	8
All-purpose flour	3 tbsp.	50 mL
Boneless beef cross rib (or blade) steak, trimmed of fat, cut into 3/4 inch (2 cm) cubes	1 lb.	454 g
Chopped onion	2 cups	500 mL
Garlic cloves, minced (or 3/4 tsp., 4 mL, powder)	3	3
Dry (or alcohol-free) red wine	1 cup	250 mL
Can of diced tomatoes (with juice)	28 oz.	796 mL
Prepared beef broth	2 cups	500 mL
Diced peeled potato	1 1/2 cups	375 mL
Diced carrot	1 cup	250 mL
Diced parsnip	1 cup	250 mL
Can of tomato paste	5 1/2 oz.	156 mL
Caraway seed	1 tsp.	5 mL
Smoked (sweet) paprika	1 tsp.	5 mL
Salt	1/2 tsp.	2 mL
Pepper	1/4 tsp.	1 mL

Cook bacon in large frying pan on medium until crisp. Transfer with slotted spoon to 3 1/2 to 4 quart (3.5 to 4 L) slow cooker. Drain and discard all but 1 tbsp. (15 mL) drippings.

Put flour into large resealable freezer bag. Add beef. Seal bag. Toss until coated. Add beef to same frying pan on medium. Discard any remaining flour. Cook for about 5 minutes, stirring occasionally, until browned. Transfer to slow cooker.

Add onion and garlic to same frying pan. Cook for about 10 minutes, stirring often, until onion starts to soften and brown.

Add wine. Heat and stir, scraping any brown bits from bottom of pan, until boiling. Pour over beef.

Add remaining 10 ingredients. Stir. Cook, covered, on Low for 9 to 10 hours or on High for 4 1/2 to 5 hours. Makes about 10 cups (2.5 L).

1 cup (250 mL): 229 Calories; 8.4 g Total Fat (3.5 g Mono, 0.7 g Poly, 3.0 g Sat); 37 mg Cholesterol; 20 g Carbohydrate; 3 g Fibre; 14 g Protein; 762 mg Sodium

Pictured on page 40.

Fennel Chowder, left

Harvest Tabbouleh

Use up the last of your garden's late-season parsley and mint to create this bright and fresh addition to the harvest table. The root vegetables add substance and sweetness to nutty bulgur.

Bulgur, fine grind	1/2 cup	125 mL
Boiling water		
Olive oil	1 tbsp.	15 mL
Finely diced carrot	1 cup	250 mL
Finely diced parsnip	1 cup	250 mL
Finely diced red onion	1 cup	250 mL
Finely diced yellow turnip (rutabaga)	1 cup	250 mL
Finely chopped fresh parsley	1 cup	250 mL
Finely chopped tomato	1 cup	250 mL
Finely chopped fresh mint	1/4 cup	60 mL
Lemon juice	1/4 cup	60 mL
Olive oil	1 tbsp.	15 mL
Salt	3/4 tsp.	4 mL
Pepper	1/8 tsp.	0.5 mL

Put bulgur into small heatproof bowl. Add boiling water to cover. Stir. Let stand for 20 minutes until tender. Drain well. Transfer to large bowl.

Heat first amount of olive oil in large frying pan on medium. Add next 4 ingredients. Stir. Cook for about 15 minutes, stirring often, until vegetables are softened and starting to brown. Cool. Add to bulgur.

Add remaining 7 ingredients. Stir. Makes about 6 cups (1.5 L).

1 cup (250 mL): 136 Calories; 5.1 g Total Fat (3.7 g Mono, 0.6 g Poly, 0.7 g Sat); 0 mg Cholesterol; 22 g Carbohydrate; 5 g Fibre; 3 g Protein; 332 mg Sodium

Pictured below.

Top: Harvest Tabbouleh, above; Bottom: Hearty Goulash Soup, page 39

Saying Grace

Many people recite a short prayer before eating to thank a deity for the food about to be eaten. It's a tradition that's been around for a long time. No one really knows where or how it originated, but one theory claims that the mealtime prayer may have entered Christian societies with the Birkat Hamazon, a Jewish prayer of thanks recited after a meal. Even if one is not religious, saying grace is a way to express humility and gratitude for all the good things one has.

Left: Tomato Endive Salad, below; Right: Kohlrabi Spinach Salad, below

KOHLRABI SPINACH SALAD

Kohlrabi has a refreshing crunch and fresh flavour that complements the horseradish and bacon nicely. Serve it as a side, or add hearty bread to make it a meal!

Bacon slices, cut into 1 inch (2.5 cm) pieces	6	6
Fresh spinach leaves, stems removed, lightly packed	6 cups	1.5 L
Cherry tomatoes, halved	1 1/2 cups	375 mL
Thinly sliced kohlrabi, halved lengthwise and sliced crosswise	1 1/2 cups	375 mL
Thinly sliced carrot	1 cup	250 mL
CREAMY HORSERADISH DRESSING		
Mayonnaise	3 tbsp.	50 mL
Sour cream	3 tbsp.	50 mL
Prepared horseradish	2 tbsp.	30 mL
Apple cider vinegar	1 tbsp.	15 mL
Granulated sugar	1/2 tsp.	2 mL
Pepper	1/8 tsp.	0.5 mL

Cook bacon in large frying pan on medium until crisp. Transfer with slotted spoon to paper towel-lined plate to drain.

Toss next 4 ingredients in extra-large bowl. Add bacon. Toss.

Creamy Horseradish Dressing: Whisk all 6 ingredients in small bowl until smooth. Makes about 2/3 cup (150 mL). Add to spinach mixture. Toss until coated. Makes about 11 cups (2.75 L).

1 cup (250 mL): 73 Calories; 5.3 g Total Fat (0.7 g Mono, 0.3 g Poly, 1.4 g Sat); 8 mg Cholesterol; 4 g Carbohydrate; 2 g Fibre; 3 g Protein; 136 mg Sodium

Pictured above.

TOMATO ENDIVE SALAD

This a great salad for fresh-picked garden tomatoes— especially when you've got a bumper crop late in the season. Make this fresh and light dish to remind you of summer days. Serve with slices of toasted baguette.

Olive (or cooking) oil	1/4 cup	60 mL
Red wine vinegar	3 tbsp.	50 mL
Dijon mustard	1 tsp.	5 mL
Granulated sugar	1 tsp.	5 mL
Garlic powder	1/4 tsp.	1 mL
Salt	1/4 tsp.	1 mL
Pepper	1/8 tsp.	0.5 mL
Medium tomatoes, cut into 6 wedges each	8	8
Sliced Belgian endive, cut crosswise	2 cups	500 mL
Sliced red onion	1/4 cup	60 mL

Whisk first 7 ingredients in large bowl.

Add remaining 3 ingredients. Stir. Serve with slotted spoon. Makes about 8 cups (2 L).

1 cup (250 mL): 96 Calories; 7.3 g Total Fat (4.2 g Mono, 2.3 g Poly, 0.6 g Sat); 0 mg Cholesterol; 8 g Carbohydrate; 3 g Fibre; 2 g Protein; 89 mg Sodium

Pictured above.

Apple Cheddar Walnut Salad

Every bite of this fresh and inviting salad is unique—there's sweet vinegar tang, crunchy apple and distinctive cheese and walnut. This recipe is part of a suggested menu on page 166.

Cut or torn romaine lettuce, lightly packed	10 cups	2.5 L
Thinly sliced unpeeled tart apple (such as Granny Smith)	1 1/2 cups	375 mL
Grated sharp Cheddar cheese	1/2 cup	125 mL
Walnut pieces, toasted (see Tip, page 93)	1/3 cup	75 mL
Thinly sliced red onion	1/4 cup	60 mL
Cooking oil	1/4 cup	60 mL
Dijon mustard	3 tbsp.	50 mL
Balsamic vinegar	2 tbsp.	30 mL
Liquid honey	2 tbsp.	30 mL
Lemon juice	2 tsp.	10 mL
Salt	1/8 tsp.	0.5 mL
Pepper	1/8 tsp.	0.5 mL

Toss first 5 ingredients in extra-large bowl.

Whisk remaining 7 ingredients in small bowl. Add to lettuce mixture. Toss until coated. Makes about 12 cups (3 L).

1 cup (250 mL): 112 Calories; 8.6 g Total Fat (3.5 g Mono, 3.1 g Poly, 1.6 g Sat); 5 mg Cholesterol; 8 g Carbohydrate; 2 g Fibre; 2 g Protein; 107 mg Sodium

Pictured below.

Parsnip Slaw

This harvest salad's crisp, winter-white look will bring to mind the first snowflakes of the year—a different look to accompany an autumn feast. Earthy parsnip is a perfect partner for juicy green apples and sweet grapes. This recipe is part of a suggested menu on page 166.

Buttermilk	1/4 cup	60 mL
Sour cream	1/4 cup	60 mL
Granulated sugar	1/2 tsp.	2 mL
Lemon juice	1/2 tsp.	2 mL
Celery seed	1/4 tsp.	1 mL
Salt	1/4 tsp.	1 mL
Grated parsnip	3 cups	750 mL
Diced unpeeled tart apple (such as Granny Smith)	1 1/2 cups	375 mL
Halved seedless red grapes	1 cup	250 mL
Chopped fresh parsley (or 1 1/2 tsp., 7 mL, flakes)	2 tbsp.	30 mL
Sliced green onion	2 tbsp.	30 mL
Chopped walnuts, toasted (see Tip, page 93), optional	1/4 cup	60 mL

Whisk first 6 ingredients in large bowl.

Add next 5 ingredients. Stir.

Sprinkle with walnuts. Makes about 5 cups (1.25 L).

1 cup (250 mL): 164 Calories; 6.5 g Total Fat (0.7 g Mono, 2.9 g Poly, 2.0 g Sat); 9 mg Cholesterol; 25 g Carbohydrate; 5 g Fibre; 3 g Protein; 140 mg Sodium

Pictured below.

Left: Apple Cheddar Walnut Salad, above; Right: Parsnip Slaw, above

Fruity Wild Rice Salad, below

FRUITY WILD RICE SALAD

Curried yogurt dressing enhances the appealing colours, tastes and textures of chewy wild rice, crunchy vegetables and distinctive bits of sweet fig. Cilantro adds freshness to a mostly sweet mix.

Water	2 1/2 cups	625 mL
Salt	1/4 tsp.	1 mL
Wild rice	1 cup	250 mL
Diced peeled jicama	1 cup	250 mL
Diced unpeeled cooking apple (such as McIntosh)	1 cup	250 mL
Chopped dried apricot	1/3 cup	75 mL
Chopped dried figs	1/3 cup	75 mL
Grated carrot	1/3 cup	75 mL
Raisins	1/3 cup	75 mL
Diced red pepper	1/4 cup	60 mL
Sliced green onion	2 tbsp.	30 mL
Plain yogurt	2/3 cup	150 mL
Lemon juice	1 tbsp.	15 mL
Mango chutney, larger pieces chopped	1 tbsp.	15 mL
Hot curry paste	1 tsp.	5 mL
Salt	3/4 tsp.	4 mL
Chopped fresh cilantro (or parsley)	1 tbsp.	15 mL

Combine water and salt in medium saucepan. Bring to a boil. Add rice. Stir. Reduce heat to medium-low. Simmer, covered, for about 75 minutes, without stirring, until tender. Drain any remaining liquid. Transfer to large bowl. Cool.

Add next 8 ingredients. Stir.

Stir next 5 ingredients in small bowl until smooth. Add to rice mixture. Stir. Chill, covered, for 1 hour to blend flavours.

Sprinkle with cilantro. Makes about 6 1/2 cups (1.6 L).

1 cup (250 mL): 210 Calories; 0.7 g Total Fat (0.1 g Mono, 0.3 g Poly, 0.1 g Sat); 1 mg Cholesterol; 46 g Carbohydrate; 5 g Fibre; 6 g Protein; 440 mg Sodium

Pictured on page 30 and above.

SOUPS & SALADS

Toasted Barley Salad

Mildly flavoured harvest fruit and vegetables allow the nutty, toasted flavour of the barley to shine. With a variety of tastes and textures, this salad is perfect to offer at a late-season barbecue.

Pearl barley	1 cup	250 mL
Water	3 cups	750 mL
Salt	1/8 tsp.	0.5 mL
Bay leaf	1	1
Chopped onion	1/2 cup	125 mL
Bacon slices, diced	2	2
Garlic clove, minced	1	1
(or 1/4 tsp., 1 mL, powder)		
Diced unpeeled cooking apple	1 cup	250 mL
(such as McIntosh)		
Diced zucchini (with peel)	1 cup	250 mL
Sliced fresh white mushrooms	1 cup	250 mL
Finely sliced green onion	3 tbsp.	50 mL
Apple cider	1/3 cup	75 mL
Cooking oil	1/4 cup	60 mL
Apple cider vinegar	3 tbsp.	50 mL
Dijon mustard	1 1/2 tsp.	7 mL
Salt	1/4 tsp.	1 mL
Pepper	1/4 tsp.	1 mL

Heat and stir barley in medium frying pan on medium for about 10 minutes until golden brown.

Combine next 3 ingredients in large saucepan. Bring to a boil. Slowly add barley. Stir. Reduce heat to medium-low. Simmer, covered, for about 30 minutes, without stirring, until barley is tender and liquid is absorbed. Remove and discard bay leaf. Rinse with cold water. Drain well. Transfer to large bowl.

Add next 3 ingredients to same frying pan. Cook on medium for about 7 minutes, stirring often, until onion is softened. Add to barley.

Add next 4 ingredients. Stir.

Whisk remaining 6 ingredients in small bowl. Add to barley mixture. Stir. Makes about 6 cups (1.5 L).

1 cup (250 mL): 268 Calories; 13.5 g Total Fat (7.0 g Mono, 3.2 g Poly, 1.8 g Sat); 5 mg Cholesterol; 33 g Carbohydrate; 6 g Fibre; 5 g Protein; 185 mg Sodium

Pictured at left.

Spiced Beet Couscous Salad

Add a splash of colour to your meal with this intriguingly pink couscous blend, complete with earthy flavours and a touch of chili heat.

Diced fresh peeled beets	2 cups	500 mL
(see Tip, page 154)		
Chopped onion	1 cup	250 mL
Diced carrot	1 cup	250 mL
Olive (or cooking) oil	1 tbsp.	15 mL
Garlic cloves, sliced	2	2
Salt	1/2 tsp.	2 mL
Prepared vegetable broth	1 1/2 cups	375 mL
Couscous	1 cup	250 mL
Pine nuts, toasted	1/2 cup	125 mL
(see Tip, page 93)		
Chopped fresh parsley	3 tbsp.	50 mL
(or 2 1/4 tsp., 11 mL, flakes)		
Lemon juice	1/3 cup	75 mL
Olive (or cooking) oil	2 tbsp.	30 mL
Liquid honey	1 tbsp.	15 mL
Dried crushed chilies	1/2 tsp.	2 mL
Ground cumin	1/2 tsp.	2 mL
Salt	1/4 tsp.	1 mL
Coarsely ground pepper	1/4 tsp.	1 mL

Put first 6 ingredients in medium bowl. Toss. Arrange in single layer on greased baking sheet with sides. Bake in 400°F (205°C) oven for about 20 minutes until vegetables are tender. Transfer to large bowl. Cool.

Bring broth to a boil in medium saucepan. Add couscous. Stir. Remove from heat. Let stand, covered, for about 5 minutes until liquid is absorbed. Fluff with fork. Cool. Add to beet mixture.

Add pine nuts and parsley. Stir.

Whisk remaining 7 ingredients in small bowl. Drizzle over couscous mixture. Stir until combined. Makes about 5 1/2 cups (1.4 L).

1 cup (250 mL): 341 Calories; 16.7 g Total Fat (7.8 g Mono, 5.6 g Poly, 1.6 g Sat); 0 mg Cholesterol; 42 g Carbohydrate; 5 g Fibre; 8 g Protein; 503 mg Sodium

Pictured at left.

Top: Spiced Beet Couscous Salad, above
Bottom: Toasted Barley Salad, above

Rosemary Turkey Scaloppine, page 76

MAIN COURSES

As family and friends arrive at your home, the scent of a delicious main course hints that a wonderful meal is in store. Hearty and succulent beef, game, pork and lamb dishes will warm you to the core, while chicken and turkey are classic comfort foods. Fish and seafood make for dinners that are light yet filling, and vegetarian selections satisfy with a wealth of harvest goodness. A special main course guarantees that everyone will leave the table contented— and isn't that what entertaining is all about?

VENISON CRANBERRY STEW

A rich, dark and intense stew infused with subtly sweet and tangy flavours. Cranberries and balsamic vinegar lend sweetness to tender bites of venison.

Venison (or beef) stewing meat, trimmed of fat	1 lb.	454 g
Salt	1/4 tsp.	1 mL
Pepper	1/2 tsp.	2 mL
Cooking oil	2 tsp.	30 mL
Tomato paste (see Tip, page 82)	1 tbsp.	15 mL
Prepared beef broth	2 cups	500 mL
Dry (or alcohol-free) red wine	1 cup	250 mL
Bay leaves	2	2
Ground cloves	1/8 tsp.	0.5 mL
Cooking oil	1 tsp.	5 mL
Chopped onion	2 cups	500 mL
Fresh (or frozen) cranberries	1 1/2 cups	375 mL
Sliced carrot	1 1/2 cups	375 mL
Sliced celery	1 1/2 cups	375 mL
Garlic cloves, minced (or 1/2 tsp., 2 mL, powder)	2	2
Salt	1/2 tsp.	2 mL
All-purpose flour	1 tbsp.	15 mL
Brown sugar, packed	3 tbsp.	50 mL
Balsamic vinegar	2 tbsp.	30 mL

Sprinkle venison with salt and pepper.

Heat first amount of cooking oil in large saucepan on medium-high. Add venison. Cook for about 5 minutes, stirring occasionally, until browned. Add tomato paste. Heat and stir for 30 seconds.

Add next 4 ingredients. Heat and stir, scraping any brown bits from bottom of pan, until boiling. Reduce heat to medium-low. Simmer, covered, for 1 1/2 hours.

Heat second amount of cooking oil in large frying pan on medium. Add next 6 ingredients. Cook for about 10 minutes, stirring often, until onion starts to soften.

Add flour. Heat and stir for 1 minute. Add to venison mixture. Stir well. Cook, covered, for about 45 minutes until vegetables are tender.

Stir brown sugar and vinegar in small cup until brown sugar is dissolved. Add to venison mixture. Stir. Makes about 4 1/2 cups (1.1 L).

1 cup (250 mL): 315 Calories; 5.9 g Total Fat (2.6 g Mono, 1.5 g Poly, 1.3 g Sat); 86 mg Cholesterol; 30 g Carbohydrate; 4 g Fibre; 25 g Protein; 1024 mg Sodium

Pictured below.

Venison Cranberry Stew, above

HUNTING TRADITION

Some enjoy taking advantage of fall's abundant game by practicing hunting traditions that are a part of this time of year. For the hunters among us, and for those who enjoy the unique taste of wild meat, we have included this delicious recipe filled with ingredients that evoke the many flavours and colours of the season.

GIVING THANKS FOR THE HARVEST

Obzhynky (ob-ZIN-key) is Ukrainian Thanksgiving, a harvest celebration that takes place in mid-August, traditionally on the last day of the harvest. The root of the word means "to cut" in reference to the scythes and sickles once used to cut grain. Wreaths of grains, sometimes decorated with flowers and ribbons, were traditionally prepared from the last sheaves of the best grain. A single clump of grain was always left unharvested. It was braided into a single sheaf and left as an offering to the spirits of ancestors believed to inhabit the fields. Sometimes foods such as bread were also left under the sheaf as tributes to these ancestral spirits. It was hoped the offerings would ensure the benevolence of the spirits and protection of the fields. After this ceremony, a harvest feast was held, followed by dancing, singing, games or sports competitions. Special harvest songs were sung about the grain, the hand implements, the birds living in the grain, the toil of the harvest and the hopes for continuing abundant harvests in years to come.

Wild Mushroom Meatloaf, right

WILD MUSHROOM MEATLOAF

Mushroom fans will love this rustic meatloaf, complete with a rich sauce—earthy mushroom flavours are enhanced with a hint of thyme. Serve with potatoes and salad.

Large eggs, fork-beaten	2	2
Chopped portobello mushrooms	2 cups	500 mL
Fine dry bread crumbs	1 cup	250 mL
Sour cream	1/2 cup	125 mL
Dijon mustard	1/4 cup	60 mL
Tomato sauce	1/4 cup	60 mL
Dried thyme	1 tsp.	5 mL
Lean ground beef	2 lbs.	900 g
WILD MUSHROOM SAUCE		
Butter (or hard margarine)	2 tbsp.	30 mL
Chopped fresh oyster mushrooms	1 cup	250 mL
Chopped fresh shiitake mushrooms	1 cup	250 mL
Chopped onion	1/4 cup	60 mL
All-purpose flour	1/4 cup	60 mL
Dried thyme	1/4 tsp.	1 mL
Salt	1/4 tsp.	1 mL
Pepper	1/4 tsp.	1 mL
Prepared beef broth	1 1/2 cups	375 mL

Combine first 7 ingredients in large bowl.

Add ground beef. Mix well. Shape into 5 x 9 inch (12.5 x 23 cm) loaf. Place on greased baking sheet with sides. Cook in 375°F (190°C) oven for about 55 minutes until internal temperature reaches 160°F (71°C). Cut into 8 slices. Transfer to serving dish. Cover to keep warm.

Wild Mushroom Sauce: Melt butter in medium frying pan on medium. Add next 3 ingredients. Cook for about 10 minutes, stirring often, until onion is softened and liquid has evaporated.

Add next 4 ingredients. Heat and stir for 1 minute.

Slowly add broth, stirring constantly until smooth. Heat and stir for about 2 minutes until boiling and thickened. Makes about 1 3/4 cups. Drizzle over meatloaf. Serves 8.

1 serving: 403 Calories; 24.5 g Total Fat (1.2 g Mono, 0.3 g Poly, 10.7 g Sat); 148 mg Cholesterol; 16 g Carbohydrate; 2 g Fibre; 27 g Protein; 655 mg Sodium

Pictured at left.

BISON STIR-FRY

Lean bison steak goes well with root vegetables in a sweet and spicy Asian-inspired sauce—try serving it over barley or wild rice for an interesting twist. If bison meat is hard to find, try substituting tender beef steak.

Prepared beef broth	1/2 cup	125 mL
Orange juice	1/4 cup	60 mL
Soy sauce	1/4 cup	60 mL
Apricot jam	2 tbsp.	30 mL
Cornstarch	1 tbsp.	15 mL
Chili paste (sambal oelek)	1/4 tsp.	1 mL
Cooking oil	2 tsp.	10 mL
Bison steak, thinly sliced	1 lb.	454 g
Thinly sliced carrot	1 1/2 cups	375 mL
Thinly sliced fennel bulb (white part only)	1 1/2 cups	375 mL
Water	2 tbsp.	30 mL
Garlic cloves, thinly sliced	3	3
Sesame (or cooking) oil	1 tsp.	5 mL
Broccoli florets	1 cup	250 mL
Sliced red pepper	1 cup	250 mL
Sliced zucchini (with peel), halved lengthwise and sliced crosswise	1 cup	250 mL
Water	1/4 cup	60 mL
Finely grated ginger root (or 1/4 tsp., 1 mL, ground ginger)	1 tsp.	5 mL
Sesame seeds, toasted (see Tip, page 93)	1 tbsp.	15 mL

Stir first 6 ingredients in small bowl until smooth.

Heat cooking oil in large frying pan or wok on medium-high until very hot. Add bison. Stir-fry for about 1 minute until browned. Transfer to plate. Cover to keep warm.

Add next 5 ingredients to same frying pan. Stir-fry for about 2 minutes until vegetables start to soften.

Add next 5 ingredients. Stir-fry for about 4 minutes until broccoli is tender-crisp. Add bison. Stir broth mixture. Pour over top. Heat and stir for about 1 minute until boiling and thickened.

Sprinkle with sesame seeds. Makes about 5 1/2 cups (1.4 L).

1 cup (250 mL): 206 Calories; 5.7 g Total Fat (1.8 g Mono, 0.7 g Poly, 1.2 g Sat); 54 mg Cholesterol; 17 g Carbohydrate; 3 g Fibre; 22 g Protein; 1152 mg Sodium

Pictured above.

REDCURRANT POT ROAST

A one-pot meal—tender beef roast and harvest vegetables cook up just right. The sweet redcurrant sauce gets a bit of bite from prepared horseradish. Looks pretty with a garnish of rosemary sprigs.

Cooking oil	1 tbsp.	15 mL
Boneless beef cross-rib roast	3 lbs.	1.4 kg
Cooking oil	1 tbsp.	15 mL
Chopped onion	2 cups	500 mL
Garlic cloves, sliced	3	3
Dried rosemary, crushed	1/2 tsp.	2 mL
Dried thyme	1/4 tsp.	1 mL
Salt	1/2 tsp.	2 mL
Pepper	1/4 tsp.	1 mL
Chopped carrot	1 cup	250 mL
Chopped yellow turnip (rutabaga)	1 cup	250 mL
Prepared beef broth	1 cup	250 mL
Redcurrant jelly	1 cup	250 mL
Apple cider vinegar	1/4 cup	60 mL
Baby potatoes, larger ones halved	1 lb.	454 g
All-purpose flour	3 tbsp.	50 mL
Prepared horseradish	1/2 tsp.	2 mL

Heat first amount of cooking oil in Dutch oven on medium-high. Add roast. Cook for about 3 minutes per side until browned. Transfer to large plate.

Heat second amount of cooking oil in same Dutch oven. Reduce heat to medium. Add next 6 ingredients. Cook for about 5 minutes, stirring often, until onion is softened.

Add carrot and turnip. Cook for 5 minutes, stirring occasionally.

Add next 3 ingredients. Heat and stir, scraping any brown bits from bottom of pan, until boiling.

Add roast and potatoes. Cook, covered, in 300°F (150°C) oven for about 2 1/2 hours until beef and vegetables are tender. Transfer roast to cutting board. Let stand, tented with foil, for 10 minutes. Slice thinly. Arrange on serving platter. Remove vegetables with slotted spoon to same serving platter. Cover to keep warm. Skim and discard fat from cooking liquid.

Stir 3 tbsp. (50 mL) cooking liquid into flour in small cup until smooth. Bring remaining cooking liquid to a boil. Slowly add flour mixture, stirring constantly until boiling and thickened. Add horseradish. Stir. Serve with roast and vegetables. Serves 8.

1 serving: 596 Calories; 31.4 g Total Fat (14.1 g Mono, 2.1 g Poly, 11.3 g Sat); 115 mg Cholesterol; 45 g Carbohydrate; 2 g Fibre; 32 g Protein; 391 mg Sodium

Pictured below.

Redcurrant Pot Roast, above

The term "jack o' lantern" refers to a carved and lit up pumpkin. The origin of this word, and of the tradition of lighting up a carved gourd or root vegetable, is in the strange lights that sometimes flicker over peat bogs or marshes, referred to as *ignis fatuus* (foolish fire). According to folk tales, these lights are mischievous spirits, lost souls or ghosts; however, scientists believe the lights are caused by methane gas lighting up or bioluminescence (living things that naturally give off light, like the glow worm).

Beef Stew and Dumplings, below

BEEF STEW AND DUMPLINGS

Hearty beef and vegetables are cooked in a savoury sauce for a satisfying one-dish meal. But the real stars of this dish are the fluffy, thyme-flavoured dumplings. Add a fresh salad on the side to round out the meal.

All-purpose flour	1/4 cup	60 mL
Dried oregano	1/2 tsp.	2 mL
Dried thyme	1/2 tsp.	2 mL
Salt	1 tsp.	5 mL
Pepper	1/4 tsp.	1 mL
Stewing beef, trimmed of fat	1 1/2 lbs.	680 g
Chopped carrot	2 cups	500 mL
Chopped yellow turnip (rutabaga)	2 cups	500 mL
Sliced fresh brown (or white) mushrooms	2 cups	500 mL
Chopped celery	1 cup	250 mL
Chopped peeled potato	1 cup	250 mL
Sliced onion	1 cup	250 mL
Can of condensed beef broth	10 oz.	284 mL
Can of diced tomatoes (with juice)	14 oz.	398 mL
Worcestershire sauce	1 tsp.	5 mL
Biscuit mix	1 1/2 cups	375 mL
Chopped fresh thyme	1 1/2 tsp.	7 mL
Buttermilk (or soured milk, see Tip, page 107)	1/2 cup	125 mL

Combine first 5 ingredients in large resealable freezer bag. Add beef. Seal bag. Toss until coated. Transfer beef to greased 4 quart (4 L) casserole or small roasting pan. Reserve remaining flour mixture.

Scatter next 6 ingredients over beef mixture.

Whisk broth and remaining flour mixture in medium bowl until combined. Add tomatoes and Worcestershire sauce. Stir. Pour over vegetables. Cook, covered, in 350°F (175°C) oven for 2 hours.

Combine biscuit mix and thyme in small bowl. Make a well in centre.

Add buttermilk to well. Stir until just moistened. Remove beef mixture from oven. Stir. Drop biscuit mixture onto beef mixture in 8 mounds, using about 2 tbsp. (30 mL) for each. Bake, covered, for about 20 minutes until wooden pick inserted in centre of dumpling comes out clean. Serves 8.

1 serving: 351 Calories; 13.9 g Total Fat (4.8 g Mono, 0.5 g Poly, 5.1 g Sat); 53 mg Cholesterol; 35 g Carbohydrate; 3 g Fibre; 21 g Protein; 1164 mg Sodium

Pictured above.

BEEF AND HERB RAGOUT

A rich, flavourful and filling pasta sauce infused with fresh rosemary. Serve it over your favourite long pasta, with a green salad and garlic bread on the side.

Cooking oil	1 tsp.	5 mL
Chopped celery	1 cup	250 mL
Chopped onion	1 cup	250 mL
Cooking oil	2 tsp.	10 mL
Boneless beef blade steak, trimmed of fat, cut into 1 inch (2.5 cm) cubes	1 1/2 lbs.	680 g
Dry (or alcohol-free) white wine	1 cup	250 mL
Can of crushed tomatoes	14 oz.	398 mL
Chopped carrot	1 cup	250 mL
Chopped purple-topped turnip	1 cup	250 mL
Chopped fresh rosemary (or 3/4 tsp., 4 mL, dried, crushed)	1 tbsp.	15 mL
Bay leaf	1	1
Garlic clove, minced (or 1/4 tsp., 1 mL, powder)	1	1
Salt	1/2 tsp.	2 mL
Pepper	1/2 tsp.	2 mL
Grated Parmesan cheese	1/4 cup	60 mL
Half-and-half cream	3 tbsp.	50 mL
Chopped fresh parsley (or 3/4 tsp., 4 mL, flakes)	1 tbsp.	15 mL
Chopped fresh rosemary	1 tsp.	5 mL
Grated orange zest	1/4 tsp.	1 mL

Heat first amount of cooking oil in large frying pan on medium. Add celery and onion. Cook for about 8 minutes, stirring often, until onion is softened. Transfer to 3 1/2 to 4 quart (3.5 to 4 L) slow cooker.

Heat second amount of cooking oil in same frying pan on medium-high. Add beef. Cook, in 2 batches, for about 5 minutes, stirring occasionally, until browned. Add to celery mixture.

Add wine to same frying pan. Heat and stir, scraping any brown bits from bottom of pan, until boiling. Pour over beef.

Add next 8 ingredients to slow cooker. Stir. Cook, covered, on Low for 7 to 8 hours or on High for 3 1/2 to 4 hours. Remove and discard bay leaf.

Add remaining 5 ingredients. Stir. Makes about 5 cups (1.25 L).

1 cup (250 mL): 402 Calories; 20.2 g Total Fat (7.7 g Mono, 1.7 g Poly, 7.1 g Sat); 97 mg Cholesterol; 16 g Carbohydrate; 4 g Fibre; 31 g Protein; 600 mg Sodium

Pictured at right.

BEEF AND SQUASH CURRY

A rich coconut curry to spoon over steamed rice. Butternut squash adds mellow colour while curry paste gives just enough heat to this rustic, earthy dish.

Cooking oil	2 tbsp.	30 mL
Thinly sliced shallots (or red onion)	1/4 cup	60 mL
Thai red curry paste	2 tbsp.	30 mL
Beef strip loin steak, thinly sliced crosswise (see Note)	3/4 lb.	340 g
Can of coconut milk	14 oz.	398 mL
Chopped butternut squash (3/4 inch, 2 cm, pieces)	2 cups	500 mL
Small cauliflower florets	2 cups	500 mL
Brown sugar, packed	1 tbsp.	15 mL
Lime juice	1 tbsp.	15 mL
Soy sauce	1 tbsp.	15 mL
Finely shredded fresh basil	2 tbsp.	30 mL

Heat cooking oil in large saucepan pan on medium-high. Add shallots. Cook for about 3 minutes, stirring often, until golden. Transfer with slotted spoon to paper towel-lined plate to drain. Reduce heat to medium.

Add curry paste to same pot. Heat and stir for about 30 seconds until fragrant.

Add beef. Cook for about 3 minutes, stirring occasionally, until starting to brown.

Add coconut milk. Stir.

Add next 5 ingredients. Stir. Cook, covered, for about 12 minutes, stirring occasionally, until squash and cauliflower are tender. Transfer to serving bowl.

Sprinkle with basil and shallots. Makes about 5 cups (1.25 L).

1 cup (250 mL): 428 Calories; 32.7 g Total Fat (7.6 g Mono, 1.9 g Poly, 19.5 g Sat); 37 mg Cholesterol; 21 g Carbohydrate; 4 g Fibre; 18 g Protein; 712 mg Sodium

Pictured at right.

NOTE: To slice meat easily, before cutting place in freezer for about 30 minutes until just starting to freeze. If using from frozen state, partially thaw before cutting.

Top: Beef and Herb Ragout, above;
Bottom: Beef and Squash Curry, above

DARK MUSHROOM TENDERLOIN

The rich-tasting sauce is flavoured with beer and earthy wild mushrooms. Serve with herbed potatoes and grilled zucchini.

Cooking oil	2 tbsp.	30 mL
Beef tenderloin roast	2 1/2 lbs.	1.1 kg
Salt	1/4 tsp.	1 mL
Pepper	1/4 tsp.	1 mL
Dijon mustard	1 tbsp.	15 mL
Garlic cloves, minced	2	2
(or 1/2 tsp., 2 mL, powder)		
Finely chopped fresh rosemary	1 tsp.	5 mL
(or 1/4 tsp., 1 mL, dried, crushed)		
Dark beer (such as honey brown)	1 1/2 cups	375 mL
Package of dried porcini (or mixed) mushrooms	3/4 oz.	22 g
Cooking oil	1 tbsp.	15 mL
Finely chopped onion	1/2 cup	125 mL
Chopped fresh brown (or white) mushrooms	2 cups	500 mL
Prepared beef broth	1 cup	250 mL
All-purpose flour	2 tbsp.	30 mL
Whipping cream (or half-and-half cream)	1/2 cup	125 mL

Heat first amount of cooking oil in large frying pan on medium-high. Sprinkle roast with salt and pepper. Add to frying pan. Cook for about 5 minutes, turning occasionally, until browned on all sides.

Combine next 3 ingredients in small bowl. Brush over roast. Place on greased rack set in large baking sheet with sides. Cook in 425°F (220°C) oven for 15 minutes. Reduce heat to 350°F (175°C). Cook for about 45 minutes until internal temperature reaches 160°F (71°C) for medium or until roast reaches desired doneness. Transfer to cutting board. Let stand, tented with foil, for 10 minutes. Slice thinly.

Bring beer to a boil in medium saucepan. Add porcini mushrooms. Stir. Remove from heat. Let stand, uncovered, for about 20 minutes until softened. Drain, reserving any remaining beer. Transfer to cutting board. Chop.

Heat second amount of cooking oil in large saucepan on medium-high. Add onion. Cook for about 3 minutes, stirring often, until softened. Add brown and porcini mushrooms. Reduce heat to medium. Cook for about 5 minutes, stirring often, until browned. Add reserved beer. Heat and stir, scraping any brown bits from bottom of pan, until boiling.

Stir broth into flour in small cup. Slowly add to mushroom mixture, stirring constantly until boiling and thickened.

Add cream. Stir. Serve with roast. Serves 6.

1 serving: 390 Calories; 21.2 g Total Fat (8.8 g Mono, 2.4 g Poly, 7.6 g Sat); 127 mg Cholesterol; 9 g Carbohydrate; 1 g Fibre; 40 g Protein; 431 mg Sodium

Pictured below.

Dark Mushroom Tenderloin, above

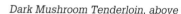

Sweet Mustard Steaks, below

Sweet Mustard Steaks

Rich, savoury steaks slow-cooked to tender perfection and flavoured with sweet maple, onion and Dijon mustard. Corn on the cob and grilled bread slices could be served on the side.

Beef cross-rib (or blade) steaks, bone-in	2 1/2 lbs.	1.1 kg
Salt	1/2 tsp.	2 mL
Pepper	1 tsp.	5 mL
Cooking oil	1 tbsp.	15 mL
Sliced onion	1 cup	250 mL
Garlic cloves, minced (or 1/2 tsp., 2 mL, powder)	2	2
Maple (or maple-flavoured) syrup	2/3 cup	150 mL
Water	1/2 cup	125 mL
White wine vinegar	1/4 cup	60 mL
Dijon mustard	2 tbsp.	30 mL
Worcestershire sauce	1 tbsp.	15 mL

Sprinkle both sides of steaks with salt and pepper.

Heat cooking oil in large frying pan on medium-high. Add steaks. Cook for about 7 minutes per side until browned. Transfer to 3 1/2 to 4 quart (3.5 to 4 L) slow cooker.

Arrange onion and garlic over steaks.

Combine remaining 5 ingredients in small bowl. Pour over top. Cook, covered, on Low for 8 to 10 hours or on High for 4 to 5 hours. Serves 8.

1 serving: 207 Calories; 6.3 g Total Fat (2.7 g Mono, 0.9 g Poly, 1.8 g Sat); 78 mg Cholesterol; 20 g Carbohydrate; trace Fibre; 17 g Protein; 287 mg Sodium

Pictured above.

Autumn vs. Fall

Ever wonder what the difference is between "autumn" and "fall"? "Autumn" comes from the Old French word *autompne* and was commonly used from the 16th century onwards to refer to the season between summer and winter. Before that, the term "harvest" was used to name that season. Over time, as people moved from farms into cities, "harvest" came to refer specifically to the activity of reaping, and "autumn" replaced it as a name for the season itself. "Fall" is an alternative to the word "autumn," used mainly in North America. Although the origin of the word is probably European, either from Old English or Old Norse, "fall" travelled to the New World with English immigrants and gradually faded from use in Britain.

Slow-Roasted Salmon, below

JAPANESE HARVEST TRADITIONS

In Japan, the rice harvest is celebrated with dances and feasts. In rural areas of the country, parades were traditionally held, featuring floats carrying symbolic gods. The Emperor would present offerings of new grains and produce to the gods to ensure continuing good harvests. In ancient times, the new rice harvested in autumn could not be eaten until after a special event was held to honour the rice spirit. People danced, sang and waved fans, and everyone in the community would join in a great feast. In modern Japan, this ritual is observed as a national holiday on November 23, a day akin to Thanksgiving Day in North America. At midnight on this day, the Emperor of Japan offers the first fruits of the autumn harvest at a special altar. *Tsumimi*, or moon-viewing, is another harvest custom observed in mid-September, around the time of the full moon. People set up tables facing the horizon to best view the moon as it rises. Offerings of autumn grasses, vegetables and rice flour dumplings (*tsukimi dango*) are placed on the table as offerings to the moon spirit.

SLOW-ROASTED SALMON

This deliciously dark-glazed salmon has sweetened salty Asian flavours with hints of red wine and lime. Transfer to a pretty platter to present for the main event. This recipe is part of a suggested menu on page 166.

Dry (or alcohol-free) red wine	1/2 cup	125 mL
Mirin (Japanese sweet cooking seasoning)	1/3 cup	75 mL
Soy sauce	1/4 cup	60 mL
Granulated sugar	1 tbsp.	15 mL
Lime juice	1 tsp.	5 mL
Pepper	1/8 tsp.	0.5 mL
Salmon fillet, any small bones removed	1 lb.	454 g

Combine first 6 ingredients in small saucepan. Bring to a boil. Reduce heat to medium. Boil gently, uncovered, for 10 to 12 minutes, stirring occasionally, until thickened to syrup consistency. Let stand for about 30 minutes until cool.

Place fillet, skin-side down, on foil-lined baking sheet with sides. Brush with 2 tbsp. (30 mL) wine mixture (see Safety Tip, below). Cook in 250°F (120°C) oven for 15 minutes. Brush with remaining wine mixture. Cook for about 10 minutes until fish flakes easily when tested with fork. Serves 4.

1 serving: 249 Calories; 7.2 g Total Fat (2.4 g Mono, 2.9 g Poly, 1.1 g Sat); 62 mg Cholesterol; 11 g Carbohydrate; trace Fibre; 24 g Protein; 1367 mg Sodium

Pictured above.

SAFETY TIP: Be sure to sanitize your brush after coating the raw salmon fillets. A second amount of wine mixture will be added once the fillets are partially cooked, so it is important that bacteria from the raw salmon do not contaminate the cooked fish.

PEANUT SHRIMP STIR-FRY

A different take on the autumn main course—creamy, spicy peanut sauce coats tender-crisp vegetables and succulent shrimp in this Malay-inspired stir-fry. Use coleslaw mix in place of the sliced cabbage and julienned carrot if you're in a hurry!

Cooking oil	2 tsp.	10 mL
Sliced green cabbage, lightly packed	2 cups	500 mL
Julienned carrot (see Note)	1 cup	250 mL
Sliced fresh brown (or white) mushrooms	1 cup	250 mL
Sliced onion	1 cup	250 mL
Thinly sliced red pepper	1 cup	250 mL
Uncooked medium shrimp (peeled and deveined)	1 lb.	454 g
Thai peanut sauce	1/2 cup	125 mL
Chopped fresh cilantro (or parsley)	2 tbsp.	30 mL
Chopped salted peanuts	2 tbsp.	30 mL

Heat large frying pan or wok on medium-high until very hot. Add cooking oil. Add next 5 ingredients. Stir-fry for about 5 minutes until vegetables are tender-crisp.

Add shrimp. Stir-fry for 2 minutes.

Add peanut sauce. Stir-fry for about 1 minute until shrimp turn pink.

Sprinkle with cilantro and peanuts. Makes about 5 1/2 cups (1.4 L).

1 cup (250 mL): 210 Calories; 9.3 g Total Fat (1.2 g Mono, 1.1 g Poly, 1.7 g Sat); 125 mg Cholesterol; 11 g Carbohydrate; 3 g Fibre; 21 g Protein; 652 mg Sodium

Pictured below.

NOTE: To julienne, cut into very thin strips that resemble matchsticks.

Peanut Shrimp Stir-Fry, above

1. Halibut Fennel Pot Pie, right
2. Squash and Seafood Stew, right
3. Tropical Fish Curry, below

TROPICAL FISH CURRY

When cooler weather has you daydreaming about tropical islands, dish up this light, sweet curry with your favourite rice or couscous. Meaty bites of tilapia pair well with sweet squash and mango.

Pineapple juice	1/4 cup	60 mL
Cornstarch	1 tbsp.	15 mL
Can of coconut milk	14 oz.	398 mL
Soy sauce	4 tsp.	20 mL
Thai red curry paste	1 tbsp.	15 mL
Granulated sugar	1 tsp.	5 mL
Cooking oil	1 tbsp.	15 mL
Cubed butternut squash (1/2 inch, 12 mm, pieces)	1 1/2 cups	375 mL
Chopped green pepper	1/2 cup	125 mL
Chopped onion	1/2 cup	125 mL
Tilapia fillets, any small bones removed, cut into 1 inch (2.5 cm) pieces	1 lb.	454 g
Frozen mango pieces	1 cup	250 mL

Stir pineapple juice into cornstarch in small bowl until smooth. Add next 4 ingredients. Stir.

Heat cooking oil in large frying pan or wok on medium-high until very hot. Add next 3 ingredients. Stir-fry for about 7 minutes until vegetables are browned and tender-crisp. Stir cornstarch mixture. Add to squash mixture. Heat and stir for about 2 minutes until boiling and slightly thickened. Reduce heat to medium.

Add fish and mango. Cook for about 5 minutes, stirring once or twice, until fish flakes easily when tested with fork. Makes about 6 1/2 cups (1.6 L).

1 cup (250 mL): 273 Calories; 17.0 g Total Fat (2.2 g Mono, 1.1 g Poly, 12.1 g Sat); 35 mg Cholesterol; 18 g Carbohydrate; 3 g Fibre; 16 g Protein; 466 mg Sodium

Pictured above.

SQUASH AND SEAFOOD STEW

A colourful and hearty cioppino-inspired stew that's chock full of squash, tomatoes and tender seafood. Serve with crusty bread to soak up the delicious sauce.

Cooking oil	1 tbsp.	15 mL
Chopped onion	1 cup	250 mL
Chopped celery	1/2 cup	125 mL
Diced butternut squash	1 1/2 cups	375 mL
Chopped red pepper	1 cup	250 mL
Garlic cloves, minced (or 1/2 tsp., 2 mL, powder)	2	2
Italian seasoning	2 tsp.	10 mL
Dried oregano	1 tsp.	5 mL
Cayenne pepper	1/4 tsp.	1 mL
Salt	1/4 tsp.	1 mL
Can of diced tomatoes (with juice)	28 oz.	796 mL
Prepared vegetable broth	1 cup	250 mL
Dry (or alcohol-free) white wine	1/2 cup	125 mL
Haddock fillets, any small bones removed, cut into 1 inch (2.5 cm) pieces	1/2 lb.	225 g
Small bay scallops	1/2 lb.	225 g
Uncooked medium shrimp (peeled and deveined)	1/2 lb.	225 g
Chopped fresh parsley (or 3/4 tsp., 4 mL, flakes)	1 tbsp.	15 mL

Heat cooking oil in large frying pan on medium. Add onion and celery. Cook for about 8 minutes, stirring often, until softened.

Add next 7 ingredients. Heat and stir for 2 minutes until garlic is fragrant.

Add next 3 ingredients. Bring to a boil. Boil gently, uncovered, for about 12 minutes until squash is tender.

Add next 3 ingredients. Cook, covered, for about 3 minutes, stirring once, until fish flakes easily when tested with fork and shrimp turn pink.

Sprinkle with parsley. Makes about 7 1/2 cups (1.9 L).

1 cup (250 mL): 181 Calories; 3.3 g Total Fat (1.2 g Mono, 1.0 g Poly, 0.3 g Sat); 73 mg Cholesterol; 15 g Carbohydrate; 3 g Fibre; 19 g Protein; 527 mg Sodium

Pictured at left.

HALIBUT FENNEL POT PIE

Dive into these inviting, pastry-topped pots, filled to the brim with a creamy, buttery and surprisingly spicy blend of meaty halibut pieces and tender vegetables.

Cooking oil	2 tsp.	10 mL
Thinly sliced fennel bulb (white part only)	1 cup	250 mL
Sliced leek (white part only)	3/4 cup	175 mL
Alfredo pasta sauce	1 cup	250 mL
Water	1/2 cup	125 mL
Lemon juice	1 tbsp.	15 mL
Halibut fillets, any small bones removed, cut into 1 inch (2.5 cm) pieces	1 lb.	454 g
Frozen peas	3/4 cup	175 mL
Grated Parmesan cheese	1 tbsp.	15 mL
Dried crushed chilies	1/4 tsp.	1 mL
Pepper	1/4 tsp.	1 mL
Package of puff pastry (14 oz., 397 g), thawed according to package directions	1/2	1/2
Large egg	1	1
Water	1 tbsp.	15 mL

Heat cooking oil in large frying pan on medium. Add fennel and leek. Cook for about 5 minutes, stirring often, until softened.

Stir next 3 ingredients in small bowl until smooth. Add to fennel mixture. Heat and stir for about 1 minute until boiling.

Add next 5 ingredients. Heat and stir for 2 minutes. Spoon into 4 ungreased 1 1/2 cup (375 mL) ramekins.

Roll out puff pastry on lightly floured surface to 12 x 12 inch (30 x 30 cm) square. Cut into 4 squares.

Whisk egg and water in small bowl. Brush top rims of ramekins with egg mixture. Place 1 pastry square over each ramekin. Press pastry onto ramekins to seal. Gently brush remaining egg mixture over top. Cut 3 slits in top of each square to allow steam to escape. Arrange ramekins on baking sheet with sides. Bake in 400°F (205°C) oven for about 15 minutes until pastry is puffed and golden. Makes 4 pot pies.

1 pot pie: 562 Calories; 34.6 g Total Fat (2.7 g Mono, 1.7 g Poly, 13.9 g Sat); 140 mg Cholesterol; 28 g Carbohydrate; 4 g Fibre; 36 g Protein; 731 mg Sodium

Pictured at left.

BAVARIAN STUFFED PORK ROAST

A festive roast that's perfect for a special Oktoberfest-themed dinner! Delicious pork loin is stuffed with a sauerkraut-style blend that has hints of bacon and tangy apple. Serve with potatoes or spaetzle, vegetables and plenty of good German beer! This recipe is part of a suggested menu on page 166.

Bacon slices, diced	5	5
Shredded green cabbage, lightly packed	1 1/2 cups	375 mL
Chopped onion	1 cup	250 mL
Chopped peeled cooking apple (such as McIntosh)	1 cup	250 mL
Caraway seed	1 tsp.	5 mL
Salt	1/2 tsp.	2 mL
Pepper	1/4 tsp.	1 mL
Apple cider vinegar	1 tbsp.	15 mL
Fresh bread crumbs	1 1/2 cups	375 mL
Chopped fresh sage (or 1/2 tsp., 2 mL, dried)	2 tsp.	10 mL
Boneless centre-cut pork loin roast	3 lbs.	1.4 kg
Dijon mustard	1 tbsp.	15 mL
Salt, sprinkle		
Pepper, sprinkle		

Cook bacon in large frying pan on medium-high until crisp. Transfer with slotted spoon to paper towel-lined plate to drain. Drain and discard all but 1 tbsp. (15 mL) drippings. Reduce heat to medium.

Add next 6 ingredients to same frying pan. Cook for about 8 minutes, stirring often, until onion is softened and starting to brown.

Add vinegar. Heat and stir for 1 minute. Remove from heat. Add bread crumbs, sage and bacon. Stir.

Butterfly roast, cutting horizontally lengthwise almost, but not quite through, to other side. Open flat. Place between 2 sheets of plastic wrap. Pound with mallet or rolling pin to 1 inch (2.5 cm) thickness.

Spread with mustard. Spoon bread crumb mixture over top, leaving 1/2 inch (12 mm) edge. Roll up from 1 long edge to enclose filling. Tie with butcher's string.

Sprinkle with salt and pepper. Place seam-side down on greased rack set in medium roasting pan. Cook in 400°F (205°C) oven for 20 minutes. Reduce heat to 325°F (160°C). Cook for about 50 minutes until browned and internal temperature of pork (not stuffing) reaches 155°F (68°C). Transfer to cutting board. Cover with foil. Let stand for 10 minutes. Internal temperature should rise to at least 160°F (71°C). Remove and discard string. Cut roast into 1/2 inch (12 mm) slices. Serves 10.

1 serving: 311 Calories; 12.7 g Total Fat (5.3 g Mono, 1.0 g Poly, 4.3 g Sat); 82 mg Cholesterol; 16 g Carbohydrate; 2 g Fibre; 31 g Protein; 395 mg Sodium

Pictured at left.

ERNTEDANKFEST

In North America, Thanksgiving Day is a secular festival, but the primary harvest festival in Germany, known as Erntedankfest (harvest gratitude festival), has strong religious undercurrents and tends to be celebrated more in rural areas. On the day of the festival, often the first Sunday in October, German churches are decorated with fruits, vegetables, sheaves of grain and baked goods. Goose is the main dish of choice at the dinner table. Farmer's markets and fairgrounds will feature dances, displays, beer tents and other festivities. In grape-growing regions of Germany, vintners present new wines at public wine tastings. In addition to Erntedankfest, Oktoberfest is a 16-day festival held from late September to early October in Munich. Founded in 1810 to commemorate a royal wedding, this festival has grown into one of the world's largest and has spawned similar festivals in cities worldwide. The festival is held on the *Theresienwiese* (field, or meadow, of Therese). In addition to drinking various kinds of beer in traditional beer tents and enjoying a festive atmosphere, festival goers are treated to such foods as potato pancakes, butter cheese, sausages, cabbage, potato dumplings and roast meats.

Bavarian Stuffed Pork Roast, above

APPLE HERB-GLAZED HAM

Create a feast by glazing this moist ham with apple and aromatic fresh herbs and serving it with your favourite side dishes—don't forget some oven-fresh buns! Slices of apples make a nice garnish. Use the leftover ham bone to make Homestyle Pea Soup, page 33.

Partially cooked bone-in ham	**8 lbs.**	**3.6 kg**
Apple jelly	**1/2 cup**	**125 mL**
Chopped fresh mint	**1 tbsp.**	**15 mL**
(or 3/4 tsp., 4 mL, dried)		
Dijon mustard	**2 tsp.**	**10 mL**
Chopped fresh oregano	**1 tsp.**	**5 mL**
(or 1/4 tsp., 1 mL, dried)		
Chopped fresh thyme	**1 tsp.**	**5 mL**
(or 1/4 tsp., 1 mL, dried)		
Lemon juice	**1 tsp.**	**5 mL**

Place ham, fat-side up, on greased wire rack set in large roasting pan. Bake, uncovered, in 325°F (160°C) oven for 1 hour.

Stir remaining 6 ingredients in small bowl until smooth. Brush 3 tbsp. (50 mL) over ham. Bake, uncovered, for about 1 hour and 40 minutes, brushing occasionally with remaining jelly mixture, until internal temperature reaches 160°F (71°C). Transfer to cutting board. Cover with foil. Let stand for 10 minutes. Slice thinly. Serves 12.

1 serving: 453 Calories; 28.9 g Total Fat (13.6 g Mono, 3.1 g Poly, 10.3 g Sat); 107 mg Cholesterol; 9 g Carbohydrate; trace Fibre; 37 g Protein; 2057 mg Sodium

Pictured below.

Apple Herb-Glazed Ham, above

Chipotle Chili Lamb, below

CHIPOTLE CHILI LAMB

Create an elegant autumn meal. Tender lamb is brushed with a simple cumin and chipotle glaze and roasted to lightly-spiced perfection. Try serving with baby potatoes and wilted spinach.

Cooking oil	1 tsp.	5 mL
Racks of lamb (about 1 lb., 454 g, each)	2	2
Liquid honey	3 tbsp.	50 mL
Balsamic vinegar	1 1/2 tsp.	7 mL
Cumin seed	1 tsp.	5 mL
Chipotle chili powder	1/2 tsp.	2 mL
Ground cinnamon	1/8 tsp.	0.5 mL
Salt	1/8 tsp.	0.5 mL

Heat cooking oil in large frying pan on medium-high. Add lamb, meat-side down. Cook for about 3 minutes until browned. Place, meat-side up, on greased baking sheet with sides.

Combine remaining 6 ingredients in small bowl. Cook lamb in 375°F (190°C) oven for 15 minutes. Brush with half of honey mixture. Cook for about 10 minutes until internal temperature reaches 145°F (63°C) for medium-rare or until lamb reaches desired doneness. Transfer to cutting board. Brush with remaining honey mixture. Cover with foil. Let stand for 10 minutes. Cut into 2-bone portions. Serves 4.

1 serving: 550 Calories; 41.9 g Total Fat (17.1 g Mono, 2.0 g Poly, 20.1 g Sat); 114 mg Cholesterol; 13 g Carbohydrate; trace Fibre; 28 g Protein; 188 mg Sodium

Pictured above.

Spanish Pork and Tomatoes, below

SPANISH PORK AND TOMATOES

Tender pork is a great match for tangy gazpacho-inspired flavours—the zesty sauce is rich with tomatoes and vegetables and is perfect for spooning over rice or potatoes.

Cooking oil	2 tsp.	10 mL
Pork tenderloin, trimmed of fat, cut into 1/4 inch (6 mm) slices	1 lb.	454 g
Seasoned salt	1/2 tsp.	2 mL
Cooking oil	1 tsp.	5 mL
Chopped onion	1 cup	250 mL
Chopped red pepper	1 cup	250 mL
Chopped zucchini (with peel), 1/2 inch (12 mm) pieces	1 cup	250 mL
Can of diced tomatoes (with juice)	14 oz.	398 mL
Red wine vinegar	2 tbsp.	30 mL
Liquid honey	1 tbsp.	15 mL
Dried oregano	1/2 tsp.	2 mL
Garlic powder	1/2 tsp.	2 mL
Salt	1/4 tsp.	1 mL
Pepper	1/4 tsp.	1 mL

Heat first amount of cooking oil in large frying pan on medium-high. Add pork. Sprinkle with seasoned salt. Cook for about 2 minutes per side until starting to brown. Transfer to bowl. Cover to keep warm.

Heat second amount of cooking oil in same frying pan on medium. Add next 3 ingredients. Cook for about 5 minutes, stirring often, until onion is softened.

Add remaining 7 ingredients. Bring to a boil. Add pork. Cook for about 3 minutes, stirring occasionally, until pork is no longer pink inside. Makes about 4 1/2 cups (1.1 L).

1 cup (250 mL): 211 Calories; 6.8 g Total Fat (3.4 g Mono, 1.4 g Poly, 1.5 g Sat); 66 mg Cholesterol; 14 g Carbohydrate; 2 g Fibre; 23 g Protein; 546 mg Sodium

Pictured above.

AUTUMN LEAVES

We all know that the leaves of deciduous trees change colour in the fall, but did you know that Canada is among just a few countries famous for their beautiful fall leaf colour? We share this honour with the U.S. and eastern Asian countries such as China, Japan and Korea. Leaves change colour in response to decreasing amounts of daylight and cooler temperatures, which prompt trees to stop producing chlorophyll and go into a dormant state for winter. Once the green disappears, the other colours present in the leaves—yellow, red, orange and brown—can be seen.

PORK, BEER AND FRUIT STEW

A saucy blend of tender pork morsels and sweet fruit bites in a dark beer-infused gravy that will make anyone cozy up to the table. This rich and flavourful stew can be served over rice or couscous.

All-purpose flour	1/4 cup	60 mL
Salt, sprinkle		
Boneless pork shoulder blade steak, trimmed of fat, cut into 3/4 inch (2 cm) pieces	2 lbs.	900 g
Cooking oil	4 tsp.	20 mL
Cooking oil	2 tsp.	10 mL
Chopped onion	1 1/2 cups	375 mL
Garlic cloves, minced (or 1/2 tsp., 2 mL, powder)	2	2
Ground coriander	1/2 tsp.	2 mL
Ground cumin	1/4 tsp.	1 mL
Salt	1/4 tsp.	1 mL
Prepared chicken broth	1 cup	250 mL
Dark beer (such as honey brown)	1 cup	250 mL
Apple juice	1/2 cup	125 mL
Dijon mustard	1 tbsp.	15 mL
Dried apricots, halved	1 cup	250 mL
Pitted prunes, halved	1/2 cup	125 mL

Combine flour and salt in large resealable freezer bag. Add half of pork. Seal bag. Toss until coated. Transfer pork to plate. Add remaining pork to flour mixture. Seal bag. Toss until coated. Transfer pork to plate. Reserve any remaining flour mixture.

Heat 2 tsp. (10 mL) of first amount of cooking oil in large frying pan on medium. Cook pork, in 2 batches, for about 5 minutes, stirring occasionally, adding more cooking oil if necessary, until browned. Transfer to 3 1/2 to 4 quart (3.5 to 4 L) slow cooker.

Heat second amount of cooking oil in same frying pan. Add onion. Cook for about 5 minutes, stirring often, until starting to soften.

Add next 4 ingredients and reserved flour mixture. Heat and stir for 1 minute.

Slowly add broth, stirring constantly until smooth.

Add next 3 ingredients. Heat and stir, scraping any brown bits from bottom of pan, until boiling and thickened. Pour over pork. Stir.

Scatter apricots and prunes over top. Cook, covered, on Low for 8 to 10 hours or on High for 4 to 5 hours. Stir. Makes about 6 cups (1.5 L).

1 cup (250 mL): 428 Calories; 14.3 g Total Fat (7.1 g Mono, 2.5 g Poly, 3.6 g Sat); 98 mg Cholesterol; 37 g Carbohydrate; 3 g Fibre; 33 g Protein; 394 mg Sodium

Pictured below.

Pork, Beer and Fruit Stew, above

PORK VEGETABLE PAPRIKASH

Comforting and delicious, this saucy dish can be served over broad egg noodles or barley—a widely appealing meal that the whole family will enjoy.

Cooking oil	1 tbsp.	15 mL
Boneless pork shoulder blade steak, trimmed of fat, cut into 1 inch (2.5 cm) cubes	1 1/2 lbs.	680 g
Cooking oil	1 tbsp.	15 mL
Diced kohlrabi	2 cups	500 mL
Sliced fresh brown (or white) mushrooms	2 cups	500 mL
Chopped onion	1 cup	250 mL
Diced red pepper	1/2 cup	125 mL
Prepared vegetable broth	1 1/2 cups	375 mL
Ketchup	1/4 cup	60 mL
Worcestershire sauce	1 1/2 tbsp.	25 mL
Paprika	4 tsp.	20 mL
Pepper	1/2 tsp.	2 mL
Water	1/4 cup	60 mL
All-purpose flour	1 tbsp.	15 mL
Sour cream	1/2 cup	125 mL

Heat first amount of cooking oil in Dutch oven on medium-high. Add pork. Cook for about 5 minutes, stirring occasionally, until starting to brown. Transfer to large plate. Reduce heat to medium.

Heat second amount of cooking oil in same pot. Add next 4 ingredients. Cook for about 10 minutes, stirring often, until onion is softened.

Add next 5 ingredients and pork. Stir. Bring to a boil. Reduce heat to medium-low. Simmer, covered, for about 1 hour until pork is tender.

Stir water into flour in small bowl until smooth. Add to pork mixture. Heat and stir for about 1 minute until boiling and thickened.

Add sour cream. Stir. Makes about 5 cups (1.25 L).

1 cup (250 mL): 372 Calories; 22.1 g Total Fat (8.5 g Mono, 2.9 g Poly, 7.6 g Sat); 88 mg Cholesterol; 17 g Carbohydrate; 4 g Fibre; 26 g Protein; 418 mg Sodium

Pictured at right.

CURRIED LAMB PATTIES

These are hearty and filling, and nicely seasoned with fragrant cumin and curry. Butternut squash is blended in for added moistness. Great served in buns with mango chutney and a side of sweet potato fries.

Cooking oil	1 tsp.	5 mL
Chopped onion	1/2 cup	125 mL
Curry powder	1/2 tsp.	2 mL
Ground cumin	1/2 tsp.	2 mL
Ground allspice	1/4 tsp.	1 mL
Large egg, fork-beaten	1	1
Fine dry bread crumbs	1/2 cup	125 mL
Grated butternut squash	1/4 cup	60 mL
Garlic cloves, minced (or 1/2 tsp., 2 mL, powder)	2	2
Salt	1 tsp.	5 mL
Pepper	1/2 tsp.	2 mL
Lean ground lamb	1 lb.	454 g
Cooking oil	2 tsp.	10 mL

Heat first amount of cooking oil in small frying pan on medium. Add next 4 ingredients. Cook for about 5 minutes, stirring often, until onion is softened. Transfer to large bowl.

Add next 6 ingredients. Stir.

Add lamb. Mix well. Divide into 4 equal portions. Shape into 4 inch (10 cm) patties.

Heat second amount of cooking oil in large frying pan on medium. Add patties. Cook for 4 to 5 minutes per side until internal temperature reaches 160°F (71°C). Makes 4 patties.

1 patty: 344 Calories; 20.8 g Total Fat (9.0 g Mono, 2.3 g Poly, 6.9 g Sat); 128 mg Cholesterol; 15 g Carbohydrate; 2 g Fibre; 23 g Protein; 769 mg Sodium

Pictured at right.

Top: Pork Vegetable Paprikash, above
Bottom: Curried Lamb Patties, above

GREEK PEASANT PARCELS

Harvest ingredients are put to good use in this rustic take on a popular Greek dish called Bandit's Lamb. Serve an individual packet for each guest, along with plenty of crusty white bread or fresh pita for dipping.

Boneless leg of lamb, trimmed of fat, cut into 1 1/2 inch (3.8 cm) pieces	1 1/2 lbs.	680 g
Chopped onion	2 cups	500 mL
Chopped tomato	2 cups	500 mL
Chopped celery root (1 inch, 2.5 cm, pieces)	1 1/2 cups	375 mL
Chopped parsnip (1 inch, 2.5 cm, pieces)	1 1/2 cups	375 mL
Chopped peeled potato (1 inch, 2.5 cm, pieces)	1 1/2 cups	375 mL
Crumbled feta cheese	3/4 cup	175 mL
Lemon juice	1/4 cup	60 mL
Butter (or hard margarine), melted	3 tbsp.	50 mL
Chopped fresh oregano (or 1 1/2 tsp., 7 mL, dried)	2 tbsp.	30 mL
Chopped fresh rosemary (or 3/4 tsp., 4 mL, dried)	1 tbsp.	15 mL
Garlic cloves, thinly sliced	3	3
Salt	1/4 tsp.	1 mL
Coarsely ground pepper	1 tsp.	5 mL

Combine all 14 ingredients in extra-large bowl. Cut 6 sheets of heavy-duty (or double layer of regular) foil about 14 inches (35 cm) long. Spoon lamb mixture in centre of each sheet. Fold edges of foil together over mixture to enclose. Fold ends to seal completely. Arrange packets, seam-side up, on ungreased baking sheet with sides. Bake in 325°F (160°C) oven for about 2 hours until lamb and vegetables are tender. Makes 6 parcels.

1 parcel: 357 Calories; 14.9 g Total Fat (4.4 g Mono, 1.0 g Poly, 8.2 g Sat); 104 mg Cholesterol; 28 g Carbohydrate; 5 g Fibre; 29 g Protein; 465 mg Sodium

Pictured below.

Greek Peasant Parcels, above

Port Wine Chops With Figs, below

PORT WINE CHOPS WITH FIGS

Gather around the table for sophisticated yet family-friendly flavours—pepper-speckled chops with a sweet port and fig glaze. Serve these richly flavoured chops with rice pilaf or mashed potatoes.

Bone-in pork chops, trimmed of fat	6	6
Salt	1/2 tsp.	2 mL
Coarsely ground pepper	1 tsp.	5 mL
Cooking oil	1 tbsp.	15 mL
Cooking oil	1 tsp.	5 mL
Finely chopped red onion	2 tbsp.	30 mL
Port wine	1 cup	250 mL
Dried figs, quartered	12	12
Red wine vinegar	1/4 cup	60 mL
Finely chopped fresh rosemary (or 1/8 tsp., 0.5 mL, dried, crushed)	3/4 tsp.	4 mL
Whipping cream	3 tbsp.	50 mL
Cornstarch	1/2 tsp.	2 mL

Sprinkle both sides of pork with salt and pepper. Heat first amount of cooking oil in large frying pan on medium. Cook pork, in 2 batches, for 4 to 5 minutes per side until no longer pink inside. Transfer to serving platter. Cover to keep warm.

Add second amount of cooking oil to same frying pan. Add onion. Cook for about 2 minutes, stirring often, until softened.

Add next 4 ingredients. Heat and stir until boiling. Boil gently, uncovered, for about 5 minutes until liquid is reduced by half.

Stir whipping cream into cornstarch in small cup until smooth. Add to fig mixture. Heat and stir for about 1 minute until boiling and thickened. Serve with pork. Serves 6.

1 serving: 361 Calories; 15.0 g Total Fat (6.5 g Mono, 1.9 g Poly, 5.2 g Sat); 63 mg Cholesterol; 31 g Carbohydrate; 4 g Fibre; 18 g Protein; 255 mg Sodium

Pictured above.

ST. LUCIA'S DAY

In Sweden, folk tradition dictates that December 13 is the day that follows the longest night of the year. To honour St. Lucia, on this day the eldest daughter of a family dons a white dress with a red sash and wears a wreath of lit candles on her head.

CHICKEN SWEET POTATO PIE

This picadillo-inspired pie will warm you on a cool evening—the topping hides a rich layer of chicken chili and green olives. Try it with a spinach side salad.

Cooking oil	2 tsp.	10 mL
Lean ground chicken	1 lb.	454 g
Chopped fresh white mushrooms	1 cup	250 mL
Chopped onion	1 cup	250 mL
Chili powder	2 tsp.	10 mL
Garlic cloves, minced (or 1/2 tsp., 2 mL, powder)	2	2
Dried oregano	1 tsp.	5 mL
Can of tomato sauce	14 oz.	398 mL
Chopped pecans, toasted (see Tip, page 93)	1 cup	250 mL
Sliced green olives	1 cup	250 mL
Chili sauce	1/4 cup	60 mL
Chopped peeled orange-fleshed sweet potato	1 1/2 cups	375 mL
Chopped peeled potato	1 1/2 cups	375 mL
Large egg, fork-beaten	1	1
Butter (or hard margarine)	2 tbsp.	30 mL
Ground cumin	1/4 tsp.	1 mL
Salt	1/4 tsp.	1 mL
Pepper	1/4 tsp.	1 mL
Finely chopped pecans, toasted (see Tip, page 93)	1/2 cup	125 mL

Heat cooking oil in large frying pan on medium-high. Add chicken. Scramble-fry for about 5 minutes until no longer pink. Reduce heat to medium.

Add next 5 ingredients. Cook for about 5 minutes, stirring often, until onion is softened and liquid is evaporated.

Add next 4 ingredients. Stir. Spread in greased 9 inch (23 cm) deep dish pie plate.

Pour water into large saucepan until about 1 inch (2.5 cm) deep. Add sweet potato and potato. Bring to a boil. Reduce heat to medium. Boil gently, covered, for 12 to 15 minutes until tender. Drain. Return to same pot.

Add next 5 ingredients. Mash.

Add pecans. Stir. Spread over chicken mixture. Using fork, score decorative pattern on top. Bake in 375°F (190°C) oven for about 30 minutes until sweet potato mixture is firm. Cuts into 6 wedges.

1 wedge: 550 Calories; 38.3 g Total Fat (17.6 g Mono, 7.7 g Poly, 6.9 g Sat); 95 mg Cholesterol; 39 g Carbohydrate; 8 g Fibre; 19 g Protein; 1486 mg Sodium

Pictured at right.

SOUPER CHICKEN STEW

This recipe is hearty like a stew, and rich and creamy like a soup—if you can't decide which comfort food you're in the mood for, this gives you both!

Cooking oil	2 tsp.	10 mL
Bone-in chicken thighs, skin removed (5 – 6 oz., 140 – 170 g, each)	8	8
Chopped carrot	2 cups	500 mL
Chopped celery	2 cups	500 mL
Chopped fresh white mushrooms	1 cup	250 mL
Chopped onion	1/2 cup	125 mL
Dried thyme	1/2 tsp.	2 mL
Paprika	1/2 tsp.	2 mL
Pepper	1/2 tsp.	2 mL
Ground allspice	1/4 tsp.	1 mL
Water	1 1/2 cups	375 mL
Can of condensed cream of chicken soup	10 oz.	284 mL
Can of condensed tomato soup	10 oz.	284 mL
Dry sherry	1/2 cup	125 mL
Balsamic vinegar	2 tbsp.	30 mL
Bay leaf	1	1
Fresh (or frozen) whole green beans, quartered	2 cups	500 mL

Heat cooking oil in Dutch oven or large pot on medium-high. Add chicken. Cook for about 3 minutes per side until browned. Transfer to plate.

Add next 8 ingredients to same pot. Cook for about 8 minutes, stirring often, until onion is softened.

Stir next 5 ingredients in medium bowl until smooth. Add to carrot mixture.

Add bay leaf and chicken. Stir. Bring to a boil. Reduce heat to medium-low. Simmer, covered, for about 45 minutes, stirring occasionally, until chicken is tender and no longer pink inside.

Add green beans. Stir. Cook, uncovered, for about 10 minutes until green beans are tender-crisp. Remove and discard bay leaf. Makes about 9 cups (2.25 L).

1 cup (250 mL): 248 Calories; 9.9 g Total Fat (3.6 g Mono, 2.6 g Poly, 2.4 g Sat); 68 mg Cholesterol; 18 g Carbohydrate; 3 g Fibre; 20 g Protein; 617 mg Sodium

Pictured at right.

Top: Souper Chicken Stew, above;
Bottom: Chicken Sweet Potato Pie, above

Chicken Fennel Stew, below

CHICKEN FENNEL STEW

A rustic, one-pot meal with lots of veggies and chicken pieces—the rich tomato broth takes on the delicate licorice flavour of fennel. Serve with fresh whole-wheat bread for dipping.

Cooking oil	2 tbsp.	30 mL
Bone-in chicken thighs, skin removed (5 – 6 oz., 140 – 170 g, each)	8	8
Salt, sprinkle		
Pepper, sprinkle		
Sliced onion	2 cups	500 mL
Bacon slices, diced	5	5
Garlic cloves, minced (or 1/2 tsp., 2 mL, powder)	2	2
Sliced fennel bulb (white part only)	3 cups	750 mL
Can of stewed tomatoes	19 oz.	540 mL
Coarsely chopped carrot	2 cups	500 mL
Prepared chicken broth	2 cups	500 mL
White baby potatoes, larger ones halved	1 lb.	454 g
Dry (or alcohol-free) white wine	1/2 cup	125 mL

Heat cooking oil in Dutch oven or large pot on medium-high. Add chicken. Sprinkle with salt and pepper. Cook for about 3 minutes per side until browned. Transfer to large bowl.

Add next 3 ingredients to same pot on medium. Cook for about 8 minutes, stirring often, until bacon is browned and onion is softened. Transfer with slotted spoon to same large bowl.

Add fennel to pot. Cook for about 10 minutes, stirring occasionally, until softened and browned.

Add remaining 5 ingredients. Heat and stir, scraping any brown bits from bottom of pot. Add chicken mixture using slotted spoon. Discard any remaining liquid in bowl. Stir. Bring to a boil. Reduce heat to medium-low. Simmer, covered, for about 40 minutes until chicken is no longer pink inside and vegetables are tender. Makes about 12 cups (3 L).

1 cup (250 mL): 239 Calories; 10.7 g Total Fat (4.5 g Mono, 2.1 g Poly, 2.9 g Sat); 55 mg Cholesterol; 16 g Carbohydrate; 2 g Fibre; 17 g Protein; 385 mg Sodium

Pictured above.

Classic Chicken Pot Pie

This familiar-tasting pot pie is the ultimate in comfort food—the perfect meal choice for a blustery day. This recipe is part of a suggested menu on page 166.

Boneless, skinless chicken thighs	1 lb.	454 g
Prepared chicken broth	2 1/2 cups	625 mL
Butter (or hard margarine)	2 tbsp.	30 mL
Sliced fresh white mushrooms	2 cups	500 mL
Sliced leek (white part only)	2 cups	500 mL
Thinly sliced carrot	1 1/2 cups	375 mL
Thinly sliced celery	3/4 cup	175 mL
All-purpose flour	1/4 cup	60 mL
Dried rosemary, crushed	1/4 tsp.	1 mL
Dried thyme	1/4 tsp.	1 mL
Salt	1/2 tsp.	2 mL
Pepper	1/4 tsp.	1 mL
Dry sherry	3 tbsp.	50 mL
Package of puff pastry (14 oz., 397 g), thawed according to package directions	1/2	1/2
Large egg, fork-beaten	1	1

Put chicken and broth in medium saucepan. Bring to a boil. Reduce heat to low. Simmer, covered, for about 15 minutes until chicken is no longer pink inside. Transfer chicken with slotted spoon to cutting board, reserving broth. Cut into 3/4 inch (2 cm) pieces.

Melt butter in large frying pan on medium. Add next 4 ingredients. Cook for about 10 minutes, stirring occasionally, until vegetables are tender-crisp.

Add next 5 ingredients. Heat and stir for 1 minute.

Slowly add sherry and reserved broth, stirring constantly until smooth. Heat and stir for about 5 minutes until boiling and thickened. Add chicken. Stir. Transfer to greased 2 quart (2 L) baking dish. Let stand for about 30 minutes until cool.

Roll out puff pastry on lightly floured surface to fit baking dish. Place over baking dish. Press pastry against sides to seal.

Gently brush egg over pastry. Cut several small vents in top to allow steam to escape. Bake in 400°F (205°C) oven for about 25 minutes until filling is bubbling and pastry is puffed and golden. Serves 4.

1 serving: 544 Calories; 29.5 g Total Fat (5.2 g Mono, 2.5 g Poly, 10.0 g Sat); 144 mg Cholesterol; 36 g Carbohydrate; 3 g Fibre; 33 g Protein; 1268 mg Sodium

Pictured below.

Classic Chicken Pot Pie, above

THYME SWEET POTATO BAKE

The distinct flavour of thyme is a highlight of this creamy sweet potato casserole, complete with a tasty topping of melted cheese.

Peeled orange-fleshed sweet potatoes, cut into 1/4 inch (6 mm) slices	2 lbs.	900 g
Prepared chicken broth	1 cup	250 mL
Thinly sliced onion	1 cup	250 mL
Butter (or hard margarine)	1 tbsp.	15 mL
All-purpose flour	3 tbsp.	50 mL
Milk	1 cup	250 mL
Prepared chicken broth	1 cup	250 mL
Chopped cooked chicken (see Note)	2 cups	500 mL
Chopped fresh thyme (or 1/4 tsp., 1 mL, dried)	1 tsp.	5 mL
Pepper	1/4 tsp.	1 mL
Butter (or hard margarine)	1 tbsp.	15 mL
Fine dry bread crumbs	2/3 cup	150 mL
Grated sharp Cheddar cheese	1/3 cup	75 mL

Put first 3 ingredients in large saucepan. Bring to a boil. Reduce heat to medium-low. Simmer, covered, for about 15 minutes until sweet potato is tender. Drain. Spread in greased 2 quart (2 L) baking dish.

Melt first amount of butter in medium saucepan on medium. Add flour. Heat and stir for 1 minute.

Slowly add milk, stirring constantly until smooth. Add second amount of broth. Heat and stir for about 5 minutes until boiling and thickened.

Add next 3 ingredients. Stir. Spread over sweet potato mixture.

Melt second amount of butter in small saucepan on medium. Remove from heat. Add bread crumbs and cheese. Mix well. Sprinkle over chicken mixture. Bake in 375°F (190°C) oven for about 25 minutes until browned and heated through. Serves 4.

1 serving: 568 Calories; 16.5 g Total Fat (4.8 g Mono, 1.7 g Poly, 7.6 g Sat); 91 mg Cholesterol; 69 g Carbohydrate; 8 g Fibre; 34 g Protein; 845 mg Sodium

Pictured below.

NOTE: Don't have any leftover chicken? Start with 2 boneless, skinless chicken breast halves (4 – 6 oz., 113 – 117 g, each). Place in large frying pan with 1 cup (250 mL) water or chicken broth. Simmer, covered, for 12 to 14 minutes until no longer pink inside. Drain. Chop. Makes about 2 cups (500 mL) of cooked chicken.

Thyme Sweet Potato Bake, above

Autumn Aromas Roast Chicken, below

AUTUMN AROMAS ROAST CHICKEN

A succulent roast chicken meal to bring the family together—this would be wonderful served as Thanksgiving dinner for a smaller group. The delicious stuffing is flavourful with root vegetables, while earthy hazelnuts add a nice crunch. This recipe is part of a suggested menu on page 166.

Cooking oil	1 tbsp.	15 mL
Chopped carrot	1 cup	250 mL
Chopped onion	1 cup	250 mL
Chopped yellow turnip (rutabaga)	1 cup	250 mL
Prepared chicken broth	3/4 cup	175 mL
Coarsely chopped hazelnuts (filberts), toasted (see Tip, page 93)	1/2 cup	125 mL
Chopped fresh parsley (or 3/4 tsp., 4 mL, dried)	1 tbsp.	15 mL
Chopped fresh thyme (or 1/4 tsp., 1 mL, dried)	1 tsp.	5 mL
Ground cumin	1/2 tsp.	2 mL
Seasoned croutons	4 cups	1 L
Lemon juice	1 tbsp.	15 mL
Whole chicken	4 lbs.	1.8 kg

Cooking oil	1 tbsp.	15 mL
Garlic powder	1 tsp.	5 mL
Smoked (sweet) paprika	1 tsp.	5 mL
Ground cumin	1/2 tsp.	2 mL
Salt	1/4 tsp.	1 mL
Pepper	1/8 tsp.	0.5 mL

Heat first amount of cooking oil in large frying pan on medium. Add next 3 ingredients. Cook for about 10 minutes, stirring often, until vegetables are softened.

Add next 5 ingredients. Stir. Remove from heat.

Add croutons. Stir until coated.

Brush lemon juice over surface of chicken. Loosely fill body cavity of chicken with crouton mixture. Secure with wooden picks or small metal skewers. Tie wings with butcher's string close to body. Tie legs to tail. Place on greased wire rack set in medium roasting pan.

Combine remaining 6 ingredients in small bowl. Rub over surface of chicken. Cook, covered, in 400°F (205°C) oven for 20 minutes. Reduce heat to 325°F (160°C). Cook, covered, for about 1 1/2 hours until meat thermometer inserted in thickest part of thigh reaches 180°F (82°C). Temperature of stuffing should reach at least 165°F (74°C). Transfer chicken to cutting board. Remove and discard string. Cover with foil. Let stand for 10 minutes. Internal temperature of chicken should rise to at least 185°F (85°C). Transfer stuffing to serving dish. Serves 6.

1 serving: 482 Calories; 24.4 g Total Fat (12.8 g Mono, 4.9 g Poly, 4.6 g Sat); 105 mg Cholesterol; 26 g Carbohydrate; 4 g Fibre; 39 g Protein; 655 mg Sodium

Pictured above.

Rosemary Turkey Scaloppine, below

ROSEMARY TURKEY SCALOPPINE

A delicious and impressive meal! Festive peppers and zucchini form a colourful bed for turkey scaloppine slices, beautifully browned and seasoned with aromatic rosemary.

Finely chopped fresh rosemary (or 1/2 tsp., 2 mL, dried, crushed)	2 tsp.	10 mL
Salt	1/4 tsp.	1 mL
Pepper	1/4 tsp.	1 mL
Turkey scaloppine (halved crosswise)	1 lb.	454 g
Cooking (or olive) oil	1 tbsp.	15 mL
Cooking (or olive) oil	1 tbsp.	15 mL
Chopped Asian eggplant (with peel)	1 cup	250 mL
Chopped zucchini (with peel)	1 cup	250 mL
Sliced green pepper	1 cup	250 mL
Sliced onion	1 cup	250 mL
Sliced red pepper	1 cup	250 mL
Sliced yellow pepper	1 cup	250 mL
Balsamic vinegar	1 tbsp.	15 mL
Chopped fresh rosemary (or 1/2 tsp., 2 mL, dried, crushed)	2 tsp.	10 mL
Salt	1/2 tsp.	2 mL
Pepper	1/4 tsp.	1 mL

Combine first 3 ingredients in small cup. Sprinkle over both sides of turkey.

Heat 1 tsp. (5 mL) of first amount of cooking oil in large frying pan on medium-high. Cook turkey, in 3 batches, for about 45 seconds per side, adding more oil if necessary, until no longer pink inside. Transfer to large plate. Cover to keep warm.

Heat second amount of cooking oil in same pan. Add remaining 10 ingredients. Cook for about 6 minutes, stirring often, until vegetables are tender-crisp. Transfer to serving dish. Arrange turkey over top. Serves 4.

1 serving: 249 Calories; 9.0 g Total Fat (4.2 g Mono, 2.3 g Poly, 0.6 g Sat); 45 mg Cholesterol; 15 g Carbohydrate; 5 g Fibre; 30 g Protein; 511 mg Sodium

Pictured on page 46 and left.

SPICED ROAST TURKEY

A traditional, spice-speckled bird that will be the centerpiece of your feast. No turkey dinner is complete without stuffing, so serve it with Herb and Fruit Stuffing, page 103. This recipe is part of a suggested menu on page 166.

Granulated sugar	1 tbsp.	15 mL
Ground cumin	1 1/2 tsp.	7 mL
Salt	1 tbsp.	15 mL
Pepper	1 1/2 tsp.	7 mL
Garlic powder	1 tsp.	5 mL
Ground allspice	3/4 tsp.	4 mL
Chopped onion	1 cup	250 mL
Whole turkey, giblets and neck removed (not self-basting)	12 lbs.	5.4 kg
Cooking oil	2 tbsp.	30 mL

Combine first 6 ingredients in small cup. Transfer 1 tbsp. (15 mL) to small bowl.

Add onion to same small bowl. Stir. Spoon into body cavity of turkey. Tie wings with butcher's string close to body. Tie legs to tail. Place on greased wire rack set in large roasting pan.

Add cooking oil to remaining spice mixture. Rub over surface of turkey. Cover with greased foil. Cook in 325°F (160°C) oven for 3 hours. Remove foil. Cook for about 30 minutes until browned and meat thermometer inserted in thickest part of thigh reaches 180°F (82°C). Transfer to cutting board. Remove and discard string. Cover with foil. Let stand for 20 minutes. Internal temperature should rise to at least 185°F (85°C). Serves 12.

1 serving: 571 Calories; 27.5 g Total Fat (9.6 g Mono, 7.1 g Poly, 7.5 g Sat); 212 mg Cholesterol; 3 g Carbohydrate; 1 g Fibre; 73 g Protein; 758 mg Sodium

Pictured on front cover, page 2 and at right.

Left: Harvest Chicken Chili, below; Right: Spiced Roast Turkey, left

HARVEST CHICKEN CHILI

A thick chicken chili that will please traditionalists, yet offers special appeal to the adventurous. Sweet corn, cranberries and spinach add personality to this dish. This recipe is part of a suggested menu on page 166.

Cooking oil	2 tsp.	10 mL
Lean ground chicken	1 1/2 lbs.	680 g
Chopped onion	1 cup	250 mL
Chili powder	2 tbsp.	30 mL
Garlic clove, minced (or 1/4 tsp., 1 mL, powder)	1	1
Ground cumin	1 tsp.	5 mL
Salt	3/4 tsp.	4 mL
Can of diced tomatoes (with juice)	28 oz.	796 mL
Can of black beans, rinsed and drained	19 oz.	540 mL
Cubed butternut squash (3/4 inch, 2 cm, pieces)	1 1/2 cups	375 mL
Frozen kernel corn	1/2 cup	125 mL
Prepared chicken broth	1/2 cup	125 mL
Tomato paste (see Tip, page 82)	2 tbsp.	30 mL
Ketchup	1 tbsp.	15 mL
Chopped fresh spinach leaves, lightly packed	2 cups	500 mL
Dried cranberries	1/2 cup	125 mL

Heat cooking oil in large frying pan on medium-high. Add chicken. Scramble-fry for about 5 minutes until no longer pink.

Add next 5 ingredients. Cook for about 5 minutes, stirring often, until onion is softened. Transfer to 4 to 5 quart (4 to 5 L) slow cooker.

Add next 7 ingredients. Stir. Cook, covered, on Low for 6 to 7 hours or on High for 3 to 3 1/2 hours.

Add spinach and cranberries. Stir. Makes about 9 1/2 cups (2.4 L).

1 cup (250 mL): 227 Calories; 7.4 g Total Fat (0.6 g Mono, 0.8 g Poly, 1.7 g Sat); 47 mg Cholesterol; 24 g Carbohydrate; 6 g Fibre; 17 g Protein; 663 mg Sodium

Pictured above.

If you know anyone who enjoys cross country skiing in the winter months, they may be interested in the legend behind the Birkebeiner ski race. The Birkebeiner is a major 55 km (34 mile) Nordic ski race held in only a few places in the world every year: between Lillehammer and Rena in Norway, in Haywood, Wisconsin, near Edmonton, Alberta and in Japan. It is run to remember two Birkebeiner warriors who, in 1206, risked their lives to rescue the very young prince of Norway from being killed in the civil war battles raging at that time. The Birkebeiners, so named because of the birch bark footwear they wore, carried the infant prince on their backs as they skied over two mountain ranges, from the Gudbrandsdal Valley near Lillehammer to the Osterdal Valley near Rena. Their dramatic flight is commemorated by thousands of skiers every year who ski a 55 km (34 mile) distance with a 3.5 kg (8 lb) weight on their backs to represent the young prince. The prince grew up to become King Haakon Haakonsson, who helped bring peace and prosperity to Norway.

Greek Bean Medley, right

GREEK BEAN MEDLEY

A comforting bean dish with the zing of fresh lemon, marinated artichokes and sharp feta, and it's quick to assemble, too. Serve it as a main course or bring it along as a potluck offering.

Cans of chickpeas (garbanzo beans),19 oz., 540 mL, each, rinsed and drained	2	2
Cans of romano beans (19 oz., 540 mL, each), rinsed and drained	2	2
Can of crushed tomatoes	14 oz.	398 mL
Can of diced tomatoes (with juice)	14 oz.	398 mL
Diced carrot	1 cup	250 mL
Diced fennel bulb (white part only)	1 cup	250 mL
Diced parsnip	1 cup	250 mL
Balsamic vinegar	2 tbsp.	30 mL
Greek seasoning	1 tbsp.	15 mL
Garlic cloves, minced (or 1/2 tsp., 2 mL, powder)	2	2
Salt	1/2 tsp.	2 mL
Pepper	1/8 tsp.	0.5 mL
Grated lemon zest	1 tsp.	5 mL
Jar of marinated artichoke hearts, drained and chopped	6 oz.	170 mL
Chopped tomato	1/3 cup	75 mL
Crumbled feta cheese	1/3 cup	75 mL
Chopped fresh parsley (or 3/4 tsp., 4 mL, flakes)	1 tbsp.	15 mL

Combine first 12 ingredients in 4 to 5 quart (4 to 5 L) slow cooker. Cook on Low for 6 to 8 hours or on High for 3 to 4 hours.

Add lemon zest. Stir. Transfer to serving bowl.

Scatter remaining 4 ingredients over top. Makes about 9 2/3 cups (2.4 L).

1 cup (250 mL): 253 Calories; 3.4 g Total Fat (0.7 g Mono, 1.1 g Poly, 0.9 g Sat); 5 mg Cholesterol; 44 g Carbohydrate; 14 g Fibre; 14 g Protein; 885 mg Sodium

Pictured at left.

LENTIL PASTA SAUCE

Loaded with delicious and nutritious lentils, this thick, rich sauce is great to use in lasagna, or to simply spoon over your favourite pasta. Store in an airtight container in the refrigerator for up to five days, or freeze it for up to six months.

Cooking oil	2 tsp.	10 mL
Chopped onion	2 cups	500 mL
Diced carrot	2 cups	500 mL
Diced celery	1 cup	250 mL
Dried basil	1 tbsp.	15 mL
Dried oregano	1 tbsp.	15 mL
Garlic powder	1 tsp.	5 mL
Prepared vegetable broth	4 cups	1 L
Water	1 cup	250 mL
Dried red split lentils, rinsed and drained	2 cups	500 mL

Can of crushed tomatoes	28 oz.	796 mL
Can of diced tomatoes (with juice)	28 oz.	796 mL
Can of tomato paste	5 1/2 oz.	156 mL
Granulated sugar	2 tsp.	10 mL
Salt	1/2 tsp.	2 mL
Pepper	1/2 tsp.	2 mL

Heat cooking oil in Dutch oven on medium. Add next 6 ingredients. Cook for about 15 minutes, stirring often, until onion is softened.

Add broth and water. Bring to a boil. Add lentils. Stir. Reduce heat to medium-low. Cook, covered, for about 20 minutes until lentils are tender.

Add remaining 6 ingredients. Stir. Bring to a boil on medium. Boil gently, covered, for 20 minutes, stirring occasionally, to blend flavours. Makes about 13 cups (3.25 L).

1 cup (250 mL): 187 Calories; 1.8 g Total Fat (0.5 g Mono, 0.4 g Poly, 0.1 g Sat); 0 mg Cholesterol; 33 g Carbohydrate; 8 g Fibre; 11 g Protein; 487 mg Sodium

Pictured below.

Lentil Pasta Sauce, above

BROCCOLI SOUFFLÉ

A lovely golden-brown soufflé that you can be proud to serve. The flavours of broccoli and Asiago blend well to create a creamy and light-tasting dish.

Finely grated Asiago cheese	1/4 cup	60 mL
Small broccoli florets	1 1/2 cups	375 mL
Salt	1/2 tsp.	5 mL
Ice water		
Finely chopped roasted red pepper	2 tbsp.	30 mL
Butter (or hard margarine)	1/4 cup	60 mL
All-purpose flour	1/4 cup	60 mL
Lemon pepper	1/2 tsp.	2 mL
Milk	1/2 cup	125 mL
Grated Asiago cheese	1/2 cup	125 mL
Egg whites (large), room temperature	4	4
Egg yolks (large)	4	4

Preheat oven to 325°F (160°C), see Note. Sprinkle greased 6 cup (1.5 L) soufflé dish with first amount of cheese until bottom and sides are coated. Set aside.

Pour water into small saucepan until about 1 inch (2.5 cm) deep. Bring to a boil. Reduce heat to medium. Add broccoli and salt. Boil gently, covered, for about 2 minutes until bright green. Drain.

Plunge broccoli into ice water in small bowl. Let stand for 10 minutes until cold. Drain well. Transfer to cutting board. Chop coarsely. Transfer to medium bowl.

Add red pepper. Stir.

Melt butter in medium saucepan on medium. Add flour and lemon pepper. Heat and stir for 1 minute. Slowly add milk, stirring constantly until boiling and thickened. Remove from heat.

Add second amount of cheese. Stir until smooth. Add to broccoli mixture. Stir.

Beat egg whites in separate medium bowl until stiff peaks form.

Beat egg yolks with same beaters in separate small bowl until frothy. Add to broccoli mixture. Stir. Fold in egg whites until just combined. Carefully pour into prepared dish. Bake for about 50 minutes until puffed and golden. Serve immediately. Serves 4.

1 serving: 309 Calories; 23.0 g Total Fat (5.0 g Mono, 1.2 g Poly, 12.7 g Sat); 256 mg Cholesterol; 11 g Carbohydrate; 1 g Fibre; 14 g Protein; 481 mg Sodium

Pictured below.

NOTE: A preheated oven contributes to a soufflé rising successfully. Once the soufflé is prepared, immediately place it in preheated oven to help preserve its "breath." Do not open the door while the soufflé is baking.

Broccoli Soufflé, above

CHEESY GARDEN MACARONI

This fusion of two classic dishes—macaroni and cheese and vegetables au gratin—creates an attractive, crumb-topped casserole full of vegetables harvested from the garden. This recipe is part of a suggested menu on page 166.

Water	10 cups	2.5 L
Salt	1 tsp.	5 mL
Elbow macaroni	2 cups	500 mL
Sliced carrot	1 cup	250 mL
Chopped broccoli	1 cup	250 mL
Chopped cauliflower	1 cup	250 mL
Frozen kernel corn	1 cup	250 mL
Butter (or hard margarine)	3 tbsp.	50 mL
All-purpose flour	3 tbsp.	50 mL
Dried crushed chilies (optional)	1/2 tsp.	2 mL
Salt	1/4 tsp.	1 mL
Milk	2 1/2 cups	625 mL
Grated sharp Cheddar cheese	2 cups	500 mL
Fine dry bread crumbs	1/3 cup	75 mL
Grated Parmesan cheese	1/4 cup	60 mL
Butter (or hard margarine), melted	2 tbsp.	30 mL

Combine water and salt in Dutch oven. Bring to a boil. Add pasta and carrot. Cook, uncovered, for 6 minutes until carrot is tender-crisp.

Add next 3 ingredients. Bring to a boil. Cook, uncovered, for about 3 minutes until pasta is tender but firm. Drain. Return to same pot. Cover to keep warm.

Melt butter in large saucepan on medium. Add next 3 ingredients. Heat and stir for 1 minute. Slowly add milk, stirring constantly until smooth. Heat and stir for about 5 minutes until boiling and thickened. Remove from heat.

Add Cheddar cheese. Stir until smooth. Pour over pasta mixture. Stir until coated. Transfer to greased 3 quart (3 L) casserole.

Combine remaining 3 ingredients in small bowl. Sprinkle over top. Bake in 350°F (175°C) oven for about 25 minutes until golden. Makes about 8 cups (2 L).

1 cup (250 mL): 391 Calories; 19.1 g Total Fat (4.9 g Mono, 0.7 g Poly, 11.5 g Sat); 56 mg Cholesterol; 38 g Carbohydrate; 3 g Fibre; 17 g Protein; 457 mg Sodium

Pictured at right.

Cheesy Garden Macaroni, left

THE KIDS' TABLE

Autumn and winter are usually great seasons for family gatherings, which might make you a little nostalgic for one of the fun traditions of the big family dinner—the kids' table. It might have involved Grandma spreading a blanket on the living room floor and treating the kids to an indoor picnic while they watched their favourite shows. Mom and Dad might have set up a special table in a separate room or the basement, where all the kids could eat, play and socialize without having the boring adults around! Wherever and however it was done, the kids' table is a fond memory for many, recalling a casual and laid-back time in life when all there was to do was stuff yourself silly with food and laugh and have a good time with your friends.

ZUCCHINI LASAGNA

The abundant zucchini from your garden replaces noodles in this meatless option for lasagna lovers! It's rich and filling with tomato sauce, satisfying lentils and, of course, plenty of melted cheese.

Medium zucchini (with peel), cut diagonally into 1/4 inch (6 mm) slices	2	2
Salt, sprinkle		
Cooking oil	2 tsp.	10 mL
Cooking oil	1 tbsp.	15 mL
Chopped onion	2 cups	500 mL
Finely chopped fresh white mushrooms	1 1/2 cups	375 mL
Garlic cloves, minced (or 1/2 tsp., 2 mL, powder)	2	2
Dried crushed chilies	1/2 tsp.	2 mL
Salt	1/2 tsp.	2 mL
Pepper	1/2 tsp.	2 mL
Can of tomato sauce	25 oz.	680 mL
Can of lentils, rinsed and drained	19 oz.	540 mL
Package of veggie ground round (see Note)	12 oz.	340 g
Tomato paste (see Tip, right)	1/4 cup	60 mL
Medium sherry	2 tbsp.	30 mL
Chopped fresh thyme (or 3/4 tsp., 4 mL, dried)	1 tbsp.	15 mL
Large eggs	2	2
Ricotta cheese	3 cups	750 mL
Chopped fresh parsley (or 1 tsp., 5 mL, flakes)	1/4 cup	60 mL
Ground nutmeg	1/8 tsp.	0.5 mL
Grated mozzarella cheese	2 cups	500 mL
Grated Asiago cheese	1/2 cup	125 mL

Sprinkle both sides of zucchini slices with salt. Arrange on wire rack set in baking sheet with sides. Let stand for 20 minutes. Rinse. Blot dry.

Brush both sides of zucchini slices with first amount of cooking oil. Arrange in single layer on greased baking sheets with sides. Broil on top rack in oven for about 10 minutes until golden. Turn. Broil for about 5 minutes until golden.

Heat second amount of cooking oil in large frying pan on medium. Add next 6 ingredients. Cook for about 12 minutes, stirring often, until onion is softened and liquid is evaporated.

Add next 6 ingredients. Stir. Heat for about 5 minutes until heated through.

Combine next 4 ingredients in medium bowl. To assemble, layer ingredients in greased 9 x 13 inch (23 x 33 cm) baking dish as follows:

1. Half of tomato sauce mixture

2. 1/3 of ricotta cheese mixture

3. Half of zucchini slices

4. Remaining tomato sauce mixture

5. 1/3 of ricotta cheese mixture

6. Remaining zucchini slices

7. Remaining ricotta cheese mixture

Sprinkle with mozzarella and Asiago cheese. Bake, uncovered, in 350°F (175°C) oven for about 45 minutes until heated through and cheese is melted and golden. Let stand for 10 minutes. Cuts into 12 pieces.

1 piece: 288 Calories; 12.5 g Total Fat (1.5 g Mono, 0.8 g Poly, 6.4 g Sat); 68 mg Cholesterol; 18 g Carbohydrate; 6 g Fibre; 25 g Protein; 921 mg Sodium

Pictured at right.

TIP

Try freezing tomato paste for 30 minutes before opening both ends and pushing the tube out. You'll be able to slice off what you need and wrap the rest for later.

Left: Zucchini Lasagna, left; Right: Mexican "Spaghetti" and Sauce, below

MEXICAN "SPAGHETTI" AND SAUCE

This fun and unique recipe makes a large portion—perfect for casual entertaining! Spaghetti squash is topped with spicy Mexican tomato sauce and a savoury sprinkling of cilantro.

Spaghetti squash	3 lbs.	1.4 kg
Water	2 tbsp.	30 mL
Cooking oil	1 tbsp.	15 mL
Chopped red onion	1 cup	250 mL
Diced red pepper	1 cup	250 mL
Fresh (or frozen, thawed) kernel corn	1 cup	250 mL
Chili powder	1 tbsp.	15 mL
Ground cumin	1 1/2 tsp	7 mL
Garlic clove, minced (or 1/4 tsp., 1 mL, powder)	1	1
Salt	1/2 tsp.	2 mL
Cayenne pepper	1/8 tsp.	0.5 mL
Can of diced tomatoes (with juice)	28 oz.	796 mL
Canned black beans, rinsed and drained	1 cup	250 mL
Grated jalapeño Monterey Jack cheese	2 cups	500 mL
Chopped fresh cilantro (or parsley)	2 tbsp.	30 mL

Cut squash in half lengthwise. Remove seeds. Place, cut-side down, in large ungreased microwave-safe 2 quart (2 L) casserole. Add water. Microwave, covered, on High for about 15 minutes until tender (see Tip, page 136). Drain. Shred squash pulp with fork. Transfer to serving platter. Cover to keep warm. Discard shells.

Heat cooking oil in large frying pan on medium. Add next 8 ingredients. Cook for about 10 minutes, stirring often, until onion is softened.

Add tomatoes and beans. Stir. Cook for about 5 minutes, stirring occasionally, until heated through.

Sprinkle squash with cheese. Spoon tomato mixture over top. Sprinkle with cilantro. Makes about 10 cups (2.5 L).

1 cup (250 mL): 171 Calories; 9.3 g Total Fat (0.9 g Mono, 0.8 g Poly, 4.2 g Sat); 20 mg Cholesterol; 16 g Carbohydrate; 3 g Fibre; 8 g Protein; 545 mg Sodium

Pictured above.

Red Pepper Quiche

A classic, colourful quiche with an abundance of red pepper, tomato and sharp Gruyère—the result is a family-friendly brunch item to please everyone in your crowd. Try serving with a tossed salad to round out the meal.

Pastry for 9 inch (23 cm) deep dish pie shell		
Grated Gruyére (or Swiss) cheese	1 cup	250 mL
Cooking oil	1 tsp.	5 mL
Chopped onion	1 cup	250 mL
Garlic cloves, minced (or 1/2 tsp., 2 mL, powder)	2	2
Chopped roasted red pepper, blotted dry	1/2 cup	125 mL
Chopped seeded tomato	1/2 cup	125 mL
Large eggs	4	4
Half-and-half cream	1 cup	250 mL
Chopped fresh parsley (or 3/4 tsp., 4 mL, flakes)	1 tbsp.	15 mL
Salt	1/4 tsp.	1 mL
Pepper	1/4 tsp.	1 mL

Roll out pastry on lightly floured surface to 1/8 inch (3 mm) thickness. Line 9 inch (23 cm) deep dish pie plate with pastry. Trim, leaving 1/2 inch (12 mm) overhang. Roll under and crimp decorative edge. Sprinkle cheese into pie shell.

Heat cooking oil in medium frying pan on medium. Add onion and garlic. Cook for about 5 minutes, stirring often, until onion is softened. Transfer to small bowl. Let stand for 10 minutes.

Add red pepper and tomato. Stir. Scatter over cheese.

Whisk remaining 5 ingredients in medium bowl. Pour over onion mixture. Bake on bottom rack in 375°F (190°C) oven for about 50 minutes until knife inserted in centre comes out clean. Cuts into 6 wedges.

1 wedge: 370 Calories; 23.9 g Total Fat (4.9 g Mono, 1.2 g Poly, 11.4 g Sat); 182 mg Cholesterol; 25 g Carbohydrate; 1 g Fibre; 13 g Protein; 450 mg Sodium

Pictured at left.

Stuffed Acorn Squash

Guests will delight in these charming stuffed squash. The delicious dark stuffing is seasoned with sage and packed with sweet and crunchy cranberries and seeds. This recipe is part of a suggested menu on page 166.

Acorn squash (about 1 1/2 lbs., 680 g, each)	4	4
Pumpernickel bread cubes	7 cups	1.75 L
Dried cranberries	1/2 cup	125 mL
Chopped raw cashews, toasted (see Tip, page 93)	1/4 cup	60 mL
Raw pumpkin seeds, toasted (see Tip, page 93)	1/4 cup	60 mL
Raw sunflower seeds, toasted (see Tip, page 93)	1/4 cup	60 mL
Chopped fresh sage (or 1 tsp., 5 mL, dried)	4 tsp.	20 mL
Chopped fresh rosemary (or 3/4 tsp., 4 mL, dried)	1 tbsp.	15 mL
Chopped fresh thyme (or 1/2 tsp., 2 mL, dried)	2 tsp.	10 mL
Butter (or hard margarine)	1/4 cup	60 mL
Cooking oil	2 tbsp.	30 mL
Chopped onion	1 cup	250 mL
Finely chopped celery	2/3 cup	150 mL
Salt	1/2 tsp.	2 mL
Coarsely ground pepper	1/2 tsp.	2 mL
White wine vinegar	1 tbsp.	15 mL
Garlic clove, minced (or 1/4 tsp., 1 mL, powder)	1	1

Cut 1 1/2 inches (3.8 cm) off stem end of each squash. Set aside. Remove and discard seeds. Trim opposite end of each squash to make flat, without piercing cavity. Arrange squash, trimmed-side down, on greased baking sheet with sides.

Combine next 8 ingredients in large bowl.

Heat butter and cooking oil in large frying pan on medium. Add next 4 ingredients. Cook for about 8 minutes, stirring often, until onion is softened.

Add vinegar and garlic. Heat and stir for about 1 minute until garlic is fragrant. Add to bread mixture. Mix well. Pack each squash with bread mixture. Replace stem ends. Cook in 400°F (205°C) oven for about 1 hour until squash is tender. Makes 4 stuffed squash.

1 stuffed squash: 733 Calories; 33.0 g Total Fat (7.3 g Mono, 3.1 g Poly, 10.3 g Sat); 30 mg Cholesterol; 107 g Carbohydrate; 15 g Fibre; 15 g Protein; 614 mg Sodium

Pictured on page 1 and at left.

Top: Stuffed Acorn Squash, above
Bottom: Red Pepper Quiche, above

Garlic Mashed Potatoes, page 93

SIDES

Humble side dishes are no longer the unsung heroes of the dinner table. Richly flavoured and vibrant sides are where your garden-fresh fruits and vegetables really get a chance to shine, in all their colour and variety. Most of these side dishes are prepared with a light hand, simply enhancing the natural flavours of fresh ingredients. Create delicious accompaniments to complement your main course, and enjoy a seasonal feast that's bound to impress.

POTATO KOHLRABI SCALLOP

Delicious and cheesy with classic Italian flavours.
A traditional offering made unique with a harvest
vegetable you may not have tried. This recipe is part of
a suggested menu on page 166.

Butter (or hard margarine)	2 tbsp.	30 mL
Chopped onion	1/2 cup	125 mL
Italian seasoning	1 tsp.	5 mL
All-purpose flour	2 tbsp.	30 mL
Salt	1/4 tsp.	1 mL
Pepper	1/4 tsp.	1 mL
Milk	1 3/4 cups	425 mL
Grated Italian cheese blend	1 cup	250 mL
Thinly sliced peeled baking potato (see Note)	2 1/4 cups	550 mL
Thinly sliced kohlrabi (see Note)	1 1/2 cups	375 mL
Grated Italian cheese blend	1 cup	250 mL

Melt butter in medium saucepan on medium. Add onion and Italian seasoning. Cook for about 5 minutes, stirring often, until onion is softened.

Add next 3 ingredients. Heat and stir for 1 minute. Slowly add milk, whisking constantly until smooth. Heat and stir for about 3 minutes until boiling and thickened.

Add first amount of cheese. Remove from heat. Stir until cheese is melted.

Combine potato, kohlrabi and cheese mixture in large bowl. Spoon into greased 2 quart (2 L) casserole.

Sprinkle second amount of cheese over top. Cook, covered, in 350°F (175°C) oven for about 1 hour until potato is tender. Cook, uncovered, for about 10 minutes until golden. Let stand for 5 minutes. Serves 6.

1 serving: *195 Calories; 6.7 g Total Fat (1.3 g Mono, 0.2 g Poly, 4.2 g Sat); 21 mg Cholesterol; 20 g Carbohydrate; 3 g Fibre; 16 g Protein; 459 mg Sodium*

Pictured below.

NOTE: Evenly sliced vegetables are one of the secrets to a good scallop. Use a mandoline slicer or food processor to ensure equal thickness.

Potato Kohlrabi Scallop, above

CELERY ROOT PURÉE

A unique stand-in for the usual mashed potatoes. This simple recipe allows celery root's delicate flavour to come through in a light and creamy purée.

Chopped celery root	7 cups	1.75 L
Chopped peeled potato	3 cups	750 mL
Milk	1/2 cup	125 mL
Butter (or hard margarine)	1/4 cup	60 mL
Salt	1/2 tsp.	2 mL
White pepper (or black), sprinkle		

Pour water into Dutch oven until about 1 inch (2.5 cm) deep. Add celery root and potato. Bring to a boil. Reduce heat to medium. Boil gently, covered, for 12 to 15 minutes until tender. Drain. Cover to keep warm.

Combine remaining 4 ingredients in small saucepan. Bring to a boil. Add to celery root mixture. Stir. Carefully process in food processor in batches until smooth (see Safety Tip, below). Makes about 6 1/2 cups (1.6 L).

1 cup (250 mL): *200 Calories; 7.8 g Total Fat (2.0 g Mono, 0.5 g Poly, 4.7 g Sat); 20 mg Cholesterol; 30 g Carbohydrate; 4 g Fibre; 4 g Protein; 572 mg Sodium*

Pictured below.

SAFETY TIP: Follow manufacturer's instructions for processing hot liquids.

Celery Root Purée, above

Autumn Dijon Vegetables, below

AUTUMN DIJON VEGETABLES

Colourful and deliciously roasted root vegetables are mixed with flavourful mustard and fresh chives for a delightful, seasonal side.

Chopped peeled orange-fleshed sweet potato (3/4 inch, 2 cm, pieces)	3 1/2 cups	875 mL
Chopped yellow turnip (rutabaga), 3/4 inch (2 cm) pieces	3 cups	750 mL
Chopped fennel bulb (white part only), 3/4 inch (2 cm) pieces	2 1/2 cups	625 mL
Chopped unpeeled tart apple (such as Granny Smith), 1/2 inch (12 mm) pieces	1 3/4 cups	425 mL
Cooking oil	1 tbsp.	15 mL
Salt	1/4 tsp.	1 mL
Pepper	1/8 tsp.	0.5 mL
Water	3/4 cup	175 mL
Dijon mustard	3 tbsp.	50 mL
Chopped fresh chives (or 3/4 tsp., 4 mL, dried)	1 tbsp.	15 mL

Combine first 7 ingredients in large bowl. Spread in greased 9 x 13 inch (23 x 33 cm) baking dish.

Pour water over vegetable mixture. Cook, covered, in 350°F (175°C) oven for 45 minutes. Remove cover. Cook for about 45 minutes, stirring occasionally, until vegetables are tender and lightly browned.

Add mustard and chives. Stir until coated. Makes about 6 cups (1.5 L).

1 cup (250 mL): 136 Calories; 2.6 g Total Fat (1.4 g Mono, 0.8 g Poly, 0.2 g Sat); 0 mg Cholesterol; 28 g Carbohydrate; 6 g Fibre; 2 g Protein; 300 mg Sodium

Pictured above.

TOMATO ZUCCHINI LINGUINE

A simple yet flavourful side that's rich with herbs, Parmesan cheese and toothsome veggie morsels. Throw it together with fresh tomatoes and zucchini from your garden for the best possible flavour.

Water	12 cups	3 L
Salt	1 1/2 tsp.	7 mL
Linguine	8 oz.	225 g
Olive (or cooking) oil	1 tbsp.	15 mL
Garlic cloves, minced (or 1/2 tsp., 2 mL, powder)	2	2
Diced tomato	2 cups	500 mL
Sliced zucchini (with peel), halved lengthwise and sliced crosswise	2 cups	500 mL
Sliced fresh white mushrooms	1 cup	250 mL
Dried basil	1 tsp.	5 mL
Dried oregano	1 tsp.	5 mL
Dried marjoram	1/2 tsp.	2 mL
Salt	1/2 tsp.	2 mL
Pepper	1/4 tsp.	1 mL
Grated Parmesan cheese	1/4 cup	60 mL

Combine water and salt in Dutch oven. Bring to a boil. Add pasta. Boil, uncovered, for 9 to 11 minutes, stirring occasionally, until tender but firm. Drain. Return to same pot. Cover to keep warm.

Heat olive oil in large frying pan on medium. Add garlic. Heat and stir for about 30 seconds until fragrant.

Add next 8 ingredients. Cook for about 7 minutes, stirring occasionally, until mushrooms and zucchini are softened. Add to pasta. Toss.

Sprinkle with cheese. Makes about 6 cups (1.5 L).

1 cup (250 mL): 201 Calories; 4.5 g Total Fat (1.4 g Mono, 0.8 g Poly, 1.0 g Sat); 3 mg Cholesterol; 3 g Carbohydrate; 3 g Fibre; 9 g Protein; 287 mg Sodium

Pictured at left.

NUTTY LENTILS AND WHEAT

Earthy flavours of lentils and wheat berries are combined with sweet apricot. Serve this lovely textured side with roasted game, pork or ham, or broiled fish. This recipe is part of a suggested menu on page 166.

Water	1 1/2 cups	375 mL
Salt	1/8 tsp.	0.5 mL
Hard red wheat, soaked in water overnight and drained	1/2 cup	125 mL
Cooking oil	2 tsp.	10 mL
Chopped onion	1 cup	250 mL
Finely diced carrot	1 cup	250 mL
Finely diced celery	1 cup	250 mL
Chopped fresh sage (or 1/4 tsp., 1 mL, dried)	1 tsp.	5 mL
Chopped fresh thyme (or 1/4 tsp., 1 mL, dried)	1 tsp.	5 mL
Salt	1/2 tsp.	2 mL
Pepper	1/8 tsp.	0.5 mL
Can of lentils, rinsed and drained	19 oz.	540 mL
Chopped dried apricot	1/2 cup	125 mL
Slivered almonds, toasted (see Tip, page 93)	1/2 cup	125 mL
Sliced green onion	1/4 cup	60 mL

Combine water and first amount of salt in small saucepan. Bring to a boil. Add wheat. Stir. Reduce heat to medium-low. Simmer, covered, for about 1 1/2 hours, without stirring, until wheat is tender. Cover to keep warm.

Heat cooking oil in large frying pan on medium. Add next 7 ingredients. Cook for about 10 minutes, stirring often, until vegetables are tender.

Add remaining 4 ingredients and wheat. Heat and stir for about 2 minutes until heated through. Makes about 5 1/4 cups (1.3 L).

1 cup (250 mL): 274 Calories; 6.8 g Total Fat (4.0 g Mono, 1.8 g Poly, 0.6 g Sat); 0 mg Cholesterol; 43 g Carbohydrate; 13 g Fibre; 12 g Protein; 434 mg Sodium

Pictured at left.

Top: Nutty Lentils and Wheat, above
Bottom: Tomato Zucchini Linguine, above

WILD RICE MEDLEY

Enjoy the natural nuttiness of wild rice enhanced with vegetables, bacon and a little Asian accent. A show-stopping side dish for roasted or braised meats.

Water	2 cups	500 mL
Salt	1/8 tsp.	0.5 mL
Wild rice	2/3 cup	150 mL
Bacon slices, chopped	4	4
Chopped fresh white mushrooms	2 cups	500 mL
Chopped onion	1 cup	250 mL
Diced carrot	1 cup	250 mL
Diced celery	1 cup	250 mL
Hoisin sauce	2 tbsp.	30 mL
Finely grated ginger root (or 3/4 tsp., 4 mL, ground ginger)	1 tbsp.	15 mL
Soy sauce	1 tbsp.	15 mL
Dried crushed chilies, just a pinch		
Raw pumpkin seeds, toasted (see Tip, right)	1/4 cup	60 mL

Combine water and salt in small saucepan. Bring to a boil. Add rice. Stir. Reduce heat to medium-low. Simmer, covered, for about 1 hour and 10 minutes, without stirring, until rice is tender. Drain any remaining liquid.

Cook bacon in large frying pan on medium until crisp. Transfer with slotted spoon to paper towel-lined plate to drain. Drain and discard all but 1 tbsp. (15 mL) drippings.

Add next 8 ingredients. Cook on medium-high for about 7 minutes, stirring often, until carrot is tender-crisp and liquid is almost evaporated. Add rice. Heat and stir for 1 minute. Transfer to serving bowl.

Sprinkle with pumpkin seeds and bacon. Makes about 5 cups (1.25 L).

1 cup (250 mL): 235 Calories; 9.4 g Total Fat (2.2 g Mono, 0.8 g Poly, 2.4 g Sat); 8 mg Cholesterol; 31 g Carbohydrate; 3 g Fibre; 9 g Protein; 702 mg Sodium

Pictured below.

Wild Rice Medley, above

Garlic Mashed Potatoes, below

GARLIC MASHED POTATOES

Smooth, creamy potatoes lightly seasoned with savoury garlic—a classic side that always has a place at family gatherings.

Chopped peeled potato	6 cups	1.5 L
Butter (or hard margarine)	1/4 cup	60 mL
Garlic cloves, minced	6	6
Milk	1/3 cup	75 mL
Salt	1/2 tsp.	2 mL

Pour water into large saucepan until about 1 inch (2.5 cm) deep. Add potato. Bring to a boil. Reduce heat to medium. Boil gently, covered, for 12 to 15 minutes until tender. Drain. Mash. Cover to keep warm.

Melt butter in small frying pan on medium. Add garlic. Heat and stir for 3 to 5 minutes until garlic is softened and fragrant.

Add milk and salt. Heat and stir until heated through. Add to potato. Stir. Makes about 4 1/2 cups (1.1 L).

1 cup (250 mL): 238 Calories; 10.3 g Total Fat (2.7 g Mono, 0.4 g Poly, 6.5 g Sat); 28 mg Cholesterol; 37 g Carbohydrate; 4 g Fibre; 6 g Protein; 340 mg Sodium

Pictured on page 86 and above.

Maple Sprouts

Browned, roasted Brussels sprouts are tossed with tart lemon and maple syrup for a simple and inviting addition to the harvest table. This recipe is part of a suggested menu on page 166.

Fresh Brussels sprouts, trimmed, larger ones halved	4 cups	1 L
Cooking oil	1 tbsp.	15 mL
Salt	1/2 tsp.	2 mL
Pepper	1/4 tsp.	1 mL
Maple syrup	1 tbsp.	15 mL
Lemon juice	2 tsp.	10 mL

Toss first 4 ingredients in large bowl. Arrange in single layer on greased baking sheet with sides. Cook in 400°F (205°C) oven for about 20 minutes, stirring occasionally, until tender and starting to brown. Return to same large bowl.

Add maple syrup and lemon juice. Toss until coated. Makes about 3 cups (750 mL).

1 cup (250 mL): 110 Calories; 5.0 g Total Fat (2.8 g Mono, 1.6 g Poly, 0.4 g Sat); 0 mg Cholesterol; 15 g Carbohydrate; 5 g Fibre; 4 g Protein; 418 mg Sodium

Pictured at right.

A Celebration of Survival

Sukkot (meaning huts or booths) is a seven-day religious harvest festival that commemorates the years that the Jews spent journeying through the desert on their way to the Promised Land, and celebrates the way God protected them under difficult conditions. Its origins are in the Hebrew Book of Leviticus. During the festival, huts are erected in synagogues and in people's gardens, and families gather in them to share meals and to sleep. It is important that the hut have a roof of branches and leaves and be quite flimsy and open to the sky to remind people both of their vulnerability to the elements and of their faith in God to keep them safe. Celebrants also take branches of four different plants (citron, palm, myrtle and willow) and wave and shake them around as they rejoice. Sukkot is said to be a way to acknowledge living with fear and insecurity and yet still be able to celebrate life. This festival also recollects the shelters shepherds and farmers lived in during the harvesting of grapes and fruits in ancient times.

Root Vegetable Latkes

Tender, golden potato and veggie cakes make a versatile side. Enlist the aid of your food processor to make light work of the prep, and garnish with sour cream or applesauce.

Grated peeled potato	1 1/2 cups	375 mL
Grated carrot	3/4 cup	175 mL
Grated parsnip	3/4 cup	175 mL
Large egg, fork-beaten	1	1
All-purpose flour	1/4 cup	60 mL
Lemon juice	1 1/2 tsp.	7 mL
Small garlic clove, minced (or 1/8 tsp., 0.5 mL, powder)	1	1
Dried thyme	1/4 tsp.	1 mL
Salt	1/4 tsp.	1 mL
Pepper	1/8 tsp.	0.5 mL
Cooking oil	1/4 cup	60 mL

Combine first 3 ingredients in fine sieve. Let stand over medium bowl for 15 minutes. Squeeze potato mixture to remove excess moisture. Transfer to large bowl.

Combine next 7 ingredients in small bowl. Add to potato mixture. Stir well.

Heat 2 tbsp. (30 mL) cooking oil in large frying pan on medium. Drop 4 portions of potato mixture into pan, using 1/4 cup (60 mL) for each. Press down lightly to 3 inch (7.5 cm) rounds. Cook for 3 to 4 minutes per side until browned. Transfer to paper towel-lined plate to drain. Cover to keep warm. Repeat with remaining cooking oil and potato mixture. Makes 8 latkes.

1 latke: 99 Calories; 4.2 g Total Fat (2.3 g Mono, 1.1 g Poly, 0.5 g Sat); 26 mg Cholesterol; 15 g Carbohydrate; 2 g Fibre; 3 g Protein; 90 mg Sodium

Pictured at right.

Top: Maple Sprouts, above;
Bottom: Root Vegetable Latkes, above

GLAZED CARROTS AND PARSNIPS

A classic side dish with a tangy-sweet glaze and savoury hints of thyme. Serve alongside roasted meats.

Sliced carrot	3 cups	750 mL
Sliced parsnip	3 cups	750 mL
Brown sugar, packed	3 tbsp.	50 mL
Butter (or hard margarine)	3 tbsp.	50 mL
Balsamic vinegar	4 tsp.	20 mL
Finely chopped fresh thyme	2 tsp.	10 mL
(or 1/2 tsp., 2 mL, dried)		

Pour water into large saucepan until about 1 inch (2.5 cm) deep. Add carrot and parsnip. Bring to a boil. Reduce heat to medium. Boil gently, covered, for about 10 minutes until tender-crisp. Drain. Return to same pot on medium.

Add remaining 4 ingredients. Heat and stir until sugar is dissolved and vegetables are coated. Makes about 5 cups (1.25 L).

1 cup (250 mL): *182 Calories; 7.2 g Total Fat (1.9 g Mono, 0.4 g Poly, 4.4 g Sat); 18 mg Cholesterol; 30 g Carbohydrate; 6 g Fibre; 2 g Protein; 111 mg Sodium*

Pictured below.

FINNISH CHRISTMAS SAUNAS

Although many Finns partake of saunas at all times of the year, having a sauna in preparation for Christmas Eve is a special Finnish winter tradition. It is common for a family to have a light lunch first, then go to the sauna and afterwards have a quick, bracing dip in a nearby lake or a roll in the snow! The sauna allows the whole family to socialize, bathe and relax before settling down with guests to a festive Christmas Eve dinner later in the evening.

Glazed Carrots and Parsnips, above

POLENTA SPINACH TRIANGLES

These colourful triangles make a bold statement, and have big flavour to match. Spinach and Asiago cheese blend with tender, grainy polenta for a tasty combination.

Prepared vegetable broth	4 cups	1 L
Yellow cornmeal	1 1/2 cups	375 mL
Salt	1/8 tsp.	0.5 mL
Pepper	1/2 tsp.	2 mL
Chopped fresh spinach leaves, lightly packed	2 cups	500 mL
Grated Asiago cheese	3/4 cup	175 mL
Chopped fresh oregano (or 1/8 tsp., 0.5 mL, dried)	1/2 tsp.	2 mL
Finely chopped fresh rosemary (or 1/8 tsp., 0.5 mL, dried, crushed)	1/2 tsp.	2 mL
Cooking oil	1 tsp.	5 mL

Bring broth to a boil in large saucepan. Reduce heat to medium. Add next 3 ingredients. Cook for about 5 minutes, whisking constantly, until mixture thickens and pulls away from side of pan.

Add next 4 ingredients. Stir. Spread in greased foil-lined 9 x 9 inch (23 x 23 cm) baking pan. Let stand for about 30 minutes until set. Invert onto cutting board. Cut into 4 squares. Cut squares into triangles. Transfer to greased baking sheet with sides.

Brush with cooking oil. Broil on top rack in oven for about 5 minutes per side until golden. Makes 8 triangles.

1 triangle: 155 Calories; 4.7 g Total Fat (0.5 g Mono, 0.4 g Poly, 2.0 g Sat); 9 mg Cholesterol; 25 g Carbohydrate; 2 g Fibre; 5 g Protein; 374 mg Sodium

Pictured above.

Dressed-Up Vegetable Medley, below

DRESSED-UP VEGETABLE MEDLEY

A slow-cooked blend of late-harvested veggies with a hint of spice and zesty lemon. Throw them in the slow cooker and you've got all afternoon (and space in the oven!) to prepare the rest of your meal.

Cooking oil	3 tbsp.	50 mL
Liquid honey	1 tbsp.	15 mL
Finely grated ginger root (or 1/4 tsp., 1 mL, ground ginger)	1 tsp.	5 mL
Garlic clove, minced (or 1/4 tsp., 1 mL, powder)	1	1
Salt	1 1/4 tsp.	11 mL
Coarsely ground pepper	1/2 tsp.	2 mL
Ground coriander	1/2 tsp.	2 mL
Ground cumin	1/2 tsp.	2 mL
Sliced carrot (1/2 inch, 12 mm, slices)	3 cups	750 mL
Sliced parsnip (1/2 inch, 12 mm, slices)	3 cups	750 mL
Small onions, quartered (roots intact)	4	4
Cubed yellow turnip (rutabaga)	5 cups	1.25 L
Lemon juice	1 tbsp.	15 mL
Chopped fresh parsley	1/4 cup	60 mL

Combine first 8 ingredients in small cup. Transfer 2 tbsp. (30 mL) to large bowl.

Add carrot and parsnip. Toss until coated. Transfer to greased 4 to 5 quart (4 to 5 L) slow cooker.

Add onion and 1 tbsp. (15 mL) cooking oil mixture to same large bowl. Toss until coated. Arrange over parsnip mixture.

Add turnip and remaining cooking oil mixture to same large bowl. Toss until coated. Arrange over onion. Do not stir. Cook, covered, on High for 4 to 4 1/2 hours until vegetables are tender. Transfer with slotted spoon to serving bowl. Discard cooking liquid.

Drizzle with lemon juice. Sprinkle with parsley. Makes about 11 cups (2.75 L).

1 cup (250 mL): 91 Calories; 2.2 g Total Fat (1.2 g Mono, 0.7 g Poly, 0.2 g Sat); 0 mg Cholesterol; 17 g Carbohydrate; 4 g Fibre; 2 g Protein; 333 mg Sodium

Pictured above.

PUMPKIN GNOCCHI

These attractive gnocchi (pronounced NYOH-kee) are the same colour as fallen leaves—something different for Sunday dinner in the fall or winter. Delicious served with tomato sauce, or simply tossed with butter and herbs.

Medium unpeeled baking potato (about 1/2 lb., 225 g)	1	1
Canned pure pumpkin (no spices), see Tip, page 23	3/4 cup	175 mL
Garlic powder	1/8 tsp.	0.5 mL
Ground nutmeg	1/8 tsp.	0.5 mL
Salt	1/8 tsp.	0.5 mL
Pepper	1/8 tsp.	0.5 mL
All-purpose flour	3/4 cup	175 mL
Water	8 cups	2 L
Salt	2 tsp.	10 mL

Prick potato in several places with fork. Microwave, uncovered, on High for about 8 minutes, turning at halftime, until tender (see Tip, page 136). Wrap in tea towel. Let stand for 5 minutes. Unwrap. Let stand until cool enough to handle. Cut potato in half lengthwise. Scoop pulp into large bowl. Discard shells. Mash pulp (see Note 1). Let stand for about 8 minutes until lukewarm. Make a well in centre.

Add next 5 ingredients to well. Stir.

Add flour, 1/4 cup (60 mL) at a time, mixing lightly with fork until soft dough forms. Turn out onto lightly floured surface. Knead gently 6 times until ball forms. Divide into 4 portions. Roll 1 portion into 3/4 inch (2 cm) thick rope, keeping remaining portions covered. Cut into 1/2 inch (12 mm) pieces. Arrange gnocchi in single layer on lightly floured baking sheet. Repeat with remaining portions. Makes about 96 gnocchi (see Note 2).

Combine water and second amount of salt in Dutch oven. Bring to a boil. Cook gnocchi in 2 batches, for about 2 minutes, stirring occasionally, until gnocchi float to top. Cook for 1 minute. Remove with slotted spoon to sieve. Drain. Transfer to serving bowl. Makes about 3 cups (750 mL).

1 cup (250 mL): 173 Calories; 0.2 g Total Fat (trace Mono, trace Poly, 0.1 g Sat); 0 mg Cholesterol; 40 g Carbohydrate; 4 g Fibre; 6 g Protein; 100 mg Sodium

Pictured below.

NOTE 1: The finer and fluffier you can mash the cooked potato, the better the texture of the gnocchi. Try running them through a potato ricer.

NOTE 2: To store, freeze uncooked gnocchi in a single layer on a lightly floured baking sheet. Store in a resealable freezer bag for up to 3 months. For best results, cook from frozen. Gnocchi can also be pre-cooked in a little cooking oil or melted butter and chilled. Reheat in boiling water for about 3 minutes. Drain well. Add your favourite sauce.

Pumpkin Gnocchi, above

FRENCH ONION BREAD PUDDING

Rich comfort food in a savoury side. Indulge in sweet onion flavour and wonderfully warming custard and cheese. Yesterday's onion buns work best for this recipe, but white or whole-wheat bread could be substituted. This recipe is part of a suggested menu on page 166.

Butter (or hard margarine)	1/4 cup	60 mL
Sliced sweet onion	4 cups	1 L
Granulated sugar	1 tbsp.	15 mL
Salt	1 tsp.	5 mL
Medium sherry	2 tbsp.	30 mL
Cubed onion buns (1 inch, 2.5 cm, pieces)	8 cups	2 L
Grated Swiss (or Gruyère) cheese	2 cups	500 mL
Large eggs	4	4
Half-and-half cream	2 cups	500 mL
Dijon mustard (with whole seeds)	1 tbsp.	15 mL
Pepper	1/2 tsp.	2 mL
Dried thyme	1/4 tsp.	1 mL

Melt butter in large frying pan on medium. Add next 3 ingredients. Cook for about 30 minutes, stirring occasionally, until onion is caramelized.

Add sherry. Heat and stir, scraping any brown bits from bottom of pan, until boiling. Transfer to large bowl.

Add bun cubes and cheese. Toss.

Whisk next 5 ingredients in medium bowl. Pour over bun mixture. Stir until moistened. Spread in greased shallow 2 quart (2 L) baking dish. Let stand for 15 minutes until buns are softened. Bake in 325°F (160°C) oven for about 50 minutes until set and knife inserted in centre comes out clean. Let stand for 10 minutes. Serves 8.

1 serving: 409 Calories; 24.5 g Total Fat (6.4 g Mono, 1.1 g Poly, 14.1 g Sat); 168 mg Cholesterol; 30 g Carbohydrate; 2 g Fibre; 17 g Protein; 678 mg Sodium

Pictured at left.

ROASTED HARVEST "RATATOUILLE"

The natural flavours of roasted vegetables come through in this rustic, versatile and subtly seasoned mix. Each vegetable offers its own unique flavour.

Olive (or cooking) oil	1/3 cup	75 mL
Balsamic vinegar	3 tbsp.	50 mL
Chopped fresh rosemary (or 1/2 tsp., 2 mL, dried, crushed)	2 tsp.	10 mL
Garlic cloves, minced (or 1/2 tsp., 2 mL, powder)	2	2
Salt	1 tsp.	5 mL
Coarsely ground pepper	1 tsp.	5 mL
Fresh Brussels sprouts, trimmed and halved	4 cups	1 L
Cubed peeled eggplant (1 inch, 2.5 cm, pieces)	3 cups	750 mL
Chopped red pepper (3/4 inch, 2 cm, pieces)	2 cups	500 mL
Sliced small zucchini (with peel), 3/4 inch (2 cm) slices	2 cups	500 mL
Chopped red onion (1 inch, 2.5 cm, pieces)	1 1/2 cups	375 mL
Cubed yellow turnip (rutabaga), 1/2 inch (12 mm) pieces	1 1/2 cups	375 mL
Sliced carrot (1/2 inch, 12 mm, slices)	1 1/2 cups	375 mL
Balsamic vinegar	1 tsp.	5 mL

Whisk first 6 ingredients in large bowl.

Add next 7 ingredients. Toss until coated. Arrange in single layer on large greased baking sheets with sides. Cook in 425°F (220°C) oven for about 35 minutes, stirring occasionally, until vegetables are browned and tender. Transfer to serving bowl.

Drizzle with second amount of vinegar. Makes about 8 cups (2 L).

1 cup (250 mL): 160 Calories; 9.8 g Total Fat (7.2 g Mono, 1.1 g Poly, 1.4 g Sat); 0 mg Cholesterol; 17 g Carbohydrate; 5 g Fibre; 3 g Protein; 342 mg Sodium

Pictured on front cover, page 2 and at left.

Top: French Onion Bread Pudding, above
Bottom: Roasted Harvest "Ratatouille," above

Corn and Quinoa Pilaf, below

CORN AND QUINOA PILAF

The whole-grain goodness of quinoa (pronounced KEEN-wah) is the star of this healthy, colourful side—some mild heat is nicely balanced by sweet corn. This makes a great side for poultry dishes.

Prepared vegetable broth	1 1/2 cups	375 mL
Quinoa, rinsed and drained	1 cup	250 mL
Cooking oil	2 tsp.	10 mL
Chopped onion	1 cup	250 mL
Finely chopped kale leaves, lightly packed (see Tip, page 37)	1/2 cup	125 mL
Fresh (or frozen, thawed) kernel corn	1 cup	250 mL
Finely chopped red pepper	1/4 cup	60 mL
Liquid honey	2 tsp.	10 mL
Garlic clove, minced (or 1/4 tsp., 1 mL, powder)	1	1
Grated lemon zest	1/2 tsp.	2 mL
Ground coriander	1/2 tsp.	2 mL
Ground cumin	1/4 tsp.	1 mL
Salt	1/8 tsp.	0.5 mL
Pepper	1/4 tsp.	1 mL
Sliced natural almonds, toasted (see Tip, page 93)	1/4 cup	60 mL
Chopped fresh parsley (or 1 1/2 tsp., 7 mL, dried)	2 tbsp.	30 mL

Bring broth to a boil in medium saucepan. Add quinoa. Stir. Reduce heat to medium-low. Simmer, covered, for about 20 minutes, without stirring, until quinoa is tender and liquid is absorbed. Fluff with fork. Transfer to large bowl. Cover to keep warm.

Heat cooking oil in large frying pan on medium. Add onion and kale. Cook for about 8 minutes, stirring often, until onion is softened.

Add next 9 ingredients. Cook for about 5 minutes, stirring often, until corn is tender-crisp. Add to quinoa mixture. Stir.

Add almonds and parsley. Stir. Makes about 5 cups (1.25 L).

1 cup (250 mL): 234 Calories; 6.7 g Total Fat (3.2 g Mono, 2.0 g Poly, 0.5 g Sat); 0 mg Cholesterol; 38 g Carbohydrate; 4 g Fibre; 7 g Protein; 210 mg Sodium

Pictured above.

HERB AND FRUIT STUFFING

A colourful French bread stuffing with a hint of sweetness from apples and cranberries goes divinely with Spiced Roast Turkey, page 77. Vermouth enhances the herbs, but an equal amount of chicken broth may be used instead.

French bread cubes	5 cups	1.25 L
Butter (or hard margarine)	1/4 cup	60 mL
Chopped onion	1 1/2 cups	375 mL
Sliced celery	1 cup	250 mL
Dried thyme	1 tsp.	5 mL
Dried rosemary, crushed	1/2 tsp.	2 mL
Dried sage	1/2 tsp.	2 mL
Diced unpeeled cooking apple (such as McIntosh)	1 cup	250 mL
Dried cranberries, chopped	1/4 cup	60 mL
Prepared chicken broth	3/4 cup	175 mL
Vermouth	1/4 cup	60 mL

Arrange bread cubes in single layer on ungreased baking sheet with sides. Bake in 325°F (160°C) oven for about 20 minutes until edges are dry. Transfer to large bowl.

Melt butter in large frying pan on medium. Add next 5 ingredients. Cook for about 12 minutes, stirring often, until celery is softened.

Add apple and cranberries. Stir. Add to bread.

Drizzle broth and vermouth over top. Stir until moistened. Spoon into greased 2 quart (2 L) casserole. Bake, covered, for 20 minutes. Bake, uncovered, for about 20 minutes until browned. Makes about 6 1/2 cups (1.6 L).

1 cup (250 mL): 195 Calories; 8.1 g Total Fat (2.2 g Mono, 0.5 g Poly, 4.7 g Sat); 19 mg Cholesterol; 26 g Carbohydrate; 2 g Fibre; 4 g Protein; 316 mg Sodium

Pictured on front cover, page 2 and below.

Herb and Fruit Stuffing, above

ORANGE BALSAMIC BEETS

Roasting whole beets takes time, but the sweet natural flavour, complemented by a tangy-sweet sauce, is well worth it! Place them in the oven alongside your roast beef or turkey.

Fresh medium beets, scrubbed clean and trimmed	2 lbs.	900 g
Medium onion (with skin)	1	1
Orange juice	1/2 cup	125 mL
Balsamic vinegar	1/3 cup	75 mL
Brown sugar, packed	1 tbsp.	15 mL
Star anise	1	1
Salt	1/8 tsp.	0.5 mL
Pepper	1/8 tsp.	0.5 mL

Place each beet on small sheet of greased heavy-duty (or double layer of regular) foil. Fold edges of foil together over beet to enclose.

Place onion on small sheet of greased heavy-duty (or double layer of regular) foil. Fold edges of foil together over onion to enclose. Arrange beets and onion on centre rack in 400°F (205°C) oven. Cook beets for about 1 hour and 20 minutes and onion for about 1 hour until tender. Transfer to cutting board. Carefully remove foil. Let stand until cool enough to handle. Peel beets (see Tip, page 154). Cut each beet into 8 wedges. Peel onion. Cut in half. Slice thinly.

Combine remaining 6 ingredients in medium saucepan. Bring to a boil. Reduce heat to medium. Cook, uncovered, for about 10 minutes, stirring occasionally, until reduced by half. Remove and discard star anise. Add beet and onion. Stir until heated through. Makes about 5 1/2 cups (1.4 L).

1 cup (250 mL): 107 Calories; 0.4 g Total Fat (0.1 g Mono, 0.1 g Poly, 0.1 g Sat); 0 mg Cholesterol; 24 g Carbohydrate; 5 g Fibre; 3 g Protein; 187 mg Sodium

Pictured below.

WAVES OF SHIMMERING LIGHT

An aurora, named for the Roman goddess of the dawn, is an atmospheric phenomenon caused by the interaction of charged solar particles, atmospheric gases and the earth's magnetic field. It appears as glowing waves or curtains of shimmering colours in the sky, most commonly at high northern and southern latitudes, known as aurora borealis and aurora australis respectively. One of the best times of year to see the aurora borealis is in early fall, from September to October. The closer you are to the earth's magnetic north pole, the more spectacular the lights will be. Known by many as the northern lights, the aurora borealis is also called the "Dance of the Spirits" by the Cree people.

Orange Balsamic Beets, above

Top: Blue-Crumble Cauliflower, below; Bottom: Roasted Fennel Gratin, below

ROASTED FENNEL GRATIN

Roasting creates wonderfully textured fennel, perfectly seasoned and topped with herbs and cheese. A decadent side that will complement your roast beef or holiday turkey. This recipe is part of a suggested menu on page 166.

Medium fennel bulbs (white part only), cut into 1/2 inch (12 mm) wedges	4	4
Cooking oil	3 tbsp.	50 mL
Lemon pepper	1/2 tsp.	2 mL
Dried sage	1/4 tsp.	1 mL
Salt	1/4 tsp.	1 mL
Dried thyme	1/8 tsp.	0.5 mL
Grated Italian cheese blend	1 cup	250 mL

Toss first 6 ingredients in large bowl. Transfer to greased 9 x 13 inch (23 x 33 cm) baking dish. Cook, uncovered, in 400°F (205°C) oven for about 50 minutes, stirring at halftime, until fennel is tender.

Sprinkle with cheese. Cook for about 10 minutes until cheese is melted and starting to brown. Serves 6.

1 serving: 144 Calories; 8.3 g Total Fat (4.1 g Mono, 2.1 g Poly, 1.2 g Sat); 3 mg Cholesterol; 12 g Carbohydrate; 5 g Fibre; 7 g Protein; 345 mg Sodium

Pictured above.

BLUE-CRUMBLE CAULIFLOWER

Blue cheese and nuts add flavourful interest to roasted cauliflower and potatoes. It makes a wonderful side to go with roast beef or pork.

Cooking oil	2 tbsp.	30 mL
Dijon mustard (with whole seeds)	1 tbsp.	15 mL
Salt	1/2 tsp.	2 mL
Pepper	1/4 tsp.	1 mL
Cauliflower florets	6 cups	1.5 L
Cubed peeled baking potato (3/4 inch, 2 cm, pieces)	3 cups	750 mL
Crumbled blue cheese	1/2 cup	125 mL
Pine nuts, toasted (see Tip, page 93)	1/2 cup	125 mL

Combine first 4 ingredients in large bowl.

Add cauliflower and potato. Toss until coated. Arrange in single layer on greased baking sheet with sides. Cook in 400°F (205°C) oven for about 35 minutes until vegetables are tender. Transfer to serving bowl.

Sprinkle with cheese and pine nuts. Makes about 8 cups (2 L).

1 cup (250 mL): 163 Calories; 12.0 g Total Fat (4.3 g Mono, 4.1 g Poly, 2.3 g Sat); 6 mg Cholesterol; 11 g Carbohydrate; 3 g Fibre; 5 g Protein; 391 mg Sodium

Pictured above.

SIDES

105

Jammy Cornbread, page 111

BREADS

Nothing soothes the soul like the scent of warm bread baking in the oven—except maybe getting a taste once it comes out! Bread is endlessly versatile, whether served as muffins for special brunches or made into a beautiful braid to offer with dessert. No feast is complete without a basket of warm dinner rolls, no tea without a slice of sweet loaf. Baked up simply or elaborately, bread is the very essence of the bounty and wholesomeness of the harvest.

SPICED SWEET POTATO MUFFINS

These fragrant, pleasantly spiced sweet potato muffins are also filled with the goodness of bran—but no one will know unless you tell them! Moist and flavourful.

All-purpose flour	2 cups	500 mL
Granulated sugar	1/2 cup	125 mL
Natural wheat bran	1/2 cup	125 mL
Baking powder	2 tsp.	10 mL
Baking soda	1/2 tsp.	2 mL
Ground cinnamon	1/2 tsp.	2 mL
Salt	1/2 tsp.	2 mL
Ground ginger	1/4 tsp.	1 mL
Ground nutmeg	1/4 tsp.	1 mL
Ground cloves	1/8 tsp.	0.5 mL
Large eggs, fork-beaten	2	2
Mashed peeled orange-fleshed sweet potato (about 3/4 lb., 340 g, uncooked)	1 cup	250 mL
Buttermilk (or soured milk, see Tip, right)	2/3 cup	150 mL
Cooking oil	1/4 cup	60 mL

Combine first 10 ingredients in large bowl. Make a well in centre.

Combine remaining 4 ingredients in small bowl. Add to well. Stir until just moistened. Fill 12 greased muffin cups 3/4 full. Bake in 375°F (190°C) oven for about 20 minutes until wooden pick inserted in centre of muffin comes out clean. Let stand in pan for 5 minutes before removing to wire rack to cool. Makes 12 muffins.

1 muffin: 176 Calories; 5.8 g Total Fat (3.2 g Mono, 1.5 g Poly, 0.8 g Sat); 36 mg Cholesterol; 29 g Carbohydrate; 2 g Fibre; 4 g Protein; 272 mg Sodium

Pictured below.

TIP

To make soured milk, measure 1 tbsp. (15 mL) white vinegar or lemon juice into a 1 cup (250 mL) liquid measure. Add enough milk to make 1 cup (250 mL). Stir. Let stand for 1 minute.

Spiced Sweet Potato Muffins, above

ROASTED SEED MUFFINS

Roasted sunflower and pumpkin seeds combine with toasted wheat germ in these light-textured muffins. The flavours are rich and nutty with a subtle hint of peanut butter.

All-purpose flour	1 1/2 cups	375 mL
Natural wheat bran	1/4 cup	60 mL
Salted, roasted shelled pumpkin seeds	1/4 cup	60 mL
Unsalted, roasted sunflower seeds	1/4 cup	60 mL
Wheat germ, toasted (see Note)	1/4 cup	60 mL
Baking powder	4 tsp.	20 mL
Salt	1/2 tsp.	2 mL
Large eggs	2	2
Milk	1 cup	250 mL
Butter (or hard margarine), melted	1/4 cup	60 mL
Liquid honey	1/4 cup	60 mL
Smooth peanut butter	1/4 cup	60 mL

Combine first 7 ingredients in large bowl. Make a well in centre.

Whisk remaining 5 ingredients in medium bowl. Add to well. Stir until just moistened. Fill 12 greased muffin cups 3/4 full. Bake in 375°F (190°C) oven for about 18 minutes until wooden pick inserted in centre of muffin comes out clean. Let stand in pan for 5 minutes before removing to wire rack to cool. Makes 12 muffins.

1 muffin: 187 Calories; 8.3 g Total Fat (2.8 g Mono, 1.2 g Poly, 3.4 g Sat); 47 mg Cholesterol; 23 g Carbohydrate; 2 g Fibre; 6 g Protein; 362 mg Sodium

Pictured at right.

NOTE: To toast wheat germ, spread in ungreased shallow frying pan. Heat and stir on medium until golden. To bake, spread in an ungreased shallow pan. Bake in 350°F (175°C) oven for 3 minutes, stirring or shaking often, until golden. Cool before adding to recipe.

BREAD PUDDING MUFFINS

Try something completely different for a harvest-themed brunch—individual bread pudding portions with Cinnamon Glaze drizzled over top! Be sure not to substitute anything for the buttermilk, as it lends a special, tangy flavour.

Large eggs, fork-beaten	4	4
Buttermilk	1 cup	250 mL
Granulated sugar	1/3 cup	75 mL
Butter (or hard margarine), melted	1/4 cup	60 mL
Almond extract	1 tsp.	5 mL
Ground cinnamon	1 tsp.	5 mL
French bread cubes	8 cups	2 L
Dried cherries, chopped	1 cup	250 mL
CINNAMON GLAZE		
Icing (confectioner's) sugar	1/2 cup	125 mL
Milk	1 tbsp.	15 mL
Ground cinnamon	1/8 tsp.	0.5 mL

Combine first 6 ingredients in large bowl.

Add bread cubes. Stir. Let stand for about 10 minutes until liquid is absorbed.

Add cherries. Stir. Fill 12 greased muffin cups full. Bake in 350°F (175°C) oven for about 28 minutes until wooden pick inserted in centre of muffin comes out clean. Let stand in pan for 5 minutes. Run knife around muffins to loosen before removing to wire rack to cool.

Cinnamon Glaze: Stir all 3 ingredients in small bowl until smooth. Drizzle over muffins. Makes 12 muffins.

1 muffin: 206 Calories; 6.7 g Total Fat (1.9 g Mono, 0.7 g Poly, 3.3 g Sat); 82 mg Cholesterol; 31 g Carbohydrate; 2 g Fibre; 5 g Protein; 229 mg Sodium

Pictured at right.

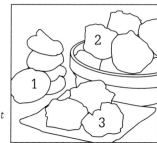

1. Sun-Dried Tomato Pretzel Twists, right
2. Roasted Seed Muffins, above
3. Bread Pudding Muffins, above

SUN-DRIED TOMATO PRETZEL TWISTS

Not your average ballpark pretzels! Everyone will love these soft, pint-sized twists, brushed with sun-dried tomato pesto and sprinkled with Asiago cheese. This recipe is part of a suggested menu on page 166.

Frozen dinner roll dough, covered, thawed in refrigerator overnight	6	6
Butter (or hard margarine), melted	1 tbsp.	15 mL
Sun-dried tomato pesto	1 tbsp.	15 mL
Grated Asiago cheese	3 tbsp.	50 mL

Cut each roll in half. Roll 1 portion into 14 inch (35 cm) long rope. Shape into loose knot. Pinch ends to seal. Repeat with remaining rolls. Arrange about 1 inch (2.5 cm) apart on greased baking sheet with sides. Let stand for 5 minutes. Bake in 400°F (205°C) oven for about 10 minutes until golden. Remove pretzels from baking sheet and arrange on wire rack to cool.

Combine butter and pesto in small cup. Brush over pretzels.

Sprinkle with cheese. Makes 12 pretzels.

1 pretzel: 73 Calories; 2.5 g Total Fat (0.3 g Mono, trace Poly, 0.9 g Sat); 4 mg Cholesterol; 10 g Carbohydrate; trace Fibre; 2 g Protein; 211 mg Sodium

Pictured below.

Whole-Wheat Seed Bread, below

WHOLE-WHEAT SEED BREAD

These attractive loaves are sprinkled with a variety of seeds, adding texture and flavour.

Caraway seed	1 tbsp.	15 mL
Fennel seed	1 tbsp.	15 mL
Poppy seeds	1 tbsp.	15 mL
Quick-cooking rolled oats	1 tbsp.	15 mL
Raw pumpkin seeds	1 tbsp.	15 mL
Raw sunflower seeds	1 tbsp.	15 mL
Sesame seeds	1 tbsp.	15 mL
Milk	1 1/4 cups	300 mL
Bulgur	1/4 cup	60 mL
Quick-cooking rolled oats	1/4 cup	60 mL
Warm water (see Tip, page 118)	1/4 cup	60 mL
Liquid honey	1/4 tsp.	1 mL
Envelope of active dry yeast (or 2 1/4 tsp., 11 mL)	1/4 oz.	8 g
Large egg, fork-beaten	1	1
Whole-wheat flour	2 cups	500 mL
Cooking oil	1/4 cup	60 mL
Liquid honey	1/4 cup	60 mL
Warm water	1/4 cup	60 mL
Salt	1 tbsp.	15 mL
All-purpose flour	2 cups	500 mL
All-purpose flour, approximately	1/3 cup	75 mL
Large egg	1	1
Water	1 tsp.	5 mL

Combine first 7 ingredients in small bowl.

Heat milk in small saucepan on medium until very hot and bubbles form around edge of saucepan. Add bulgur and oats. Stir. Transfer to large bowl. Let stand, uncovered, for about 30 minutes, stirring occasionally, until cooled to room temperature.

Combine first amount of water and first amount of honey in separate small bowl. Sprinkle yeast over top. Let stand for 10 minutes. Stir until yeast is dissolved.

Add next 6 ingredients to milk mixture. Beat with spoon until smooth. Add yeast mixture and half of caraway seed mixture. Stir.

Add first amount of all-purpose flour, 1/2 cup (125 mL) at a time, mixing until soft dough forms.

Turn out onto lightly floured surface. Knead for 5 to 10 minutes until smooth and elastic, adding second amount of all-purpose flour 1 tbsp. (15 mL) at a time, if necessary, to

(continued on next page)

prevent sticking. Place in greased extra-large bowl, turning once to grease top. Cover with greased waxed paper and tea towel. Let stand in oven with light on and door closed for about 1 hour until doubled in bulk. Punch dough down. Turn out onto lightly floured surface. Knead for about 1 minute until smooth. Divide into 2 portions. Pat each portion out to 8 inch (20 cm) round. Place about 3 inches (7.5 cm) apart on large greased baking sheet. Cover with greased waxed paper and tea towel. Let stand in oven with light on and door closed for about 30 minutes until almost doubled in size.

Whisk second egg and third amount of water in small cup. Brush over loaves. Sprinkle with remaining caraway seed mixture. Using sharp knife and starting at outside edge of 1 loaf, make shallow cut, about 1/8 inch (0.5 mL) deep, to centre of loaf. Repeat 4 more times, spacing evenly to divide bread into fifths. Repeat with second loaf. Bake in 350°F (175°C) oven for about 30 minutes until browned and hollow sounding when tapped. Remove bread from baking sheet and place on wire racks to cool. Makes 2 loaves. Each loaf cuts into 12 slices, for a total of 24 slices.

1 slice: 139 Calories; 3.9 g Total Fat (1.7 g Mono, 1.0 g Poly, 0.5 g Sat); 18 mg Cholesterol; 22 g Carbohydrate; 2 g Fibre; 4 g Protein; 306 mg Sodium

Pictured on page 4 and at left.

Jammy Cornbread

Nicely browned cornbread with a dollop of jam sweetening each piece—perfect with butter for a decadent breakfast treat or mid-morning snack. Experiment by using your favourite jam, and add a few fresh strawberries for a special treat.

Buttermilk (or soured milk, see Tip, page 107)	1 cup	250 mL
Yellow cornmeal	1 cup	250 mL
Large eggs	2	2
Butter (or hard margarine), melted	1/2 cup	125 mL
All-purpose flour	1 1/2 cups	375 mL
Brown sugar, packed	1/2 cup	125 mL
Baking powder	1/2 tsp.	2 mL
Baking soda	1/2 tsp.	2 mL
Salt	1/4 tsp.	1 mL
Strawberry jam	3 tbsp.	50 mL

Combine buttermilk and cornmeal in medium bowl. Let stand for 10 minutes.

Add eggs and butter. Whisk until well combined.

Jammy Cornbread, below

Combine next 5 ingredients in large bowl. Make a well in centre. Add buttermilk mixture to well. Stir until just moistened. Spread in greased 9 x 9 inch (23 x 23 cm) pan.

Make 9 small dents in batter with back of spoon in 3 evenly spaced rows of 3. Spoon 1 tsp. (5 mL) jam into each dent. Bake in 400°F (205°C) oven for about 30 minutes until wooden pick inserted in centre of cornbread comes out clean. Let stand in pan on wire rack for 10 minutes. Cuts into 9 pieces.

1 piece: 299 Calories; 12.0 g Total Fat (3.3 g Mono, 0.7 g Poly, 7.2 g Sat); 76 mg Cholesterol; 44 g Carbohydrate; 1 g Fibre; 6 g Protein; 276 mg Sodium

Pictured page 106 and above.

Pumpkin Wheat Bread

Impress company with these attractive, artisan-style loaves with rich pumpkin colour and mild flavour. Toast slices and use to make sandwiches with leftover roast pork or chicken.

Water	1 cup	250 mL
Canned pure pumpkin (no spices), see Tip, page 23	1/2 cup	125 mL
Brown sugar, packed	2 tbsp.	30 mL
Cooking oil	2 tbsp.	30 mL
Salt	1 1/2 tsp.	7 mL
Ground nutmeg	1/4 tsp.	1 mL
Whole-wheat flour	2 cups	500 mL
Envelope of instant yeast (or 2 1/4 tsp., 11 mL)	1/4 oz.	8 g
All-purpose flour	1 1/2 cups	375 mL
All-purpose flour, approximately	1 tbsp.	15 mL

Combine first 6 ingredients in medium saucepan. Heat and stir on medium until very warm (see Tip, page 118). Transfer to large bowl.

Add whole-wheat flour and yeast. Stir until combined.

Add first amount of all-purpose flour, 1/2 cup (125 mL) at a time, mixing until soft dough forms.

Turn out onto lightly floured surface. Knead for 5 to 10 minutes until smooth and elastic, adding second amount of all-purpose flour, if necessary, to prevent sticking. Place in greased extra-large bowl, turning once to grease top. Cover with greased waxed paper and tea towel. Let stand in oven with light on and door closed for about 1 hour until doubled in bulk. Punch dough down. Knead for about 1 minute until smooth. Divide into 2 portions. Shape into 12 inch (30 cm) long loaves. Arrange diagonally, about 3 inches (7.5 cm) apart, on greased baking sheet. Cover with greased waxed paper and tea towel. Let stand in oven with light on and door closed for about 50 minutes until doubled in size. Using sharp knife, cut 3 slashes diagonally across top of each loaf. Bake in 350°F (175°C) oven for about 35 minutes until golden brown and hollow sounding when tapped. Remove loaves from baking sheet and place on wire racks to cool. Makes 2 loaves. Each loaf cuts into 20 slices, for a total of 40 slices.

1 slice: 46 Calories; 0.8 g Total Fat (0.4 g Mono, 0.3 g Poly, 0.1 g Sat); 0 mg Cholesterol; 9 g Carbohydrate; 1 g Fibre; 1 g Protein; 88 mg Sodium

Pictured at right.

Hazelnut Crowns

Every celebration needs a basket of warm buns—these golden crowns have a homespun touch and the elegant flavour of toasted hazelnuts. They're deliciously versatile, and can be served with soups, stews or alongside the main course.

All-purpose flour	2 1/4 cups	550 mL
Granulated sugar	1 1/2 tbsp.	25 mL
Envelope of instant yeast (or 2 1/4 tsp., 11 mL)	1/4 oz.	8 g
Salt	1 tsp.	5 mL
Milk	1 cup	250 mL
Egg yolk (large)	1	1
Chopped flaked hazelnuts (filberts), toasted (see Tip, page 93)	1 cup	250 mL
Cooking oil	2 tbsp.	30 mL
All-purpose flour, approximately	1/4 cup	60 mL
Egg white (large)	1	1
Water	1 tsp.	5 mL

Combine first 4 ingredients in large bowl. Make a well in centre.

Heat milk in small saucepan on medium until very warm (see Tip, page 118). Add to well.

Add next 3 ingredients. Mix until soft dough forms.

Turn out onto lightly floured surface. Knead for 5 to 10 minutes until smooth and elastic, adding second amount of flour, 1 tbsp. (15 mL) at a time, if necessary, to prevent sticking. Place in greased extra-large bowl, turning once to grease top. Cover with greased waxed paper and tea towel. Let stand in oven with light on and door closed for about 45 minutes until almost doubled in bulk. Punch dough down. Divide into 12 portions. Roll into balls. Place in greased muffin cups. Cut '+' on top of each, about 1/2 inch (12 mm) deep, using sharp scissors. Cover with greased wax paper and tea towel. Let stand in oven with light on and door closed for about 30 minutes until doubled in size.

Whisk egg white and water in small bowl. Brush over tops. Bake in 375°F (190°C) oven for about 15 minutes until golden brown and hollow sounding when tapped. Remove rolls from pan and place on wire rack to cool. Makes 12 rolls.

1 roll: 185 Calories; 8.8 g Total Fat (6.0 g Mono, 1.5 g Poly, 0.9 g Sat); 18 mg Cholesterol; 22 g Carbohydrate; 1 g Fibre; 5 g Protein; 211 mg Sodium

Pictured at right.

QUINOA CRANBERRY MUFFINS

These nutritious muffins are ideal to serve up for breakfast, with their pleasant quinoa crunch and sweet bits of cranberry—delicious served warm with a bit of butter.

Water	3/4 cup	175 mL
Salt	1/8 tsp.	0.5 mL
Quinoa, rinsed and drained	1/2 cup	125 mL
All-purpose flour	1 cup	250 mL
Whole-wheat flour	1 cup	250 mL
Brown sugar, packed	1/3 cup	75 mL
Baking powder	1 1/2 tsp.	7 mL
Salt	3/4 tsp.	4 mL
Baking soda	1/4 tsp.	1 mL
Large egg	1	1
Buttermilk (or soured milk, see Tip, page 107)	1 1/4 cups	300 mL
Applesauce	1/3 cup	75 mL
Cooking oil	1/4 cup	60 mL
Dried cranberries, chopped	1 1/4 cups	300 mL

Combine water and salt in small saucepan. Bring to a boil. Add quinoa. Stir. Reduce heat to medium-low. Simmer, covered, for about 20 minutes, without stirring, until quinoa is tender and liquid is absorbed. Transfer to small bowl. Cool completely.

Combine next 6 ingredients in large bowl. Make a well in centre.

Whisk next 4 ingredients in medium bowl.

Add cranberries and quinoa. Stir. Add to well. Stir until just moistened. Fill 12 greased muffin cups full. Bake in 375°F (190°C) oven for about 30 minutes until wooden pick inserted in centre of muffin comes out clean. Let stand in pan for 5 minutes before removing to wire rack to cool. Makes 12 muffins.

1 muffin: 220 Calories; 6.2 g Total Fat (3.2 g Mono, 1.7 g Poly, 0.9 g Sat); 20 mg Cholesterol; 38 g Carbohydrate; 3 g Fibre; 5 g Protein; 272 mg Sodium

Pictured below.

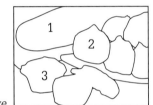

1. *Pumpkin Wheat Bread, left*
2. *Hazelnut Crowns, left*
3. *Quinoa Cranberry Muffins, above*

SWEET POTATO KNOTS

Pretty "knotted" buns with a slightly sweet flavour from sweet potato and savoury sage notes—a great way to use leftover sweet potato if you have any on hand. This recipe is part of a suggested menu on page 166.

All-purpose flour	2 cups	500 mL
Finely chopped fresh sage (or 3/4 tsp., 4 mL, dried)	1 tbsp.	15 mL
Envelope of instant yeast (or 2 1/4 tsp., 11 mL)	1/4 oz.	8 g
Salt	1 tsp.	5 mL
Onion powder	1/2 tsp.	2 mL
Mashed canned sweet potato	1/2 cup	125 mL
Water	1/2 cup	125 mL
Buttermilk (or soured milk, see Tip, page 107)	1/4 cup	60 mL
Liquid honey	2 tbsp.	30 mL
Butter (or hard margarine)	1 tbsp.	15 mL
Large egg, fork-beaten	1	1
All-purpose flour	1 cup	250 mL
All-purpose flour, approximately	2 tbsp.	30 mL
Butter (or hard margarine), melted	1 tbsp.	15 mL

Combine first 5 ingredients in large bowl. Make a well in centre.

Combine next 5 ingredients in small saucepan. Heat and stir on medium until very warm (see Tip, page 118). Add to well. Stir.

Add egg. Mix until soft, sticky dough forms.

Add second amount of flour. Mix until dough pulls away from side of bowl and is no longer sticky.

Turn out onto lightly floured surface. Knead for 5 to 10 minutes until smooth and elastic, adding third amount of flour 1 tbsp. (15 mL) at a time, if necessary, to prevent sticking. Place in greased extra-large bowl, turning once to grease top. Cover with greased waxed paper and tea towel. Let stand in oven with light on and door closed for about 1 hour until doubled in bulk. Punch dough down. Turn out onto lightly floured surface. Divide into 12 portions. Roll 1 portion into 10 inch (25 cm) long rope. Shape into simple knot. Place in greased muffin cup. Repeat with remaining portions.

Brush with second amount of butter. Cover with greased waxed paper and tea towel. Let stand in oven with light on and door closed for about 30 minutes until doubled in size. Bake in 350°F (175°C) oven for about 17 minutes until golden. Remove rolls from pan and place on wire rack to cool. Makes 12 rolls.

1 roll: 154 Calories; 2.5 g Total Fat (0.7 g Mono, 0.2 g Poly, 1.4 g Sat); 23 mg Cholesterol; 29 g Carbohydrate; 1 g Fibre; 4 g Protein; 227 mg Sodium

Pictured below.

Sweet Potato Knots, above

Potato Chive Bread, below

POTATO CHIVE BREAD

An impressive, tender-textured bread. The delicious flavour combination of potato, chives and pepper is baked right into this appetizing, homestyle loaf. A great bread for dipping into a warm bowl of soup.

Chopped peeled potato	1 1/2 cups	375 mL
Butter (or hard margarine)	1/4 cup	60 mL
Granulated sugar	1 1/2 tsp.	7 mL
Salt	1 1/2 tsp.	7 mL
All-purpose flour	3 1/2 cups	875 mL
Chopped fresh chives (or green onion)	1/4 cup	60 mL
Envelope of instant yeast (or 2 1/4 tsp., 11 mL)	1/4 oz.	8 g
Coarsely ground pepper	1/2 tsp.	2 mL
All-purpose flour, approximately	2 tbsp.	30 mL
Butter (or hard margarine), melted	1 tsp.	5 mL

Pour water into small saucepan until about 1 inch (2.5 cm) deep. Add potato. Bring to a boil. Reduce heat to medium. Boil gently, covered, for 12 to 15 minutes until tender. Drain, reserving 1 1/4 cups (300 mL) cooking water. Return potato to same pot. Mash.

Add next 3 ingredients and reserved cooking water. Stir until butter is melted. Transfer to large bowl. Let stand for about 5 minutes until slightly cooled (see Tip, page 118).

Add next 4 ingredients. Mix until soft dough forms.

Turn out onto lightly floured surface. Knead for 5 to 10 minutes until smooth and elastic, adding second amount of flour 1 tbsp. (15 mL) at a time, if necessary, to prevent sticking. Place in greased extra-large bowl, turning once to grease top. Cover with greased waxed paper and tea towel. Let stand in oven with light on and door closed for about 45 minutes until doubled in bulk. Punch dough down. Turn out onto lightly floured surface. Knead for about 1 minute until smooth. Shape into loaf. Place in greased 9 x 5 x 3 inch (23 x 12.5 x 7.5 cm) loaf pan. Cover with greased waxed paper and tea towel. Let stand in oven with light on and door closed for about 25 minutes until almost doubled in size. Bake in 350°F (175°C) oven for about 45 minutes until golden brown and hollow sounding when tapped.

Brush with second amount of butter. Remove loaf from pan and place on wire rack to cool. Cuts into 16 slices.

1 slice: 127 Calories; 3.1 g Total Fat (0.8 g Mono, 0.1 g Poly, 2.0 g Sat); 8 mg Cholesterol; 22 g Carbohydrate; 1 g Fibre; 3 g Protein; 258 mg Sodium

Pictured above.

Raisin Walnut Bread

A hearty, rustic-looking whole-wheat loaf, complete with lots of raisins and toasted walnuts for sweet and nutty flavour.

Raisins	3/4 cup	175 mL
Hot water	1 cup	250 mL
Warm water (see Tip, page 118)	1/4 cup	60 mL
Liquid honey	1/4 tsp.	1 mL
Envelope of active dry yeast (or 2 1/4 tsp., 11 mL)	1/4 oz.	8 g
Large egg, fork-beaten	1	1
Warm water	3/4 cup	175 mL
Liquid honey	3 tbsp.	50 mL
Cooking oil	2 tbsp.	30 mL
Whole-wheat flour	2 cups	500 mL
Salt	1 tsp.	5 mL
All-purpose flour	1 1/2 cups	375 mL
Walnut pieces, toasted (see Tip, page 93)	3/4 cup	175 mL
All-purpose flour, approximately	1/4 cup	60 mL

Put raisins into small bowl. Pour hot water over top. Let stand, uncovered, for 30 minutes. Drain. Set aside.

Stir warm water and honey in separate small bowl until combined. Sprinkle yeast over top. Let stand for 10 minutes. Stir until yeast is dissolved.

Combine next 4 ingredients in large bowl. Add whole-wheat flour, salt and yeast mixture. Mix well.

Add first amount of all-purpose flour, 1/2 cup (125 mL) at a time, mixing until soft dough forms. Add walnuts and raisins. Mix well.

Turn out onto lightly floured surface. Knead for 5 to 10 minutes until smooth and elastic, adding second amount of all-purpose flour 1 tbsp. (15 mL) at a time, if necessary, to prevent sticking. Place in greased extra-large bowl, turning once to grease top. Cover with greased waxed paper and tea towel. Let stand in oven with light on and door closed for about 1 hour until doubled in bulk. Punch dough down. Turn out onto lightly floured surface. Shape into 14 inch (35 cm) long log. Place on large greased baking sheet. Cover with greased waxed paper and tea towel. Let stand in oven with light on and door closed for about 45 minutes until doubled in size. Bake on centre rack in 350°F (175°C) oven for about 40 minutes until golden and hollow sounding when tapped. Remove bread from baking sheet and place on wire rack to cool. Cuts into 16 slices.

1 slice: 190 Calories; 6.0 g Total Fat (1.7 g Mono, 3.3 g Poly, 0.6 g Sat); 13 mg Cholesterol; 31 g Carbohydrate; 3 g Fibre; 5 g Protein; 154 mg Sodium

Pictured at right

Italian Cornbread Loaf

A healthy-tasting quick-bread with savoury Italian flavours—the squash adds lovely colour. Perfect for dipping into a thick, creamy Roasted Tomato Soup, page 36.

All-purpose flour	1 cup	250 mL
Whole-wheat flour	3/4 cup	175 mL
Grated Parmesan cheese	1/3 cup	75 mL
Yellow cornmeal	1/4 cup	60 mL
Baking powder	2 tsp.	10 mL
Italian seasoning	2 tsp.	10 mL
Baking soda	1 tsp.	5 mL
Salt	1/2 tsp.	2 mL
Large eggs	2	2
Mashed butternut squash (about 1 lb., 454 g, uncooked)	1 cup	250 mL
Buttermilk (or soured milk, see Tip, page 107)	1/2 cup	125 mL
Cooking oil	1/3 cup	75 mL
Chopped fresh spinach leaves, lightly packed	1 cup	250 mL
Sun-dried tomatoes in oil, blotted dry, chopped	1/4 cup	60 mL

Combine first 8 ingredients in large bowl. Make a well in centre.

Beat next 4 ingredients in medium bowl until smooth. Add to well.

Add spinach and tomatoes. Stir until just moistened. Spread in greased 9 x 5 x 3 inch (23 x 12.5 x 7.5 cm) loaf pan. Bake in 350°F (175°C) oven for about 40 minutes until wooden pick inserted in centre comes out clean. Let stand in pan for 10 minutes before removing to wire rack to cool. Cuts into 16 slices.

1 slice: 134 Calories; 6.6 g Total Fat (3.2 g Mono, 1.6 g Poly, 1.0 g Sat); 29 mg Cholesterol; 15 g Carbohydrate; 2 g Fibre; 4 g Protein; 292 mg Sodium

Pictured at right.

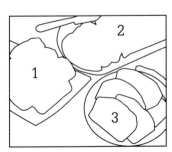

1. *Italian Cornbread Loaf, above*
2. *Raisin Walnut Bread, above*
3. *Sweet Harvest Loaf, right*

Sweet Harvest Loaf

A beautiful way to put your garden's bounty to good use—this colourful loaf is packed with zucchini, beets, carrots and apples.

All-purpose flour	2 cups	500 mL
Granulated sugar	1 cup	250 mL
Baking powder	2 tsp.	10 mL
Ground cinnamon	1 tsp.	5 mL
Baking soda	1/2 tsp.	2 mL
Salt	1/2 tsp.	2 mL
Large eggs	2	2
Cooking oil	1/2 cup	125 mL
Apple juice	3 tbsp.	50 mL
Vanilla extract	1 tsp.	5 mL

Grated carrot	1/2 cup	125 mL
Grated fresh peeled beets (see Tip, page 154)	1/2 cup	125 mL
Grated peeled cooking apple (such as McIntosh)	1/2 cup	125 mL
Grated zucchini (with peel)	1/2 cup	125 mL
Grated orange zest	1 tsp.	5 mL

Combine first 6 ingredients in large bowl. Make a well in centre.

Whisk next 4 ingredients in medium bowl. Add to well.

Add remaining 5 ingredients. Stir until just moistened. Spread in greased 9 x 5 x 3 inch (23 x 12.5 x 7.5 cm) loaf pan. Bake in 350°F (175°C) oven for about 55 minutes until wooden pick inserted in centre comes out clean. Let stand in pan for 10 minutes before removing to wire rack to cool. Cuts into 16 slices.

1 slice: 161 Calories; 7.7 g Total Fat (4.4 g Mono, 2.2 g Poly, 0.7 g Sat); 26 mg Cholesterol; 22 g Carbohydrate; 1 g Fibre; 3 g Protein; 196 mg Sodium

Pictured below.

Cardamom Pear Braid, below

Egg white (large)	1	1
Water	1 tbsp.	15 mL
Liquid honey	1 tbsp.	15 mL

Combine first 5 ingredients in large bowl. Cut in butter until mixture resembles coarse crumbs. Make a well in centre.

Combine next 3 ingredients in small bowl. Add to well. Stir until soft dough forms. Turn out onto lightly floured surface. Knead gently 8 to 10 times. Roll or pat out to 12 x 15 inch (30 x 38 cm) rectangle on large greased baking sheet.

Combine next 5 ingredients in separate small bowl. Sprinkle along centre of dough in 4 inch (10 cm) strip, leaving 1 inch (2.5 cm) space on short sides.

Arrange pear slices over almond mixture. Cut dough at angle into 1 inch (2.5 cm) strips, starting 1 inch (2.5 cm) away from sides of filling out to edge. Discard irregular pieces. Fold top and bottom edges over filling. Starting at top, cross alternating strips for each side over filling, allowing strips to overlap in middle (see diagram).

Beat egg white and water in small cup. Brush over crossed strips. Bake on centre rack in 425°F (220°C) oven for about 20 minutes until golden and firm to the touch. Let stand on baking sheet for 5 minutes.

Brush with honey. Cuts into 12 slices.

1 slice: 268 Calories; 12.2 g Total Fat (4.7 g Mono, 1.4 g Poly, 5.3 g Sat); 38 mg Cholesterol; 37 g Carbohydrate; 4 g Fibre; 6 g Protein; 255 mg Sodium

Pictured at left.

CARDAMOM PEAR BRAID

An attractive braid of tender biscuit filled with sweet pears, raisins and almonds, all infused with warm spices. A not-too-sweet treat to serve with tea on a quiet afternoon.

All-purpose flour	1 1/3 cups	325 mL
Whole-wheat flour	1 cup	250 mL
Granulated sugar	3 tbsp.	50 mL
Baking powder	2 tsp.	10 mL
Salt	1/2 tsp.	2 mL
Cold butter (or hard margarine), cut up	1/2 cup	125 mL
Large egg, fork-beaten	1	1
Chai tea concentrate	2/3 cup	150 mL
Vanilla extract	1 tsp.	5 mL
Ground almonds	1 cup	250 mL
Raisins	1/2 cup	125 mL
Brown sugar, packed	3 tbsp.	50 mL
Ground cardamom	1/2 tsp.	2 mL
Ground cinnamon	1/2 tsp.	2 mL
Thinly sliced peeled pear	2 cups	500 mL

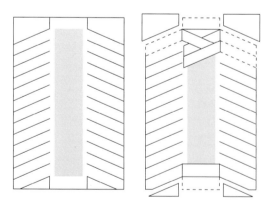

TIP

When using yeast, it is important for the liquid to be at the correct temperature. If the liquid is too cool, the yeast will not activate properly. If the liquid is too hot, the yeast will be destroyed. For best results, follow the recommended temperatures as instructed on the package.

Herb Stuffing Buns, below

HERB STUFFING BUNS

These tasty buns pack in the favourite herb flavours of stuffing, with walnuts adding a bit of texture. They make for tasty sandwiches using leftover turkey! This recipe is part of a suggested menu on page 166.

Butter (or hard margarine)	2 tsp.	10 mL
Finely diced celery	1/2 cup	125 mL
Finely diced onion	1/2 cup	125 mL
Chopped dried cherries	2 tbsp.	30 mL
Chopped walnuts, toasted (see Tip, page 93)	2 tbsp.	30 mL
Chopped fresh marjoram (or 1/2 tsp., 2 mL, dried)	2 tsp.	10 mL
Chopped fresh sage (or 1/2 tsp., 2 mL, dried)	2 tsp.	10 mL
Salt	1/4 tsp.	1 mL
Pepper	1/4 tsp.	1 mL
Warm water (see Tip, left)	3/4 cup	175 mL
Granulated sugar	1/2 tsp.	2 mL
Active dry yeast	1 1/2 tsp.	7 mL
Large egg	1	1
Cooking oil	1 tbsp.	15 mL
Salt	1/2 tsp.	2 mL
Whole-wheat flour	2 1/2 cups	625 mL
Whole-wheat flour, approximately	6 tbsp.	100 mL

Melt butter in large frying pan on medium. Add celery and onion. Cook for about 5 minutes, stirring often, until onion is softened. Remove from heat.

Add next 6 ingredients. Stir.

Stir warm water and sugar in large bowl until sugar is dissolved. Sprinkle yeast over top. Let stand for 10 minutes. Stir until yeast is dissolved.

Add next 3 ingredients. Whisk until smooth. Add celery mixture. Stir.

Add first amount of flour, 1/2 cup (125 mL) at a time, mixing until soft dough forms.

Turn out onto lightly floured surface. Knead for 5 to 10 minutes until smooth and elastic, adding second amount of flour, if necessary, to prevent sticking. Place in greased extra-large bowl, turning once to grease top. Cover with greased wax paper and tea towel. Let stand in oven with light on and door closed for about 45 minutes until doubled in bulk. Punch dough down. Knead for about 1 minute until smooth. Divide into 12 portions. Roll into balls. Arrange balls in greased 9 x 13 inch (23 x 33 cm) pan. Cover with greased wax paper and tea towel. Let stand in oven with light on and door closed for about 30 minutes until doubled in size. Bake in 375°F (190°C) oven for about 20 minutes until golden and hollow-sounding when tapped. Remove buns from pan and place on wire rack to cool. Makes 12 buns.

1 bun: 137 Calories; 3.6 g Total Fat (1.2 g Mono, 1.3 g Poly, 0.8 g Sat); 19 mg Cholesterol; 24 g Carbohydrate; 4 g Fibre; 5 g Protein; 162 mg Sodium

Pictured above.

Apple Onion Bread Ring

Caramelized onion and apple, combined with fragrant herbs, create a savoury bread ring that will become an instant favourite at family gatherings. This recipe is part of a suggested menu on page 166.

Butter (or hard margarine)	1 tbsp.	15 mL
Thinly sliced onion	3/4 cup	175 mL
Thinly sliced peeled tart apple (such as Granny Smith)	3/4 cup	175 mL
Chopped red pepper	1/4 cup	60 mL
Granulated sugar	2 tsp.	10 mL
Chopped fresh thyme (or 1/4 tsp., 1 mL, dried)	1 tsp.	5 mL
Finely chopped fresh rosemary (or 1/8 tsp., 0.5 mL, dried, crushed)	1/2 tsp.	2 mL
Salt	1/4 tsp.	1 mL
Pepper	1/8 tsp.	0.5 mL
Apple cider vinegar	1 tsp.	5 mL
Frozen whole-wheat (or white) bread dough, covered, thawed in refrigerator overnight	1	1
Butter (or hard margarine), melted	1 tsp.	5 mL

Melt butter in medium frying pan on medium. Add onion and apple. Cook for about 5 minutes, stirring often, until starting to soften.

Add next 6 ingredients. Cook for about 8 minutes, stirring often, until onion is caramelized.

Add vinegar. Heat and stir for 1 minute. Transfer to small bowl. Cool.

Roll out dough on lightly floured surface to 9 x 16 inch (23 x 40 cm) rectangle. Spread onion mixture over dough, leaving 1 inch (2.5 cm) border on long edges. Roll up from 1 long edge, jelly-roll style. Pinch seams to seal. Shape into ring. Place, seam-side down, on greased baking sheet. Pinch ends together to seal. Cut ring 16 times from outside edge to within 1/2 inch (12 mm) of centre using scissors. Turn each cut wedge on its side, all in the same direction, allowing them to overlap. Cover with greased waxed paper and tea towel. Let stand in oven with light on and door closed for about 1 hour until doubled in size. Bake in 350°F (175°C) oven for about 30 minutes until browned and hollow sounding when tapped. Let stand on baking sheet for 5 minutes.

Brush with second amount of butter. Remove bread from baking sheet and place on wire rack to cool. Cuts into 16 pieces.

1 piece: 89 Calories; 2.1 g Total Fat (0.3 g Mono, trace Poly, 0.6 g Sat); 3 mg Cholesterol; 15 g Carbohydrate; 1 g Fibre; 4 g Protein; 202 mg Sodium

Pictured at left.

Chipotle Corn Muffins

Bite into sweet corn goodness with these pretty golden muffins, enjoying the pleasing texture and lingering heat. Spread on some butter or dip one into a vegetable stew.

All-purpose flour	1 1/2 cups	375 mL
Grated havarti cheese	1 cup	250 mL
Yellow cornmeal	1 cup	250 mL
Baking powder	2 tsp.	10 mL
Baking soda	1 tsp.	5 mL
Salt	1/2 tsp.	2 mL
Chipotle chili powder (or cayenne pepper)	1/8 tsp.	0.5 mL
Large egg, fork-beaten	1	1
Fresh (or frozen, thawed) kernel corn	1/2 cup	125 mL
Milk	1/2 cup	125 mL
Sour cream	1/2 cup	125 mL
Butter (or hard margarine), melted	1/4 cup	60 mL
Liquid honey	1/4 cup	60 mL
Finely chopped onion	2 tbsp.	30 mL
Grated lime zest	1/2 tsp.	2 mL

Combine first 7 ingredients in large bowl. Make a well in centre.

Combine remaining 8 ingredients in medium bowl. Add to well. Stir until just moistened. Fill 12 greased muffin cups full. Bake in 375°F (190°C) oven for about 15 minutes until wooden pick inserted in centre of muffin comes out clean. Let stand in pan for 5 minutes before removing to wire rack to cool. Makes 12 muffins.

1 muffin: 222 Calories; 9.2 g Total Fat (1.3 g Mono, 0.3 g Poly, 5.8 g Sat); 43 mg Cholesterol; 29 g Carbohydrate; 1 g Fibre; 6 g Protein; 393 mg Sodium

Pictured at left.

Top: Chipotle Corn Muffins, above
Bottom: Apple Onion Bread Ring, above

Spiced Rum Pear Cake, page 137

DESSERTS

Fill your home with the cozy autumn aromas of warm spices, baking fruit or chocolate with these decadent desserts. Everyone looks forward to being presented with something sweet and lovingly prepared at the end of the meal—eyes will light up when you bring out a beautiful pie, cake or crumble with a stack of your best dessert plates. Follow a magnificent meal with a show-stopping sweet ending, and your guests will leave the table utterly satisfied.

CRISP AUTUMN CRUMBLE

Warm up with this delicious dessert. Tender apple and mellow pear offer a pleasingly tart contrast with the crumble topping and gingery sweetness.

Thinly sliced peeled tart apple (such as Granny Smith)	4 cups	1 L
Sliced peeled pear	2 cups	500 mL
Brown sugar, packed	1/2 cup	125 mL
Coarsely chopped dried apricot	1/4 cup	60 mL
Coarsely chopped crystallized ginger	3 tbsp.	50 mL
All-purpose flour	2 tbsp.	30 mL
GINGER TOPPING		
All-purpose flour	3/4 cup	175 mL
Brown sugar, packed	1/2 cup	125 mL
Crushed gingersnaps (about 6 gingersnaps)	1/4 cup	60 mL
Baking powder	1/2 tsp.	2 mL
Ground cinnamon	1/2 tsp.	2 mL
Cold butter (or hard margarine), cut up	1/2 cup	125 mL
Chopped pecans	1/4 cup	60 mL

Combine first 6 ingredients in large bowl. Spread in greased 2 quart (2 L) casserole.

Ginger Topping: Combine first 5 ingredients in medium bowl. Cut in butter until mixture resembles coarse crumbs.

Add pecans. Stir. Scatter over apple mixture. Bake in 375°F (190°C) oven for about 40 minutes until topping is crisp and golden and fruit is tender. Let stand on wire rack for 15 minutes. Serves 8.

1 serving: 361 Calories; 14.7 g Total Fat (4.8 g Mono, 1.3 g Poly, 7.6 g Sat); 30 mg Cholesterol; 59 g Carbohydrate; 4 g Fibre; 2 g Protein; 152 mg Sodium

Pictured below.

AUTUMN IN NEW YORK

All the vivid colour of an eastern fall and the electricity of New York City are captured in the jazz standard "Autumn in New York," composed in 1934 by Vernon Duke for the Broadway musical *Thumbs Up!* Several versions of the song have been recorded over the years by numerous musicians and singers, notably Frank Sinatra, Billie Holiday and Jo Stafford. An instrumental version recorded by guitarist Tal Farlow is regarded as superb.

Crisp Autumn Crumble, above

CARAMEL APPLE CAKE

Caramel, apples and oats—what's not to like? This whole-wheat cake is wholesome and appealing.

Diced peeled cooking apple (such as McIntosh)	2 cups	500 mL
Lemon juice	2 tbsp.	30 mL
Large flake rolled oats	1/2 cup	125 mL
Brown sugar, packed	1/4 cup	60 mL
Butter (or hard margarine), melted	3 tbsp.	50 mL
Ground cinnamon	1 tsp.	5 mL
Whole-wheat flour	1 1/4 cups	300 mL
Baking powder	1 1/2 tsp.	7 mL
Salt	1/2 tsp.	2 mL
Butter (or hard margarine), softened	1/2 cup	125 mL
Granulated sugar	1/2 cup	125 mL
Large egg	1	1
Vanilla extract	1 tsp.	5 mL
Milk	2/3 cup	150 mL
Caramel ice cream topping	1/3 cup	75 mL

Toss apple and lemon juice in medium bowl.

Stir next 4 ingredients in small bowl until mixture resembles coarse crumbs. Set aside.

Combine next 3 ingredients in separate small bowl.

Beat second amount of butter and granulated sugar in large bowl until light and fluffy.

Add egg and vanilla. Beat well. Add flour mixture in 3 additions, alternating with milk in 2 additions, stirring well after each addition until just combined. Spread in greased 9 x 9 inch (23 x 23 cm) pan. Arrange apple mixture over top.

Drizzle ice cream topping over apple mixture. Sprinkle reserved oat mixture over top. Bake in 350°F (175°C) oven for about 45 minutes until wooden pick inserted in centre comes out clean. Let stand in pan on wire rack until cool. Cuts into 16 pieces.

1 piece: 175 Calories; 8.6 g Total Fat (2.2 g Mono, 0.4 g Poly, 5.1 g Sat); 35 mg Cholesterol; 24 g Carbohydrate; 2 g Fibre; 3 g Protein; 214 mg Sodium

Pictured at right.

APPLE RHUBARB CRISP PIE

Favourite crisp flavours in the form of a pie—everyone will love this as a warm-up treat. An appetizing pie with a golden crumble top, perfect for serving with vanilla ice cream. This recipe is part of a suggested menu on page 166.

Pastry for 9 inch (23 cm) deep dish pie shell		
All-purpose flour	1/2 cup	125 mL
Brown sugar, packed	1/2 cup	125 mL
Quick-cooking rolled oats	1/2 cup	125 mL
Cold butter (or hard margarine), cut up	1/3 cup	75 mL
Thinly sliced peeled cooking apple (such as McIntosh)	5 cups	1.25 L
Chopped fresh (or frozen) rhubarb	2 cups	500 mL
Brown sugar, packed	1 cup	250 mL
All-purpose flour	2 tbsp.	30 mL
Minute tapioca	2 tbsp.	30 mL
Ground cinnamon	2 tsp.	10 mL
Ground ginger	1 tsp.	5 mL

Roll out pastry on lightly floured surface to 1/8 inch (3 mm) thickness. Line 9 inch (23 cm) deep dish pie plate with pastry. Trim, leaving 1/2 inch (12 mm) overhang. Roll under and crimp decorative edge.

Combine next 3 ingredients in medium bowl. Cut in butter until mixture resembles coarse crumbs.

Combine remaining 7 ingredients in large bowl. Transfer to pie shell. Sprinkle with flour mixture. Bake on bottom rack of 425°F (220°C) oven for 20 minutes. Reduce heat to 350°F (175°C). Bake for about 1 hour and 10 minutes until apples are tender and filling is bubbling (see Note). Let stand on wire rack until cool. Cuts into 8 wedges.

1 wedge: 428 Calories; 15.2 g Total Fat (2.0 g Mono, 0.4 g Poly, 7.8 g Sat); 25 mg Cholesterol; 73 g Carbohydrate; 3 g Fibre; 3 g Protein; 156 mg Sodium

Pictured at right

NOTE: If top browns too quickly, lay sheet of foil over top of pie to allow bottom crust to finish baking.

WARM APPLES AND RHUBARB

Sneak nutritious brown rice and rolled oats into dessert! You'll welcome the annual onslaught of rhubarb in your garden when you try this sweet-tart delight. Serve warm with ice cream.

Sliced peeled tart apple (such as Granny Smith)	3 cups	750 mL
Chopped fresh (or frozen) rhubarb	1 1/2 cups	375 mL
Cooked long-grain brown rice (about 1/3 cup, 75 mL, uncooked)	1 cup	250 mL
Brown sugar, packed	3/4 cup	175 mL
All-purpose flour	2 tbsp.	30 mL
Water	2 tbsp.	30 mL
Ground cinnamon	2 tsp.	10 mL
Brown sugar, packed	1/2 cup	125 mL
Whole-wheat flour	1/3 cup	75 mL
Ground cinnamon	1/2 tsp.	2 mL
Cold butter (or hard margarine), cut up	2 tbsp.	30 mL
Large flake rolled oats	1 cup	250 mL
Unsweetened applesauce	2 tbsp.	30 mL

Combine first 7 ingredients in large bowl. Spread in greased 2 quart (2 L) shallow baking dish.

Combine next 3 ingredients in medium bowl. Cut in butter until mixture resembles coarse crumbs.

Add oats and applesauce. Stir. Spoon over apple mixture. Bake in 375°F (190°C) oven for about 30 minutes until top is lightly browned and fruit is tender. Let stand on wire rack for 10 minutes. Serves 6.

1 serving: 346 Calories; 5.4 g Total Fat (1.1 g Mono, 0.4 g Poly, 2.5 g Sat); 10 mg Cholesterol; 74 g Carbohydrate; 5 g Fibre; 5 g Protein; 31 mg Sodium

Pictured above.

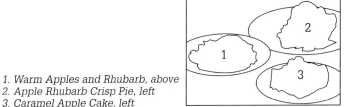

1. Warm Apples and Rhubarb, above
2. Apple Rhubarb Crisp Pie, left
3. Caramel Apple Cake, left

Chocolate Caramel Fondue, below

RHUBARB SUNDAES

During those warm autumn days, embrace comforting flavours while holding onto the carefree fun of summer. A crunchy, candied pecan topping adds wonderful texture to ice cream with rhubarb sauce.

Egg white (large)	1	1
Brown sugar, packed	1/4 cup	60 mL
Ground cinnamon	1/2 tsp.	2 mL
Ground allspice	1/4 tsp.	1 mL
Ground ginger	1/4 tsp.	1 mL
Pecan halves	1 cup	250 mL
Chopped fresh (or frozen) rhubarb	1 1/2 cups	375 mL
Water	1/2 cup	125 mL
Granulated sugar	1/3 cup	75 mL
Minced crystallized ginger	2 tbsp.	30 mL
Butterscotch ripple ice cream	3 cups	750 mL

Beat egg white in medium bowl until frothy.

Add next 4 ingredients. Stir.

Add pecans. Stir until coated. Spread on greased baking sheet with sides. Bake in 325°F (160°C) oven for about 15 minutes, stirring occasionally, until golden. Transfer to cutting board. Cool. Chop coarsely.

Combine next 4 ingredients in medium saucepan. Bring to a boil. Reduce heat to medium-low. Cook for about 20 minutes, stirring occasionally, until rhubarb is softened and mixture is thickened. Cool.

Scoop ice cream into 6 serving bowls. Spoon rhubarb mixture over ice cream. Scatter pecans over top. Makes 6 sundaes.

1 sundae: 363 Calories; 20.1 g Total Fat (7.4 g Mono, 3.9 g Poly, 6.1 g Sat); 25 mg Cholesterol; 44 g Carbohydrate; 3 g Fibre; 5 g Protein; 102 mg Sodium

Pictured at right.

FALL FROSTS

Some fruits and vegetables, such as apples, sour cherries, carrots, parsnips and kale, benefit from being left unharvested until after a light frost. Fall frosts can serve to sweeten or mellow their flavours.

CHOCOLATE CARAMEL FONDUE

Pair this decadent caramel and white chocolate dip with apple slices—candy apples with a grown-up twist! Try it with other harvest-fresh fruit such as pears or apple-pears.

Milk	1 1/2 cups	375 mL
Box of butterscotch pudding powder (not instant), 6-serving size	1	1
White chocolate baking squares (1 oz., 28 g, each), chopped	8	8

Combine milk and pudding powder in medium saucepan. Heat and stir on medium for about 6 minutes until boiling and thickened. Remove from heat.

Add chocolate. Stir until smooth. Carefully pour into fondue pot. Keep warm over low flame. Makes about 2 1/2 cups (625 mL).

1/4 cup (60 mL): 173 Calories; 3.9 g Total Fat (1.3 g Mono, 0.3 g Poly, 2.2 g Sat); 2 mg Cholesterol; 34 g Carbohydrate; 2 g Fibre; 3 g Protein; 98 mg Sodium

Pictured above.

BEET SPICE CAKE

Beets and zucchini join traditional carrots in this moist spice cake, with rich and aromatic Orange Cardamom Icing creating an inviting look. When wrapped in plastic wrap and aluminum foil, the un-iced cake will freeze well for up to two months.

All-purpose flour	2 1/2 cups	625 mL
Baking powder	1 1/2 tsp.	7 mL
Ground cinnamon	1 1/4 tsp.	6 mL
Ground ginger	1 1/4 tsp.	6 mL
Baking soda	1 tsp.	5 mL
Salt	1 tsp.	5 mL
Ground cardamom	1/2 tsp.	2 mL
Ground nutmeg	1/2 tsp.	2 mL
Large eggs	3	3
Brown sugar, packed	1 1/3 cups	325 mL
Cooking oil	2/3 cup	150 mL
Buttermilk (or soured milk, see Tip, page 107)	1/3 cup	75 mL
Grated fresh peeled beets (see Tip, page 154)	1 1/2 cups	375 mL
Grated carrot	1 cup	250 mL
Grated zucchini (with peel), squeezed dry	1 cup	250 mL

ORANGE CARDAMOM ICING

Block cream cheese, softened	4 oz.	125 g
Butter (or hard margarine), softened	1/4 cup	60 mL
Frozen concentrated orange juice, thawed	1 tbsp.	15 mL
Ground cardamom	1/4 tsp.	1 mL
Icing (confectioner's) sugar	1 cup	250 mL

Combine first 8 ingredients in large bowl. Make a well in centre.

Beat next 4 ingredients in medium bowl until smooth. Add to flour mixture. Stir until just combined.

Add next 3 ingredients. Stir well. Spread in greased 9 x 13 inch (23 x 33 cm) pan. Bake in 350°F (175°C) oven for about 30 minutes until wooden pick inserted in centre comes out clean. Let stand in pan on wire rack until cool. Transfer to serving plate.

Orange Cardamom Icing: Beat cream cheese and butter in small bowl until combined.

Add concentrated orange juice and cardamom. Beat well.

Add icing sugar. Beat for about 1 minute until spreading consistency. Spread over cake. Cuts into 15 pieces.

1 piece: 333 Calories; 16.8 g Total Fat (7.8 g Mono, 3.3 g Poly, 4.7 g Sat); 59 mg Cholesterol; 43 g Carbohydrate; 1 g Fibre; 5 g Protein; 372 mg Sodium

Pictured below.

Left: Rhubarb Sundaes, left; Right: Beet Spice Cake, above

PLUM WALNUT TART

Neat plum slices give this appetizing tart an attractive look, and creamy, cheesecake-like filling contrasts wonderfully with a nutty walnut crust. Serve slices with a garnish of whipped cream if desired.

All-purpose flour	3/4 cup	175 mL
Brown sugar, packed	1/3 cup	75 mL
Cold butter (or hard margarine), cut up	1/3 cup	75 mL
Finely chopped walnuts	1/3 cup	75 mL
Egg yolk (large)	1	1
Ice water	2 tbsp.	30 mL
Large egg	1	1
Block cream cheese, softened	8 oz.	250 g
Finely chopped walnuts	1/2 cup	125 mL
Granulated sugar	1/3 cup	75 mL
Sour cream	1/4 cup	60 mL
Lemon juice	2 tsp.	10 mL
Vanilla extract	1 tsp.	5 mL
Pitted fresh red plums, thinly sliced	3	3
Apple jelly, warmed	2 tbsp.	30 mL

Process first 4 ingredients in food processor until mixture resembles coarse crumbs.

Add egg yolk and ice water. Process with on/off motion until mixture starts to come together. Do not over process. Turn out onto lightly floured surface. Press pastry into ball. Flatten slightly into disc. Roll out to fit ungreased 9 inch (23 cm) tart pan with fluted sides and removable bottom. Carefully lift pastry and press into bottom and up side of tart pan. Trim edge. Chill for 30 minutes. Place pan on ungreased baking sheet with sides (see Note). Bake on bottom rack in 400°F (205°C) oven for about 18 minutes until golden. Cool.

Beat next 7 ingredients in small bowl until combined. Spread over crust. Bake on bottom rack in 350°F (175°C) oven for about 20 minutes until filling is set. Let stand in pan on wire rack until cool.

Arrange plum in single layer over top. Brush with apple jelly. Chill. Cuts into 10 wedges.

1 wedge: 316 Calories; 22.4 g Total Fat (5.1 g Mono, 5.4 g Poly, 10.4 g Sat); 87 mg Cholesterol; 26 g Carbohydrate; 1 g Fibre; 5 g Protein; 120 mg Sodium

Pictured at right

NOTE: Placing the tart pan on a baking sheet provides a safe way to transfer the hot pan out of the oven.

CARDAMOM PUMPKIN CRÈME BRÛLÉE

The classic fall flavours of pumpkin pie transform into a delightful grown-up treat—crisp sugar topping makes way for smooth and creamy spiced custard. An impressive make-ahead dessert that needs only a final touch before serving. Try garnishing with edible flowers.

Egg yolks (large)	6	6
Brown sugar, packed	1/2 cup	125 mL
Ground cardamom	3/4 tsp.	4 mL
Vanilla extract	1/2 tsp.	2 mL
Whipping cream	2 cups	500 mL
Canned pure pumpkin (no spices), see Tip, page 23	1/2 cup	125 mL
Brown sugar, packed	3 tbsp.	50 mL

Arrange six 3/4 cup (175 mL) ramekins in ungreased 9 x 13 inch (23 x 33 cm) pan. Whisk first 4 ingredients in small bowl until combined.

Heat cream in small saucepan on medium until hot, but not boiling. Remove from heat. Whisk 2 tbsp. (30 mL) whipping cream into egg yolk mixture. Slowly add egg yolk mixture to remaining whipping cream, whisking constantly.

Add pumpkin. Stir well. Pour into ramekins. Pour boiling water into pan until water comes halfway up sides of ramekins. Bake in 325°F (160°C) oven for about 30 minutes until custard is set along edges but centre still wobbles. Carefully remove ramekins from water. Place on wire rack to cool completely. Chill, covered, for at least 6 hours or overnight.

Spread second amount of brown sugar on ungreased baking sheet with sides. Bake in 325°F (160°C) oven for about 2 minutes until dried and crumbly. Cool completely. Press through sieve into small bowl. Sprinkle over custards. Broil on top rack in oven for 2 to 3 minutes until sugar is browned and bubbling. Let stand for 5 minutes. Makes 6 crème brûlées.

1 crème brûlée: 418 Calories; 33.8 g Total Fat (10.4 g Mono, 1.8 g Poly, 19.9 g Sat); 314 mg Cholesterol; 27 g Carbohydrate; 1 g Fibre; 5 g Protein; 39 mg Sodium

Pictured at right.

Left: Cardamom Pumpkin Crème Brûlée, above
Right: Plum Walnut Tart, above

MAPLE WALNUT COFFEE CAKE

Crunchy walnuts coated with sweet maple syrup contrast wonderfully with dense vanilla cake. Serve it with ice cream or whipped cream for dessert, or set out a plate of slices with coffee.

All-purpose flour	1/2 cup	125 mL
Ground cinnamon	1/2 tsp.	2 mL
Salt, sprinkle		
Cold butter (or hard margarine), cut up	2 tbsp.	30 mL
Chopped walnuts	1 1/2 cups	375 mL
Maple syrup	1/4 cup	60 mL
Butter (or hard margarine), softened	1/4 cup	60 mL
Granulated sugar	1 cup	250 mL
Large eggs	2	2
Vanilla extract	2 tsp.	30 mL
All-purpose flour	2 cups	500 mL
Baking powder	1 1/2 tsp.	7 mL
Salt	1/2 tsp.	2 mL
Milk	1 cup	250 mL
Maple syrup	2 tbsp.	30 mL

Combine first 3 ingredients in small bowl. Cut in first amount of butter until mixture resembles coarse crumbs.

Add walnuts and first amount of maple syrup. Stir.

Beat second amount of butter and sugar in large bowl until light and fluffy. Add eggs, one at a time, beating well after each addition. Add vanilla. Stir.

Combine next 3 ingredients in medium bowl. Add to butter mixture in 3 additions, alternating with milk in 2 additions, stirring well after each addition until just combined. Spread in greased 9 x 9 inch (23 x 23 cm) pan. Scatter walnut mixture over top. Bake in 350°F (175°C) oven for about 45 minutes until wooden pick inserted in centre comes out clean. Let stand in pan on wire rack until cool.

Drizzle with second amount of maple syrup. Cuts into 16 pieces.

1 piece: 242 Calories; 12.4 g Total Fat (2.4 g Mono, 5.6 g Poly, 3.7 g Sat); 39 mg Cholesterol; 31 g Carbohydrate; 1 g Fibre; 5 g Protein; 172 mg Sodium

Pictured at right.

PUMPKIN CARAMEL CHEESECAKE

An autumn-themed treat abounding with sophisticated taste. Light, fluffy pumpkin filling rests atop a rich gingersnap crust, all drizzled with a caramel sauce spiked with bourbon.

Crushed gingersnaps (about 35)	1 1/2 cups	375 mL
Butter (or hard margarine), melted	1/3 cup	75 mL
Brown sugar, packed	2 tbsp.	30 mL
Envelope of unflavoured gelatin (about 2 1/4 tsp., 11 mL)	1/4 oz.	7 g
Water	3 tbsp.	50 mL
Block cream cheese, softened	16 oz.	500 g
Canned pure pumpkin (no spices), see Tip, page 23	1/2 cup	125 mL
Sour cream	1/2 cup	125 mL
Brown sugar, packed	1/3 cup	75 mL
Ground ginger	1/2 tsp.	2 mL
Caramel (or butterscotch) ice cream topping	1/2 cup	125 mL
Bourbon whiskey (optional)	1 tbsp.	15 mL

Stir first 3 ingredients in medium bowl until well mixed. Press firmly in bottom of greased 9 inch (23 cm) springform pan. Bake in 350°F (175°C) oven for 10 minutes. Cool.

Sprinkle gelatin over water in small saucepan. Let stand for 1 minute. Heat and stir on medium-low for about 1 minute until gelatin is dissolved. Remove from heat.

Beat next 5 ingredients in large bowl until combined. Add gelatin mixture. Beat until smooth. Spread in crust. Chill, covered, for at least 3 hours until set. Cuts into 12 wedges.

Combine ice cream topping and bourbon in small bowl. Drizzle over wedges. Serves 12.

1 serving: 349 Calories; 21.9 g Total Fat (6.1 g Mono, 1.0 g Poly, 13.2 g Sat); 62 mg Cholesterol; 34 g Carbohydrate; 1 g Fibre; 5 g Protein; 334 mg Sodium

Pictured at right.

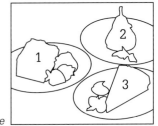

1. Maple Walnut Coffee Cake, above
2. Almond-Poached Pears, right
3. Pumpkin Caramel Cheesecake, above

ALMOND-POACHED PEARS

A light and elegant dessert—sweet, soft pears with a caramel sauce infused with warming spices. A mint garnish makes a nice final touch.

Almond liqueur	1/2 cup	125 mL
Butter (or hard margarine), melted	2 tbsp.	30 mL
Whole black peppercorns	1/8 tsp.	0.5 mL
Star anise	1	1
Whole green cardamom, bruised (see Tip, page 14)	1	1
Medium firm peeled pears, stems intact	4	4
Apple juice	2 tbsp.	30 mL
Cornstarch	2 tsp.	10 mL
Sliced almonds, toasted (see Tip, page 93)	2 tbsp.	30 mL

Combine first 5 ingredients in 4 to 5 quart (4 to 5 L) slow cooker.

Carefully remove cores from bottoms of pears using apple corer, leaving stems intact. Set pears upright in liqueur mixture. Cook, covered, on High for 2 hours. Transfer pears with slotted spoon to serving plate.

Stir apple juice into cornstarch in small cup until smooth. Add to cooking liquid. Stir. Cook, covered, on High for about 5 minutes until thickened. Remove and discard solids. Pour over pears.

Sprinkle with almonds. Serves 4.

1 serving: *276 Calories; 8.3 g Total Fat (2.4 g Mono, 0.6 g Poly, 3.7 g Sat); 15 mg Cholesterol; 40 g Carbohydrate; 4 g Fibre; 2 g Protein; 43 mg Sodium*

Pictured below.

TRIPLE GINGERBREAD WITH PEAR

With a triple hit of ginger and plenty of other fragrant spices, this pear-filled gingerbread is moist and delicious. Enjoy this on a crisp afternoon with a dollop of whipped cream, a sprinkle of raspberries and a mug of hot tea. This recipe is part of a suggested menu on page 166.

All-purpose flour	2 cups	500 mL
Ground ginger	2 tsp.	10 mL
Baking powder	1 tsp.	5 mL
Ground cinnamon	1 tsp.	5 mL
Baking soda	1/2 tsp.	2 mL
Ground allspice	1/2 tsp.	2 mL
Ground nutmeg	1/2 tsp	2 mL
Salt	1/4 tsp.	1 mL
Butter (or hard margarine), softened	1/2 cup	125 mL
Brown sugar, packed	1 cup	250 mL
Large eggs	2	2
Buttermilk (or soured milk, see Tip, page 107)	1/3 cup	75 mL
Fancy (mild) molasses	1/3 cup	75 mL
Finely grated ginger root	1 tbsp.	15 mL
Diced peeled pear	1 cup	250 mL
Minced crystallized ginger	1/4 cup	60 mL
Icing (confectioner's) sugar	1 tbsp.	15 mL

Combine first 8 ingredients in medium bowl.

Beat butter and sugar in large bowl until light and fluffy. Add eggs, 1 at a time, beating well after each addition.

Add next 3 ingredients. Beat well. Add flour mixture. Stir until just combined.

Fold in pear and crystallized ginger. Spread in greased 9 inch (23 cm) springform pan. Bake in 350°F (175°C) oven for about 55 minutes until wooden pick inserted in centre comes out clean. Let stand in pan for 10 minutes before removing to wire rack to cool.

Sprinkle with icing sugar. Cuts into 12 wedges.

1 wedge: 262 Calories; 8.7 g Total Fat (2.3 g Mono, 0.4 g Poly, 5.2 g Sat); 56 mg Cholesterol; 44 g Carbohydrate; 1 g Fibre; 4 g Protein; 224 mg Sodium

Pictured at right.

BUTTERSCOTCH MAPLE TAPIOCA

This pudding is sweet and comforting served warm, but is good when chilled, too. Topped with maple whipped cream, it offers a pretty layered look for clear dessert dishes. This recipe is part of a suggested menu on page 166.

Egg yolks (large)	2	2
Milk	2/3 cup	150 mL
Minute tapioca	3 tbsp.	50 mL
Salt	1/4 tsp.	1 mL
Evaporated milk	1 1/2 cups	375 mL
Butter (or hard margarine)	3 tbsp.	50 mL
Brown sugar, packed	2/3 cup	150 mL
Maple syrup	2 tsp.	10 mL
Vanilla extract	1 tsp.	5 mL
Whipping cream	1/2 cup	125 mL
Maple syrup	1 tbsp.	15 mL

Whisk first 4 ingredients in small bowl. Let stand for 5 minutes.

Bring evaporated milk to a boil in small saucepan. Remove from heat. Cover to keep warm.

Melt butter in medium saucepan on medium. Add brown sugar. Cook for about 4 minutes, stirring once or twice, until melted and foamy. Carefully add evaporated milk, whisking until smooth. Add egg yolk mixture. Heat and stir for about 4 minutes until boiling and starting to thicken. Remove from heat.

Add first amount of maple syrup and vanilla. Stir. Spoon into 4 serving bowls.

Beat cream in medium bowl until stiff peaks form.

Add second amount of maple syrup. Stir. Spoon over pudding. Serves 4.

1 serving: 518 Calories; 28.2 g Total Fat (7.8 g Mono, 1.3 g Poly, 17.8 g Sat); 198 mg Cholesterol; 57 g Carbohydrate; 0 g Fibre; 10 g Protein; 334 mg Sodium

Pictured at right.

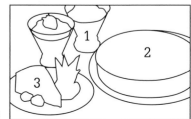

1. Butterscotch Maple Tapioca, above
2. Chocolate Orange BOO Cakes, right
3. Triple Gingerbread With Pear, above

CHOCOLATE ORANGE BOO CAKES

Fun chocolate cakes with a cream-cheesy, orange-flavoured icing baked right in. A Halloween treat perfect for a kids' party but appreciated by all ages. Mix it up with different themed designs—try jack-o'-lantern faces or bats. This recipe is part of a suggested menu on page 166.

Block cream cheese, softened	1/4 cup	60 mL
Sour cream	2 tbsp.	30 mL
Orange juice	1 tbsp.	15 mL
Granulated sugar	2 tsp.	10 mL
Drops of yellow liquid food colouring, (about 1/8 tsp., 0.5 mL)	16	16
Drops of red liquid food colouring	8	8
All-purpose flour	2 cups	500 mL
Cocoa, sifted if lumpy	1/4 cup	60 mL
Baking soda	2 tsp.	10 mL
Baking powder	1 tsp.	5 mL
Salt	1/2 tsp.	2 mL
Butter (or hard margarine), softened	1/2 cup	125 mL
Brown sugar, packed	1 1/2 cups	375 mL
Large eggs	2	2
Sour cream	3/4 cup	175 mL
Orange juice	1/2 cup	125 mL
Vanilla extract	1 tsp.	5 mL
Grated orange zest (see Tip, page 160)	1/2 tsp.	2 mL

Beat first 6 ingredients in small bowl until smooth. Set aside.

Combine next 5 ingredients in separate small bowl.

Beat butter and brown sugar in large bowl. Add eggs, 1 at a time, beating well after each addition.

Add remaining 4 ingredients. Beat well. Add flour mixture in 2 additions, mixing well after each addition, until no dry flour remains. Spread in 2 greased 9 inch (23 cm) round pans. Spoon cream cheese mixture into small resealable freezer bag. Snip off 1 corner. Pipe B-O-O letters (or any other Halloween design) across top of batter in each pan. Bake in 350°F (175°C) oven for about 30 minutes until wooden pick inserted in centre of cake comes out clean. Let stand in pans on wire racks until cool. Makes 2 cakes. Each cake cuts into 10 wedges for a total of 20 wedges.

1 wedge: 180 Calories; 8.0 g Total Fat (1.7 g Mono, 0.3 g Poly, 5.0 g Sat); 43 mg Cholesterol; 25 g Carbohydrate; 1 g Fibre; 3 g Protein; 263 mg Sodium

Pictured above.

PLUM HAZELNUT TRIFLE

A beautiful autumn trifle topped with pretty plum slices for a wonderful grand finale. For best results, make and serve on the same day. This recipe is part of a suggested menu on page 166.

Chopped fresh red plum	2 1/3 cups	575 mL
Water	1/4 cup	60 mL
Brandy	3 tbsp.	50 mL
Liquid honey	3 tbsp.	50 mL
Chinese five-spice powder	1/2 tsp.	2 mL
Ice water		
Milk	2 cups	500 mL
Egg yolks (large)	4	4
Milk	1 cup	250 mL
Granulated sugar	1/2 cup	125 mL
Cornstarch	1/4 cup	60 mL
Salt	1/4 tsp.	1 mL
Hazelnut liqueur	3 tbsp.	50 mL
Ice water		
Ladyfingers	18	18
Whipping cream	1 cup	250 mL
Fresh red plum, pitted and thinly sliced	1	1
Flaked hazelnuts (filberts), toasted (see Tip, page 93)	1/4 cup	60 mL

Combine first 5 ingredients in medium saucepan. Bring to a boil. Reduce heat to medium-low. Simmer, covered, for about 10 minutes, stirring occasionally, until plum is tender. Remove from heat. Transfer to small bowl.

Place same small bowl in large bowl of ice water. Let stand, stirring occasionally, until cool.

Heat first amount of milk in small saucepan on medium for about 5 minutes, stirring occasionally, until hot, but not boiling.

Whisk next 5 ingredients in medium bowl. Slowly add hot milk, stirring constantly with whisk. Return to saucepan. Cook on medium for about 9 minutes, stirring constantly, until boiling and thickened. Heat and stir for 1 minute.

Add liqueur. Stir. Transfer to separate medium bowl. Cover with plastic wrap directly on surface to prevent skin from forming.

Place bowl in separate large bowl of ice water. Let stand, stirring occasionally, until cool.

To assemble, layer in large glass serving bowl as follows:

1. Half of ladyfingers

2. Half of plum mixture

3. Half of milk mixture

4. Remaining ladyfingers

5. Remaining plum mixture

6. Remaining milk mixture

Beat whipping cream in separate small bowl until stiff peaks form. Spread over top. Chill, covered, for 4 hours.

Arrange plum slices over top. Sprinkle with hazelnuts. Serve immediately. Makes about 8 cups (2 L).

1 cup (250 mL): 416 Calories; 18.8 g Total Fat (7.3 g Mono, 1.5 g Poly, 9.2 g Sat); 239 mg Cholesterol; 50 g Carbohydrate; 1 g Fibre; 9 g Protein; 174 mg Sodium

Pictured at right.

BEST IN SHOWINESS

Some of the best trees for autumn leaf colour are:
- Aspen, Poplar, Birch—bright yellow
- Red and Sugar Maple—red
- Hickory—bright yellow
- Sassafras—yellow, orange and red
- Sycamore, Oak—scarlet, tan
- American Beech—golden bronze
- White Ash—purple
- Japanese Maple—purple or red
- Larch—golden yellow
- Black Gum—red

Left: Plum Hazelnut Trifle, left; Right: Hazelnut Bread Pudding, below

HAZELNUT BREAD PUDDING

A wonderful comforting dessert with just enough chocolate to satisfy—perfect with a dollop of spiced whipped cream. Enjoy by a cozy fire with close friends.

Homogenized milk	3 cups	750 mL
Granulated sugar	1/2 cup	125 mL
Vanilla bean	1	1
Dried cranberries, chopped	3/4 cup	175 mL
Orange liqueur	2 tbsp.	30 mL
Chocolate hazelnut spread	1/3 cup	75 mL
French bread slices	12	12
(1/2 inch, 12 mm, thick)		
Large eggs	4	4
Salt	1/8 tsp.	0.5 mL
Flaked hazelnuts (filberts)	1/2 cup	125 mL

Combine milk and sugar in medium saucepan. Split vanilla bean in half lengthwise. Scrape seeds from pods into milk mixture. Add pods. Heat and stir on medium for about 5 minutes until sugar is dissolved and bubbles form around edge of pan. Remove from heat. Let stand, covered, for 20 minutes. Remove and discard pods.

Put cranberries into small bowl. Pour liqueur over cranberries in small bowl. Stir until coated. Let stand, covered, for 15 minutes.

Spread hazelnut spread over 1 side of each bread slice. Cut into 1 inch (2.5 cm) pieces.

Whisk eggs and salt in large bowl. Slowly add milk mixture, whisking constantly, until well combined. Add bread pieces and cranberry mixture. Stir. Transfer to greased 2 quart (2 L) baking dish. Let stand for 10 minutes.

Scatter hazelnuts over top. Bake in 325°F (160°C) oven for about 1 hour until set and knife inserted in centre comes out clean. Let stand on wire rack for 15 minutes. Serves 8.

1 serving: 660 Calories; 17.0 g Total Fat (8.5 g Mono, 2.7 g Poly, 4.4 g Sat); 119 mg Cholesterol; 106 g Carbohydrate; 6 g Fibre; 20 g Protein; 999 mg Sodium

Pictured above.

ZUCCHINI MOLE CAKE

Mole (MOH-lay) is a Mexican sauce made with chocolate and chili spices. We've added the same flair to a moist, decadent chocolate cake with the surprising bite of cayenne. Leftover cake should be stored in the fridge because the icing contains sour cream.

Large eggs	2	2
Granulated sugar	1 3/4 cups	425 mL
Cooking oil	3/4 cup	175 mL
Buttermilk (or sour milk, see Tip, page 107)	1/2 cup	125 mL
Vanilla extract	1 tsp.	5 mL
Almond extract	1/2 tsp.	2 mL
Grated zucchini (with peel)	2 cups	500 mL
All-purpose flour	2 1/2 cups	625 mL
Cocoa, sifted if lumpy	1/3 cup	75 mL
Baking soda	1 tsp.	5 mL
Ground cinnamon	1 tsp.	5 mL
Baking powder	1/2 tsp.	2 mL
Salt	1/2 tsp.	2 mL
Cayenne pepper	1/4 tsp.	1 mL

CHOCOLATE MOLE ICING

Semi-sweet chocolate chips	1 cup	250 mL
Sour cream	1/2 cup	125 mL
Ground cinnamon	1/2 tsp.	2 mL
Cayenne pepper	1/8 tsp.	0.5 mL

Beat first 6 ingredients in large bowl until smooth. Add zucchini. Stir.

Combine next 7 ingredients in medium bowl. Add to egg mixture. Stir until well combined. Spread in greased 9 x 13 inch (23 x 33 cm) pan. Bake in 350°F (175°C) oven for about 35 minutes until wooden pick inserted in centre comes out clean. Let stand in pan on wire rack for 30 minutes. Remove cake from pan and place on wire rack.

Chocolate Mole Icing: Place chocolate chips and sour cream in small microwave-safe bowl. Microwave on Medium for about 90 seconds, stirring every 30 seconds until almost melted (see Tip, below). Stir until smooth.

Add cinnamon and cayenne. Stir. Spread over cake. Cool. Cuts into 20 pieces.

1 piece: 257 Calories; 12.8 g Total Fat (6.1 g Mono, 2.7 g Poly, 3.1 g Sat); 26 mg Cholesterol; 35 g Carbohydrate; 1 g Fibre; 3 g Protein; 152 mg Sodium

Pictured below.

Zucchini Mole Cake, above

TIP

The microwaves used in our test kitchen are 900 watts—but microwaves are sold in many different powers. You should be able to find the wattage of yours by opening the door and looking for the mandatory label. If your microwave is more than 900 watts, you may need to reduce the cooking time. If it's less than 900 watts, you'll probably need to increase the cooking time.

Spiced Rum Pear Cake, below

SPICED RUM PEAR CAKE

Sweet pears and colourful cherries make this moist spice cake a simple yet delicious dessert item that will make your afternoon cup of coffee special.

Butter (or hard margarine)	1/4 cup	60 mL
Brown sugar, packed	1/4 cup	60 mL
Diced peeled pear	2 cups	500 mL
Chopped dried cherries	1/4 cup	60 mL
Butter (or hard margarine), softened	1/3 cup	75 mL
Brown sugar, packed	2/3 cup	150 mL
Large eggs	2	2
Sour cream	1/2 cup	125 mL
Spiced rum (or orange juice)	2 tbsp.	30 mL
Grated orange zest	1/2 tsp.	2 mL
Vanilla extract	1/2 tsp.	2 mL
All-purpose flour	1 1/4 cups	300 mL
Baking powder	1/2 tsp.	2 mL
Baking soda	1/4 tsp.	1 mL
Ground cinnamon	1/4 tsp.	1 mL
Salt	1/4 tsp.	1 mL

Melt butter in medium saucepan on medium. Add first amount of brown sugar. Heat and stir until brown sugar is dissolved.

Add pear and cherries. Cook for about 5 minutes, stirring often, until pear is tender.

Beat second amount of butter and second amount of brown sugar in large bowl until light and fluffy.

Add eggs, 1 at a time, beating well after each addition. Add next 4 ingredients. Beat well.

Combine remaining 5 ingredients in medium bowl. Add to butter mixture in 2 additions, mixing well after each addition until no dry flour remains. Add pear mixture. Stir until just combined. Spread in greased 9 inch (23 cm) round pan. Bake in 350°F (175°C) oven for about 45 minutes until wooden pick inserted in centre comes out clean. Let stand in pan on wire rack until cool. Cuts into 12 wedges.

1 wedge: 237 Calories; 11.4 g Total Fat (2.6 g Mono, 0.5 g Poly, 7.0 g Sat); 65 mg Cholesterol; 31 g Carbohydrate; 1 g Fibre; 3 g Protein; 176 mg Sodium

Pictured on page 122 and above.

CANADIAN PECAN TART

Indulge in the classic look and taste of a rich pecan tart. The highlights of the smooth filling are the quintessential Canadian ingredients of maple syrup and whisky.

All-purpose flour	1 1/4 cups	300 mL
Cold butter (or hard margarine), cut up	1/3 cup	75 mL
Finely chopped pecans	1/4 cup	60 mL
Brown sugar, packed	2 tbsp.	30 mL
Salt	1/4 tsp.	1 mL
Canadian whisky (rye)	2 tbsp.	30 mL
Ice water	2 tbsp.	30 mL
Pecan halves	1 1/4 cups	300 mL
Large eggs, fork-beaten	3	3
Brown sugar, packed	1 cup	250 mL
Maple syrup	1/2 cup	125 mL
Butter (or hard margarine), melted	3 tbsp.	50 mL
Canadian whisky (rye)	3 tbsp.	50 mL

Process first 5 ingredients in food processor until mixture resembles coarse crumbs.

Add whisky and water. Process with on/off motion until mixture starts to come together. Do not over process. Turn out onto lightly floured surface. Press pastry into ball. Flatten slightly into disc. Wrap with plastic wrap. Chill for 30 minutes. Remove plastic wrap. Roll out pastry on lightly floured surface to fit ungreased 9 inch (23 cm) tart pan with fluted sides and removable bottom. Carefully lift pastry and press into bottom and up sides of tart pan. Trim edge. Poke pastry several times with fork. Chill for 1 hour. Place pan on ungreased baking sheet with sides (see Note). Bake on bottom rack in 375°F (190°C) oven for about 25 minutes until golden. Cool.

Scatter pecan halves in pie shell.

Whisk remaining 5 ingredients in medium bowl until smooth. Pour over pecans. Bake on bottom rack in 350°F (175°C) oven for about 30 minutes until golden and set. Let stand in pan on wire rack until cool. Cuts into 8 wedges.

1 wedge: 510 Calories; 28.6 g Total Fat (12.2 g Mono, 5.2 g Poly, 9.4 g Sat); 111 mg Cholesterol; 57 g Carbohydrate; 2 g Fibre; 6 g Protein; 185 mg Sodium

Pictured below.

NOTE: Placing tart pan on baking sheet provides a safe way to transfer hot pan out of oven.

Canadian Pecan Tart, above

SWEET POTATO BROWNIES

The flavours of sweet potato casserole in rich, chocolatey brownie form! Use canned or leftover sweet potato if you have any on hand. This recipe is part of a suggested menu on page 166.

Granulated sugar	1 cup	250 mL
All-purpose flour	3/4 cup	175 mL
Cocoa, sifted if lumpy	1/2 cup	125 mL
Whole-wheat flour	1/2 cup	125 mL
Baking powder	1 tsp.	5 mL
Salt	1/4 tsp.	1 mL
Semi-sweet chocolate baking squares (1 oz., 28 g, each), chopped	2	2
Large eggs	2	2
Mashed orange-fleshed sweet potato (about 3/4 lb., 340 g, uncooked)	1 cup	250 mL
Buttermilk (or soured milk, see Tip, page 107)	1/2 cup	125 mL
Cooking oil	1/4 cup	60 mL
Vanilla extract	1 tsp.	5 mL
Ground cinnamon	1/2 tsp.	2 mL
Miniature marshmallows	2 cups	500 mL
Semi-sweet chocolate chips	1/3 cup	75 mL

Combine first 6 ingredients in medium bowl. Make a well in centre.

Microwave chocolate in small microwave-safe bowl on Medium for about 90 seconds, stirring every 30 seconds until almost melted (see Tip, page 136). Stir until smooth.

Put next 6 ingredients into blender or food processor. Add chocolate. Process until smooth. Add to well. Stir until just combined. Spread in greased 9 x 9 inch (23 x 23 cm) pan. Bake in 350°F (175°C) oven for about 35 minutes until wooden pick inserted in centre comes out moist but not wet with batter. Do not overbake.

Scatter marshmallows and chocolate chips over top. Broil on centre rack in oven for 1 to 2 minutes until golden. Let stand in pan on wire rack until cool. Cuts into 36 pieces.

1 piece: 80 Calories; 2.8 g Total Fat (1.3 g Mono, 0.6 g Poly, 0.8 g Sat); 12 mg Cholesterol; 14 g Carbohydrate; 1 g Fibre; 2 g Protein; 44 mg Sodium

Pictured below.

Sweet Potato Brownies, above

Chicago-Style Popcorn, page 149

SNACKS

It is a delightful thing to nip into a big bowl of something crunchy, sweet or salty (or all three!). Bite-size nibbles make perfect after-school snacks for the first days of a new school year, or fun treats for the whole family to share on a movie or game night. They can also provide charming surprises for guests—a plate of enticing cookies set out for company, or sweet and savoury mixes wrapped up for them to take home.

CARAMEL APPLE COOKIES

*Fun sugar cookies with a crunchy caramel "apple core."
Set out a plate of these when cookie monsters drop by.
You can store them in airtight containers in the freezer
for up to two months. This recipe is part of a suggested
menu on page 166.*

All-purpose flour	1 cup	250 mL
Crushed round butter-flavoured crackers	1/2 cup	125 mL
Ground cinnamon	1/2 tsp.	2 mL
Cream of tartar	1/4 tsp.	1 mL
Grated lemon zest (see Tip, page 160)	1/4 tsp.	1 mL
Salt	1/8 tsp.	0.5 mL
Butter (or hard margarine), softened	1/2 cup	125 mL
Brown sugar, packed	1/2 cup	125 mL
Large egg	1	1
Lemon juice	1/2 tsp.	2 mL
Crushed hard caramel candies (such as Werther's), see Tip, page 17	1/4 cup	60 mL

Combine first 6 ingredients in medium bowl.

Beat butter and brown sugar in large bowl until light and fluffy.

Add egg and lemon juice. Beat well. Add flour mixture in 2 additions, beating well after each addition until no dry flour remains. Shape into flattened disc. Wrap in plastic wrap. Chill for at least 1 hour. Discard plastic wrap. Roll out dough on lightly floured surface to 1/4 inch (6 mm) thickness. Cut out shapes with lightly floured 2 1/2 inch (6.4 cm) apple-shaped (or round) cookie cutter. Arrange, about 1 inch (2.5 cm) apart, on parchment paper-lined cookie sheets. Cut out circles from centre of each apple with lightly floured 1 inch (2.5 cm) round cookie cutter. Roll out scraps to cut more shapes.

Spoon 1/2 tsp. (2 mL) candy into each cut-out circle. Bake in 375°F (190°C) oven for about 10 minutes until candy is melted and cookies are golden. Let stand on cookie sheets for 10 minutes before removing to wire racks to cool. Makes about 19 cookies.

1 cookie: 108 Calories; 5.7 g Total Fat (1.4 g Mono, 0.3 g Poly, 3.3 g Sat); 26 mg Cholesterol; 14 g Carbohydrate; trace Fibre; 1 g Protein; 74 mg Sodium

Pictured below.

Caramel Apple Cookies, above

PUMPKIN SEED COOKIES

Celebrate harvest goodness in a nutritious snack—moist, chewy pumpkin cookies are loaded with sweet fruit bites and crunchy pumpkin seeds. These will store in airtight containers in the freezer for up to two months.

Brown sugar, packed	3/4 cup	175 mL
Granulated sugar	3/4 cup	175 mL
Butter (or hard margarine), softened	1/2 cup	125 mL
Large egg	1	1
Canned pure pumpkin (no spices), see Tip, page 23	1 1/3 cups	325 mL
Quick-cooking rolled oats	1 cup	250 mL
All-purpose flour	1 1/2 cups	375 mL
Baking powder	1 tbsp.	15 mL
Ground cinnamon	3/4 tsp.	4 mL
Ground allspice	1/4 tsp.	1 mL
Salt	1/4 tsp.	1 mL
Dried cranberries	3/4 cup	175 mL
Salted, roasted shelled pumpkin seeds	3/4 cup	175 mL

Beat first 3 ingredients in large bowl until light and fluffy.

Add egg and pumpkin. Beat well.

Process rolled oats in blender or food processor until coarse powder. Transfer to medium bowl.

Add next 5 ingredients. Stir. Add to pumpkin mixture in 2 additions, mixing well after each addition until no dry flour remains.

Add cranberries and pumpkin seeds. Mix well. Drop, using 1 tbsp. (15 mL) for each, about 2 inches (5 cm) apart, onto greased cookie sheets. Bake in 375°F (190°C) oven for about 10 minutes until golden. Let stand on cookie sheets for 5 minutes before removing to wire racks to cool. Makes about 54 cookies.

1 cookie: 75 Calories; 3.2 g Total Fat (0.9 g Mono, 0.7 g Poly, 1.4 g Sat); 8 mg Cholesterol; 11 g Carbohydrate; 1 g Fibre; 1 g Protein; 73 mg Sodium

Pictured below.

Pumpkin Seed Cookies, above

Chocolate Almond Brittle, below

CHOCOLATE ALMOND BRITTLE

A crunchy delight—chocolate-flavoured hard candy melted around whole almonds. Tie a few pieces into coloured cellophane as a gift for a hard-candy lover! This will keep in an airtight container at room temperature for up to two weeks.

Whole natural almonds	1 1/2 cups	375 mL
Cocoa, sifted if lumpy	1/4 cup	60 mL
Butter (or hard margarine), melted	2 tbsp.	30 mL
Salt	1/4 tsp.	1 mL
Granulated sugar	1 cup	250 mL
White corn syrup	1/2 cup	125 mL
Water	1/4 cup	60 mL
Baking soda	2 tsp.	10 mL

Spread almonds on ungreased baking sheet with sides. Bake in 350°F (175°C) oven for about 10 minutes until darkened. Transfer to medium bowl. Cover to keep warm. Turn oven off. Return baking sheet to oven (see Note 1).

Combine next 3 ingredients in small bowl.

Combine next 3 ingredients in large saucepan. Heat and stir on medium until sugar is dissolved. Bring to a boil. Boil for 10 minutes, without stirring, brushing sides of pan with wet pastry brush to dissolve any sugar crystals until mixture reaches hard crack stage (about 300°F, 150°C) on candy thermometer (see Note 2) or until small amount dropped into very cold water separates into hard, brittle threads. Add cocoa mixture and almonds. Stir. Remove from heat.

Add baking soda. Stir well. Mixture will foam. Working quickly and carefully, pour nut mixture in thick line on warmed parchment paper-lined baking sheet. Spread with greased spatula. Let stand until cooled completely. Break into pieces. Makes about 1 lb. 5 1/8 oz. (598 g).

1 oz. (28 g): 113 Calories; 6.3 g Total Fat (3.5 g Mono, 1.3 g Poly, 1.1 g Sat); 3 mg Cholesterol; 15 g Carbohydrate; 2 g Fibre; 2 g Protein; 157 mg Sodium

Pictured above.

NOTE 1: A warm baking sheet will make it easier to spread sugar mixture. Turn off oven after toasting almonds. Line baking sheet with parchment paper and return to oven until ready to use.

NOTE 2: Test your candy thermometer before each use. Bring cold water to a boil. Candy thermometer should read 212°F (100°C) at sea level. Adjust recipe temperature up or down based on test results. For example, if your thermometer reads 206°F (97°C), subtract 6°F (43°C) from each temperature called for in the recipe.

Spiced Nut Mix, below

SING YOUR WINTER BLUES AWAY

There are lots of songs out there on the subject of winter and the many emotions and activities associated with it. Here is a short list of popular songs, both old and more recent, that are about or set in the winter season. Can you think of any others to add to the list?

"California Dreamin," *The Mamas and the Papas*
"Snowbird," *Anne Murray*
"If We Make It Through December," *Merle Haggard*
"Sleighride," *Leroy Anderson*
"I've Got My Love to Keep Me Warm," *Irving Berlin*
"Moonlight in Vermont," *Blackburn and Suessdorf*
"Winter Wonderland," *Bernard and Smith*
"Winter Romance," *Dean Martin*
"December Blue," *Duke Ellington*
"December Child," *Cyndi Lauper*
"January Rain," *David Gray*
"Hazy Shade of Winter," *Simon and Garfunkel*
"Song For A Winter's Night," *Sarah McLachlan*
"Winter," *John Denver*
"Winter Has Me In Its Grip," *Don Mclean*
"Winter Rose," *Wings*
"Looks Like A Cold Cold Winter," *Bing Crosby*
"Cold December In Your Heart," *Glenn Campbell*
"River," *Joni Mitchell*

SPICED NUT MIX

A classic mix of toasted nuts that pack some heat from garam masala—ideal for the cravings that only nuts can fulfill! This mix stores in an airtight container at room temperature for up to three weeks, or in the freezer for up to two months.

Butter (or hard margarine), melted	3 tbsp.	50 mL
Garam masala	1 tbsp.	15 mL
Ground ginger	1 tsp.	5 mL
Salt	1/8 tsp.	0.5 mL
Pecan halves	1 cup	250 mL
Walnut halves	1 cup	250 mL
Whole natural almonds	1 cup	250 mL
Salted cashews	1/2 cup	125 mL
Salted peanuts	1/2 cup	125 mL

Combine first 4 ingredients in large bowl.

Add remaining 5 ingredients. Toss until coated. Arrange in single layer on greased baking sheet with sides. Bake in 300°F (150°C) oven for about 20 minutes, stirring twice, until darkened and fragrant. Makes about 4 cups (1 L).

1/2 cup (125 mL): 468 Calories; 43.9 g Total Fat (13.7 g Mono, 12.3 g Poly, 7.5 g Sat); 11 mg Cholesterol; 12 g Carbohydrate; 5 g Fibre; 11 g Protein; 262 mg Sodium

Pictured above.

WALNUT GINGER BISCOTTI

Walnuts provide a pleasing crunch in these delicious biscotti, their flavour a lovely match with ginger—a not-too-sweet dipper for a steaming mug of coffee. These will store in an airtight container in the freezer for up to two months.

All-purpose flour	2 cups	500 mL
Chopped walnuts, toasted (see Tip, page 93)	3/4 cup	175 mL
Brown sugar, packed	1/2 cup	125 mL
Granulated sugar	1/2 cup	125 mL
Baking powder	1/4 tsp.	1 mL
Ground ginger	1/4 tsp.	1 mL
Salt	1/4 tsp.	1 mL
Large eggs, fork-beaten	3	3
Minced crystallized ginger	1/3 cup	75 mL
Cooking oil	1/4 cup	60 mL
Vanilla extract	1 tsp.	5 mL

Combine first 7 ingredients in large bowl. Make a well in centre.

Add remaining 4 ingredients to well. Mix until stiff dough forms. Turn out onto lightly floured surface. Knead 6 times. Divide into 2 portions. Shape into 8 inch (20 cm) long logs. Place crosswise, about 3 inches (7.5 cm) apart, on greased cookie sheet. Flatten slightly. Bake in 350°F (175°C) oven for about 27 minutes until golden. Let stand on cookie sheet for about 20 minutes until cool enough to handle. Cut logs diagonally with serrated knife into 1/2 inch (12 mm) slices. Arrange, cut side down, on greased cookie sheet. Bake for 10 minutes. Turn. Bake for about 5 minutes until dry and browned on bottom. Let stand on cookie sheet for 5 minutes before removing to wire racks to cool. Makes about 24 biscotti.

1 biscotti: 121 Calories; 5.4 g Total Fat (2.0 g Mono, 2.6 g Poly, 0.6 g Sat); 26 mg Cholesterol; 17 g Carbohydrate; trace Fibre; 2 g Protein; 40 mg Sodium

Pictured below.

Walnut Ginger Biscotti, above

Seed and Fruit Granola Bars

A homemade, nut-free alternative to commercial granola bars. Store in an airtight container at room temperature for up to one week, or in the freezer for up to two months.

Large flake rolled oats	2 cups	500 mL
Raw pumpkin seeds	1/2 cup	125 mL
Raw sunflower seeds	1/2 cup	125 mL
Chopped dried cherries	1/3 cup	75 mL
Dried blueberries	1/3 cup	75 mL
Golden raisins	1/3 cup	75 mL
Wheat germ	1/3 cup	75 mL
Flaxseed	1 tbsp.	15 mL
Sesame seeds	1 tbsp.	15 mL
Butter (or hard margarine)	1/3 cup	75 mL
Brown sugar, packed	1/4 cup	60 mL
Liquid honey	1/4 cup	60 mL
Maple (or maple-flavoured) syrup	1/4 cup	60 mL

Spread rolled oats on ungreased baking sheet with sides. Bake in 350°F (175°C) oven for about 18 minutes, stirring occasionally, until golden. Transfer to large bowl.

Add next 8 ingredients. Stir.

Combine remaining 4 ingredients in small saucepan. Heat and stir on medium for about 5 minutes until starting to boil. Drizzle over rolled oat mixture. Stir until coated. Press into greased 9 x 13 inch (23 x 33 cm) pan. Bake for about 15 minutes until golden. Let stand for 15 minutes to cool slightly. Run knife around inside edge of pan to loosen. Cut into 12 bars while still warm. Let stand in pan on wire rack until cool. Makes 12 bars.

1 bar: 290 Calories; 12.6 g Total Fat (1.3 g Mono, 0.2 g Poly, 4.1 g Sat); 14 mg Cholesterol; 38 g Carbohydrate; 5 g Fibre; 6 g Protein; 43 mg Sodium

Pictured below.

Seed and Fruit Granola Bars, above

Spiced Honey Macaroons, below

SPICED HONEY MACAROONS

Honey-sweet and very chewy treats reminiscent of a perfectly toasted marshmallow! These macaroons have rich coconut flavour and a hint of spice, and will keep in an airtight container in the freezer for up to two months.

Medium unsweetened coconut	1/2 cup	125 mL
All-purpose flour	2 tbsp.	30 mL
Sliced almonds	2 tbsp.	30 mL
Ground cinnamon	1/8 tsp.	0.5 mL
Ground ginger	1/8 tsp.	0.5 mL
Ground allspice, sprinkle		
Salt, sprinkle		
Egg whites (large), room temperature	2	2
Granulated sugar	1/3 cup	75 mL
Liquid honey	1 tbsp.	15 mL

Combine first 7 ingredients in small bowl.

Beat egg whites in medium bowl until soft peaks form. Slowly add sugar, beating constantly until stiff peaks form.

Add honey. Beat well. Fold in coconut mixture. Drop, using 1 tbsp. (15 mL) for each, about 2 inches (5 cm) apart onto greased cookie sheets. Bake in 350°F (175°C) oven for about 10 minutes until bottoms are golden. Let stand on cookie sheets for 5 minutes before removing to wire racks to cool. Makes about 32 macaroons.

1 macaroon: 20 Calories; 0.9 g Total Fat (0.2 g Mono, 0.1 g Poly, 0.7 g Sat); 0 mg Cholesterol; 3 g Carbohydrate; trace Fibre; trace Protein; 4 mg Sodium

Pictured above.

SNACKS

Fall Fruit Snack Mix

This wholesome, tasty snack mix incorporates dried fall fruits, honey and warm spices—it makes a big batch, so you can pack it in lunches or simply set out a bowl for the family to share. It will store in an airtight container at room temperature for up to three weeks, or in the freezer for up to two months. This recipe is part of a suggested menu on page 166.

Puffed wheat cereal	4 cups	1 L
Rice squares cereal	4 cups	1 L
"O"-shaped toasted oat cereal	2 cups	500 mL
Pecan halves	1 cup	250 mL
Raw pumpkin seeds	1 cup	250 mL
Butter (or hard margarine), melted	1/2 cup	125 mL
Liquid honey	1/4 cup	60 mL
Ground cinnamon	2 tsp.	10 mL
Ground ginger	2 tsp.	10 mL
Ground cardamom	1 tsp.	5 mL
Salt	1/2 tsp.	2 mL
Chopped dried apple	1 cup	250 mL
Chopped dried apricot	1 cup	250 mL
Dried cranberries	1 cup	250 mL

Combine first 5 ingredients in large roasting pan.

Combine next 6 ingredients in small bowl. Drizzle over cereal mixture. Stir until coated. Bake, uncovered, in 300°F (150°C) oven for about 45 minutes, stirring occasionally, until golden.

Add remaining 3 ingredients. Stir. Bake, uncovered, for 15 minutes. Let stand in pan on wire rack, stirring occasionally, until cool. Makes about 14 cups (3.5 L).

1/2 cup (125 mL): 179 Calories; 9.3 g Total Fat (2.5 g Mono, 1.1 g Poly, 2.8 g Sat); 9 mg Cholesterol; 22 g Carbohydrate; 2 g Fibre; 3 g Protein; 156 mg Sodium

Pictured at left.

Chicago-Style Popcorn

The unlikely combination of caramel popcorn and Cheddar cheese popcorn is very popular in Chicago, and makes a very tasty sweet-and-salty treat. Store this in an airtight container at room temperature for up to one week. This recipe is part of a suggested menu on page 166.

Popped corn (3/4 cup, 175 mL, unpopped)	16 cups	4 L
Butter, melted	2 tbsp.	15 mL
Cheddar-flavoured popcorn seasoning	2 tbsp.	15 mL
Brown sugar, packed	1 cup	250 mL
Butter	1/2 cup	125 mL
White corn syrup	1/4 cup	60 mL
Salt	1/2 tsp.	2 mL
Vanilla extract	1/2 tsp.	2 mL
Baking soda	1/2 tsp.	2 mL

Put 8 cups (2 L) popcorn into extra-large bowl. Drizzle with first amount of butter. Toss well.

Sprinkle with popcorn seasoning. Toss until coated. Set aside.

Put remaining popcorn into small roasting pan. Combine next 4 ingredients in medium saucepan. Heat and stir on medium for about 3 minutes until butter is melted and sugar is dissolved. Bring to a boil on medium-high. Boil for 2 minutes without stirring. Remove from heat.

Add vanilla and baking soda. Stir well. Mixture will foam. Pour over popcorn. Stir until coated. Bake, uncovered, in 200°F (95°C) oven for about 1 hour, stirring often, until popcorn is glazed. Spread on waxed paper. Let stand until dry. Add to reserved popcorn. Toss. Makes about 16 cups (4 L).

1/2 cup (125 mL): 80 Calories; 3.9 g Total Fat (1.0 g Mono, 0.2 g Poly, 2.4 g Sat); 10 mg Cholesterol; 11 g Carbohydrate; 1 g Fibre; 1 g Protein; 127 mg Sodium

Pictured on page 140 and at left.

Snowflakes

Snowflakes are formed when water vapor condenses directly into ice, and their shape and size are affected by temperature, air currents and humidity. They come in an amazing variety of shapes: needles, plates, columns and hexagons that are flat, lacy or indented. Snowflakes are truly nature's gems.

Top: Chicago-Style Popcorn, above
Bottom: Fall Fruit Snack Mix, above

Spiced Plum Jam, page 163

CONDIMENTS & PRESERVES

There is a timeless appeal about Mason jars filled with cheery, jewel-toned mixtures, or a rustic pickle mix pulled from the pantry. Chutneys and relishes add a little something special when served alongside your favourite roasted meats, and there is nothing better than homemade jam on toast to start the day. Condiments and preserves embody the age-old tradition of storing food away for the winter, reminding us to be thankful for the abundance that keeps us fed throughout the year.

APPLE SQUASH CHUTNEY

You'll love this sweet, spicy and versatile condiment. It tastes great with cheese, fruit, vegetables and cooked meats, especially pork.

Chopped ginger root	1/3 cup	75 mL
Whole black peppercorns	1 tbsp.	15 mL
Whole green cardamom, bruised (see Tip, page 14)	6	6
Bay leaf	1	1
Chopped butternut squash	3 cups	750 mL
Chopped peeled tart apple (such as Granny Smith)	3 cups	750 mL
Malt vinegar	1 1/2 cups	375 mL
Brown sugar, packed	1 cup	250 mL
Chopped onion	1 cup	250 mL
Chopped red pepper	1 cup	250 mL
Chopped dried apricot	1/2 cup	125 mL
Currants	1/2 cup	125 mL
Diced mixed peel	1/2 cup	125 mL
Salt	2 tsp.	10 mL
Dried crushed chilies	1 tsp.	5 mL
Ground cinnamon	1 tsp.	5 mL
Ground nutmeg	1/4 tsp.	1 mL
Ground cloves	1/8 tsp.	0.5 mL

Place first 4 ingredients in centre of 6 inch (15 cm) square of double-layered cheesecloth. Draw up corners and tie with butcher's string.

Combine next 10 ingredients in Dutch oven. Bring to a boil. Reduce heat to medium. Boil gently, covered, for about 20 minutes, stirring occasionally, until apple and squash are tender.

Add remaining 4 ingredients and cheesecloth bag. Stir. Reduce heat to medium-low. Simmer, covered, for 30 minutes. Remove and discard cheesecloth bag. Carefully process with hand blender or in blender, in batches, until coarsely chopped and liquid is absorbed (see Safety Tip, below). Fill 5 hot sterile 1 cup (250 mL) jars to within 1/2 inch (12 mm) of top. Remove air bubbles and adjust headspace if necessary. Wipe rims. Place hot metal lids on jars and screw on metal bands fingertip tight. Do not over-tighten. Process in boiling water bath for 15 minutes (see Note). Remove jars. Let stand at room temperature until cool. Store in refrigerator for up to 1 month after opening. Makes about 5 cups (1.25 L).

1 tbsp. (15 mL): 21 Calories; trace Total Fat (0 g Mono, trace Poly, trace Sat); 0 mg Cholesterol; 5 g Carbohydrate; 1 g Fibre; trace Protein; 58 mg Sodium

Pictured below.

SAFETY TIP: Follow manufacturer's instructions for processing hot liquids.

NOTE: Processing time is for elevations 1001 to 3000 feet (306 to 915 m) above sea level. Adjust the processing time for elevation in your area if necessary.

Apple Squash Chutney, above

CRANBERRY PLUM FREEZER JAM

Festive jam with a hint of orange and spice gives a cozy fall feeling to warm scones or slices of toast. Freezer pectin allows you to use much less sugar than traditional jam recipes, resulting in a sweet-tart spread.

Chopped peeled pear	4 cups	1 L
Chopped pitted fresh red (or black) plum	4 cups	1 L
Fresh (or frozen) cranberries, chopped	2 cups	500 mL
Water	1/4 cup	60 mL
Ground cinnamon	1/4 tsp.	1 mL
Ground cloves, just a pinch		
Granulated sugar	1 1/2 cups	375 mL
Envelope of freezer jam pectin	1 1/2 oz.	45 g
Grated orange zest	1 tbsp.	15 mL

Combine first 6 ingredients in large saucepan. Bring to a boil. Reduce heat to medium. Cook, uncovered, for about 20 minutes, stirring occasionally, until fruit is softened.

Combine remaining 3 ingredients in large bowl. Add pear mixture. Stir for 3 minutes to suspend fruit. Fill clean plastic containers to within 1/2 inch (12 mm) of top (see Note). Let stand at room temperature for about 30 minutes until cool and thickened. Cover with tight-fitting lids. Store in refrigerator for up to 3 weeks or in freezer for up to 1 year. Makes about 5 cups (1.25 L).

1 tbsp. (15 mL): 18 Calories; trace Total Fat (trace Mono, trace Poly, 0 g Sat); 0 mg Cholesterol; 5 g Carbohydrate; trace Fibre; trace Protein; trace Sodium

Pictured at right.

NOTE: Plastic freezer jars designed to store food in the freezer are available at grocery stores.

MOONCAKES

Rich, heavy, dense and round or rectangular, Chinese mooncakes are pastries traditionally filled with bean pastes and egg yolks and eaten as delicacies during the Mid-Autumn Festival in mid-August, in honour of the moon.

TOMATO TAPENADE

This spread combines tomatillos and tomatoes, both fresh and sun-dried. Serve it with cheese and crackers, or as an accompaniment for roasted pork or poultry.

Oil from sun-dried tomatoes	2 tbsp.	30 mL
Finely chopped tomatillo	2 cups	500 mL
Finely chopped shallots (or green onion)	1/2 cup	125 mL
Garlic cloves, minced (or 1 tsp., 5 mL, powder)	4	4
Dried crushed chilies	1/8 tsp.	0.5 mL
Finely chopped seeded tomato	2 cups	500 mL
Sun-dried tomatoes in oil, blotted dry, finely chopped	1/2 cup	125 mL
Balsamic vinegar	1/4 cup	60 mL
Dried oregano	1 tsp.	5 mL
Salt	1/2 tsp.	2 mL
Pepper	1/4 tsp.	1 mL

Heat sun-dried tomato oil in large frying pan on medium. Add next 4 ingredients. Cook for about 5 minutes, stirring often, until shallots are softened.

Add remaining 6 ingredients. Stir. Bring to a boil. Fill 2 sterile 1 cup (250 mL) jars to within 1/2 inch (12 mm) of top. Let stand at room temperature until cool. Cover with tight-fitting lids. Store in refrigerator for up to 2 weeks or in freezer for up to 3 months. Makes about 2 1/4 cups (550 mL).

1 tbsp. (15 mL): 18 Calories; 1.1 g Total Fat (0.7 g Mono, 0.2 g Poly, 0.2 g Sat); 0 mg Cholesterol; 2 g Carbohydrate; 1 g Fibre; 0.3 g Protein; 37 mg Sodium

Pictured at right.

Top: Cranberry Plum Freezer Jam, above
Bottom: Tomato Tapenade, above

BEET RELISH

This versatile relish is for pickled beet lovers! With speedy microwave prep, you'll be enjoying it on burgers or serving it alongside savoury roasts in no time.

Diced fresh peeled beets (see Tip, right)	2 1/3 cups	575 mL
Water	1 tbsp.	15 mL
Diced celery	1/3 cup	75 mL
Diced onion	1/3 cup	75 mL
Granulated sugar	1/3 cup	75 mL
Balsamic vinegar	1 tbsp.	15 mL
Frozen concentrated orange juice	1 tbsp.	15 mL
White vinegar	1 tbsp.	15 mL
Salt	1/4 tsp.	1 mL
Cayenne pepper	1/8 tsp.	0.5 mL

Place beet in medium microwave-safe bowl. Sprinkle with water. Microwave, covered, on High for about 5 minutes until almost tender (see Tip, page 136).

Add celery and onion. Microwave, covered, on High for about 5 minutes until celery is softened.

Combine remaining 6 ingredients in small bowl. Add to beet mixture. Stir. Microwave, covered, on High for 3 minutes. Transfer to food processor. Carefully process with on/off motion for about 30 seconds until finely chopped (see Safety Tip, below). Fill 3 sterile 1/2 cup (125 mL) jars to within 1/2 inch (12 mm) of top. Let stand at room temperature until cool. Cover with tight-fitting lids. Store in refrigerator for up to 2 weeks. Makes about 1 1/3 cups (325 mL).

1 tbsp. (15 mL): 16 Calories; trace Total Fat (trace Mono, trace Poly, trace Sat); 0 mg Cholesterol; 4 g Carbohydrate; 1 g Fibre; trace Protein; 40 mg Sodium

Pictured below.

SAFETY TIP: Follow manufacturer's instructions for processing hot liquids.

TIP

Don't get caught red-handed! Wear rubber gloves when handling beets.

Beet Relish, above

Apple Pear Chutney, below

APPLE PEAR CHUTNEY

Spoon this sweet and delicately spiced blend, reminiscent of comforting apple pie filling, next to your ham, pork or poultry.

Cooking oil	2 tsp.	10 mL
Chopped onion	1/2 cup	125 mL
Ground allspice	1/4 tsp.	1 mL
Ground cinnamon	1/4 tsp.	1 mL
Ground cloves	1/8 tsp.	0.5 mL
Ground nutmeg	1/8 tsp.	0.5 mL
Chopped peeled cooking apple (such as McIntosh)	3 cups	750 mL
Chopped peeled pear	2 cups	500 mL
Apple juice	1 cup	250 mL
Brown sugar, packed	1/3 cup	75 mL
Apple cider vinegar	1/4 cup	60 mL
Raisins	1/4 cup	60 mL

Heat cooking oil in medium saucepan on medium. Add next 5 ingredients. Cook for about 5 minutes, stirring often, until onion is caramelized.

Add remaining 6 ingredients. Bring to a boil. Boil gently, uncovered, for about 6 minutes, stirring occasionally, until apple and pear are just tender. Remove from heat. Remove 1 cup (250 mL) to blender. Carefully process with on/off motion for about 1 minute until chunky (see Safety Tip, below). Return to apple mixture. Stir. Fill 4 hot sterile 1 cup (250 mL) jars to within 1/2 inch (12 mm) of top. Wipe rims. Place sterile metal lids on jars and screw on metal bands fingertip tight. Do not over-tighten. Process in boiling water bath for 15 minutes (see Note). Remove jars. Let stand at room temperature until cool. Store in refrigerator for up to 1 month after opening. Makes about 4 1/2 cups (1.1 L).

1 tbsp. (15 mL): 14 Calories; 0.2 g Total Fat (0.1 g Mono, trace Poly, trace Sat); 0 mg Cholesterol; 3 g Carbohydrate; trace Fibre; trace Protein; 1 mg Sodium

Pictured above.

NOTE: Processing time is for elevations 1001 to 3000 feet (306 to 915 m) above sea level. Adjust the processing time for elevation in your area if necessary.

SAFETY TIP: Follow manufacturer's instructions for processing hot liquids.

Cardamom Citrus Marmalade, below

CARDAMOM CITRUS MARMALADE

Homemade marmalade makes a great gift come the holiday season—three types of citrus and aromatic floral notes make this version an elegant addition to breakfast time.

Medium oranges	4	4
Medium lemons	2	2
Small lime	1	1
Whole green cardamom, bruised (see Tip, page 14)	2	2
Water	2 cups	500 mL
Orange juice	1/2 cup	125 mL
Box of pectin crystals	2 oz.	57 g
Granulated sugar	6 cups	1.5 L

Remove rind from oranges, lemons and lime using vegetable peeler. Cut rind into 1/8 x 1 inch (0.3 x 2.5 cm) strips. Transfer to Dutch oven. Line medium bowl with 16 inch (40 cm) square of double-layered cheesecloth. Cut oranges, lemons and lime into quarters. Squeeze juice into cheesecloth-lined bowl.

Place juiced fruit pieces and cardamom in centre of cheesecloth square. Draw up corners and tie with butcher's string. Add cheesecloth bag and juice to pot.

Add water and orange juice. Stir. Bring to a boil. Reduce heat to medium. Boil gently, uncovered, for about 30 minutes, stirring occasionally, until rind is softened. Transfer cheesecloth bag to medium bowl. Let stand until cool enough to handle. Squeeze liquid from cheesecloth bag into rind mixture. Discard bag. Stir.

Add pectin. Heat and stir on high for about 4 minutes until mixture begins to boil.

Add sugar. Heat and stir until mixture comes to a hard boil. Boil for 1 minute, stirring constantly. Remove from heat. Fill 6 hot sterile 1 cup (250 mL) jars to within 1/4 inch (6 mm) of top. Remove air bubbles and adjust headspace if necessary. Wipe rims. Place hot metal lids on jars and screw on metal bands fingertip tight. Do not over-tighten. Process in boiling water bath for 15 minutes (see Note). Remove jars. Let stand at room temperature until cool. Store in refrigerator for up to 1 month after opening. Makes about 7 cups (1.75 L).

1 tbsp. (15 mL): 26 Calories; trace Total Fat (0 g Mono, 0 g Poly, 0 g Sat); 0 mg Cholesterol; 8 g Carbohydrate; trace Fibre; trace Protein; trace Sodium

Pictured above.

NOTE: Processing time is for elevations 1001 to 3000 feet (306 to 915 m) above sea level. Adjust the processing time for elevation in your area if necessary.

PINEAPPLE RHUBARB JAM

Pretty pink jam with a hit of pineapple flavour, the tang of rhubarb mixed with just a little spice. Try some on croissants for a breakfast treat.

Chopped fresh (or frozen) rhubarb	6 cups	1.5 L
Cans of crushed pineapple (14 oz., 398 mL, each), with juice	2	2
Lemon juice	1/4 cup	60 mL
Chinese five-spice powder	3/4 tsp.	4 mL
Granulated sugar	6 cups	1.5 L

Combine first 4 ingredients in Dutch oven. Bring to a boil. Reduce heat to medium-low. Simmer, uncovered, for about 20 minutes, stirring occasionally, until thickened.

Add sugar. Cook on medium, stirring often, for about 12 minutes until mixture comes to a hard boil. Boil for about 35 minutes, stirring often, until jam gels when tested on small cold plate (see Note 1). Fill 7 hot sterile 1 cup (250 mL) jars to within 1/4 inch (6 mm) of top. Remove air bubbles and adjust headspace if necessary. Wipe rims. Place hot metal lids on jars and screw on metal bands fingertip tight. Do not over-tighten. Process in boiling water bath for 15 minutes (see Note 2). Remove jars. Let stand at room temperature until cool. Store in refrigerator for up to 1 month after opening. Makes about 7 1/3 cups (1.8 L).

1 tbsp. (15 mL): 29 Calories; trace Total Fat (0 g Mono, trace Poly, 0 g Sat); 0 mg Cholesterol; 8 g Carbohydrate; trace Fibre; trace Protein; 1 mg Sodium

Pictured below.

NOTE 1: To make sure your jam has reached the gelling point, remove from heat, place a spoonful on a chilled plate and place it in the freezer until the mixture has reached room temperature. Press your finger down the middle of the mixture. If it doesn't run together into the groove you've created, the mixture has gelled. To prevent overcooking, don't leave the jam simmering on the stove while you're testing.

NOTE 2: Processing time is for elevations 1001 to 3000 feet (306 to 915 m) above sea level. Adjust the processing time for elevation in your area if necessary.

Pineapple Rhubarb Jam, above

Combine remaining 5 ingredients in medium saucepan. Bring to a boil, stirring often, until sugar is dissolved. Pour over carrot mixture. Let stand at room temperature until cool. Cover with tight-fitting lid. Chill for 1 day before opening. Store in refrigerator for up to 2 weeks after opening. Makes about 4 cups (1 L).

1/4 cup (60 mL): 39 Calories; trace Total Fat (0 g Mono, trace Poly, trace Sat); 0 mg Cholesterol; 11 g Carbohydrate; 1 g Fibre; trace Protein; 290 mg Sodium

Pictured at left.

GIARDINO REFRIGERATOR PICKLES

Giardino (gee-ar-DEE-no) means garden in Italian—fitting for this sweet and tangy pickled mix chock full of colourful veggies.

Sliced fennel bulb (white part only)	2 cups	500 mL
Sliced small zucchini (1/2 inch, 12 mm, slices)	2 cups	500 mL
Small cauliflower florets	1 1/2 cups	375 mL
Fresh green beans, cut into 1 inch (2.5 cm) pieces	1 cup	250 mL
Sliced carrot (1/4 inch, 6 mm, slices)	1 cup	250 mL
Sliced red pepper (1/4 inch, 6 mm, slices)	1 cup	250 mL
White vinegar	4 cups	1 L
Granulated sugar	1 3/4 cups	425 mL
Coarse (pickling) salt	4 tsp.	20 mL
Fennel seed	1 1/2 tsp.	7 mL
Garlic clove	1	1
Whole black peppercorns	1 tsp.	5 mL
Bay leaf	1	1

Combine first 6 ingredients in large bowl. Pack into 2 sterile 4 cup (1 L) jars.

Combine remaining 7 ingredients in large saucepan. Bring to a boil. Reduce heat to medium. Boil gently, covered, for 5 minutes to blend flavours. Pour over fennel mixture. Let stand at room temperature until cool. Cover with tight-fitting lids. Chill for 2 weeks before opening. Store in refrigerator for up to 2 weeks after opening. Makes about 8 cups (2 L).

1/4 cup (60 mL): 37 Calories; trace Total Fat (trace Mono, trace Poly, trace Sat); 0 mg Cholesterol; 9 g Carbohydrate; 1 g Fibre; trace Protein; 287 mg Sodium

Pictured at right.

Quick Carrot and Kohlrabi Pickles, below

QUICK CARROT AND KOHLRABI PICKLES

These spicy refrigerator pickles are so quick, you can have them on the table the very next day! They make a colourful addition to meals, and are a great condiment to serve with Asian-inspired menus.

Thinly sliced carrot	1 1/2 cups	375 mL
Thinly sliced kohlrabi, quartered and sliced crosswise	1 1/2 cups	375 mL
Slivered red pepper	1/2 cup	125 mL
Thinly sliced red onion	1/4 cup	60 mL
Rice vinegar	1 1/2 cups	375 mL
Granulated sugar	1 cup	250 mL
Finely grated ginger root	1 tbsp.	15 mL
Coarse (pickling) salt	2 tsp.	10 mL
Dried crushed chilies	1/2 tsp.	2 mL

Combine first 4 ingredients in medium bowl. Pack into sterile 4 cup (1 L) jar.

158

BREAD-AND-BUTTER PICKLES

For those who prefer sweet pickles to dills, these crispy cukes are delicious in sandwiches and make an attractive addition to a pickle tray.

Sliced pickling cucumbers (1/4 inch, 6 mm, slices)	16 cups	4 L
Ice cubes	4 cups	1 L
Diced red pepper	2 cups	500 mL
Sliced onion (1/4 inch, 6 mm, slices)	2 cups	500 mL
Coarse (pickling) salt	1 cup	250 mL
Apple cider vinegar	3 cups	750 mL
Granulated sugar	3 cups	750 mL
Mustard seed	2 tbsp.	30 mL
Celery seed	1 1/2 tsp.	7 mL
Turmeric	1 1/2 tsp.	7 mL
Coriander seed	1/2 tsp.	2 mL

Combine first 5 ingredients in extra-large bowl. Let stand, covered, at room temperature for 3 hours. Drain. Rinse with cold water. Drain well.

Combine remaining 6 ingredients in Dutch oven or large pot. Bring to a boil. Add cucumber mixture. Heat and stir for about 6 minutes until boiling. Fill 8 hot sterile 2 cup (500 mL) jars to within 1/2 inch (12 mm) of top. Wipe rims. Place sterile metal lids on jars and screw on metal bands fingertip tight. Do not over-tighten. Process in boiling water bath for 15 minutes (see Note). Remove jars. Let stand at room temperature until cool. Store in refrigerator for up to 1 month after opening. Makes about 17 cups (4.25 L).

1/4 cup (60 mL): 28 Calories; 0.1 g Total Fat (trace Mono, trace Poly, trace Sat); 0 mg Cholesterol; 8 g Carbohydrate; trace Fibre; trace Protein; 160 mg Sodium

Pictured below.

NOTE: Processing time is for elevations 1001 to 3000 feet (306 to 915 m) above sea level. Adjust the processing time for elevation in your area if necessary.

Left: Giardino Refrigerator Pickles, left; Right: Bread-and-Butter Pickles, above

Brandy Apple Cranberry Sauce, below

BRANDY APPLE CRANBERRY SAUCE

The addition of pomegranate and brandy bumps this apple-cranberry blend to the next level.

Bag of fresh (or frozen) cranberries	12 oz.	340 g
Grated peeled cooking apple (such as McIntosh)	1 1/2 cups	375 mL
Granulated sugar	1 cup	250 mL
Pomegranate juice	3/4 cup	175 mL
Brandy	1/4 cup	60 mL
Grated onion	2 tbsp.	30 mL
Finely grated ginger root (or 3/4 tsp., 4 mL, ground ginger)	1 tbsp.	15 mL
Coarsely ground pepper	1/2 tsp.	2 mL
Grated lemon zest	1/2 tsp.	2 mL

Combine all 9 ingredients in large saucepan. Bring to a boil. Reduce heat to medium-low. Simmer, uncovered, for about 15 minutes, stirring occasionally, until cranberries are softened and mixture is thickened. Let stand until cool. Chill. Makes about 3 cups (750 mL).

1 tbsp. (15 mL): 21 Calories; trace Total Fat (0 g Mono, 0 g Poly, 0 g Sat); 0 mg Cholesterol; 5 g Carbohydrate; trace Fibre; trace Protein; 1 mg Sodium

Pictured on front cover, page 2 and above.

TIP

When a recipe calls for grated zest and juice, it's easier to grate the fruit first, then juice it. Be careful not to grate down to the pith (white part of the peel), which is bitter and best avoided.

PEAR AND ALMOND BUTTER

A unique and tasty condiment with aromatic hints of vanilla, maple and almond—it's smooth with a pleasantly grainy texture. This versatile spread could be served with anything from spice cake to roast pork.

Chopped peeled pear	11 cups	2.75 L
Orange juice	1/3 cup	75 mL
White balsamic (or white wine) vinegar	1/4 cup	60 mL
Brown sugar, packed	1/2 cup	125 mL
Maple syrup	1/2 cup	125 mL
Ground almonds, toasted (see Tip, page 93)	1/3 cup	75 mL
Almond liqueur	2 tbsp.	30 mL
Grated orange zest (see Tip, left)	1 tsp.	5 mL
Vanilla bean	1/2	1/2
Salt, sprinkle		

Combine first 3 ingredients in Dutch oven. Bring to a boil. Reduce heat to medium. Boil gently, uncovered, for about 15 minutes, stirring occasionally, until pear is tender. Transfer to blender or food processor. Carefully process, in batches, until smooth (see Safety Tip, right). Return to same pot.

Add remaining 7 ingredients. Stir. Bring to a boil on medium. Boil gently, uncovered, for 40 minutes, stirring often. Boil gently, partially covered, for about 30 minutes, stirring often, until thickened (see Note 1). Remove and discard vanilla bean. Fill 8 hot sterile 1/2 cup (125 mL) jars to within 1/4 inch (6 mm) of top. Remove air bubbles and adjust headspace if necessary. Wipe rims. Place hot metal lids on jars and screw on metal bands fingertip tight. Do not over-tighten. Process in boiling water bath for 15 minutes (see Note 2). Remove jars. Let stand at room temperature until cool. Store in refrigerator for up to 1 month after opening. Makes about 4 1/2 cups (1.1 L).

1 tbsp. (15 mL): 30 Calories; 0.3 g Total Fat (0.2 g Mono, 0.1 g Poly, trace Sat); 0 mg Cholesterol; 7 g Carbohydrate; 1 g Fibre; trace Protein; 1 mg Sodium

Pictured below.

SAFETY TIP: Follow manufacturer's instructions for processing hot liquids.

NOTE 1: Mixture should have the consistency of softened butter.

NOTE 2: Processing time is for elevations 1001 to 3000 feet (306 to 915 m) above sea level. Adjust the processing time for elevation in your area if necessary.

Pear and Almond Butter, above

SPICED PLUM JAM

*Spices bring out the bright plum flavours in this beautiful
jewel-toned jam—try it with lamb, poultry or pork.*

Coarsely chopped fresh plums	10 cups	2.5 L
Water	1/4 cup	60 mL
Lemon juice	2 tbsp.	30 mL
Finely grated ginger root	1 tbsp.	15 mL
Fennel seed, crushed	1 tsp.	5 mL
Ground cinnamon	1 tsp.	5 mL
Coarsely ground pepper	1/2 tsp.	2 mL
Ground cardamom	1/2 tsp.	2 mL
Ground allspice	1/8 tsp.	0.5 mL
Box of pectin crystals	2 oz.	57 g
Granulated sugar	6 cups	1.5 L

Combine first 9 ingredients in Dutch oven. Bring to a boil on
medium. Boil gently, uncovered, for about 15 minutes, stirring
occasionally, until plum is softened.

Add pectin. Bring to a boil on medium-high, stirring
constantly. Add sugar. Heat and stir until mixture comes to a
hard boil. Boil for 1 minute, stirring constantly. Remove from
heat. Stir for 5 minutes to suspend fruit. Fill 8 hot sterile 1 cup
(250 mL) jars to within 1/4 inch (6 mm) of top. Remove air
bubbles and adjust headspace if necessary. Wipe rims. Place
hot metal lids on jars and screw on metal bands fingertip
tight. Do not over-tighten. Process in boiling water bath
for 15 minutes (see Note). Remove jars. Let stand at room
temperature until cool. Store in refrigerator for up to 1 month
after opening. Makes about 9 cups (2.25 L).

*1 tbsp. (15 mL): 25 Calories; trace Total Fat (trace Mono, trace Poly,
0 g Sat); 0 mg Cholesterol; 7 g Carbohydrate; trace Fibre; trace Protein;
trace Sodium*

Pictured on page 150 and at left.

NOTE: Processing time is for elevations 1001 to 3000 feet
(306 to 915 m) above sea level. Adjust the processing time
for elevation in your area if necessary.

RHUBARB GINGER CHUTNEY

*This tart, gingery chutney is a wonderful reason to get
the canner out! It uses up a goodly amount of fresh
rhubarb from your backyard patch. Enjoy it alongside
roast pork for a change from applesauce. This recipe is
part of a suggested menu on page 166.*

Cooking oil	2 tsp.	10 mL
Chopped onion	1 1/2 cups	375 mL
Chopped fresh (or frozen) rhubarb	6 cups	1.5 L
Apple cider vinegar	1 cup	250 mL
Brown sugar, packed	1 cup	250 mL
Dark raisins	1 cup	250 mL
Finely chopped ginger root	1/3 cup	75 mL
Dry mustard	2 tsp.	10 mL
Ground cinnamon	1/2 tsp.	2 mL
Ground coriander	1/2 tsp.	2 mL
Ground allspice	1/4 tsp.	1 mL
Salt	1/4 tsp.	1 mL
Pepper	1/4 tsp.	1 mL
Minced crystallized ginger	1/3 cup	75 mL

Heat cooking oil in Dutch oven on medium. Add onion. Cook
for about 10 minutes, stirring often, until softened.

Add next 11 ingredients. Stir. Bring to a boil on medium. Boil
gently, uncovered, for about 20 minutes until rhubarb
is tender.

Add crystallized ginger. Stir well. Fill 5 hot sterile 1 cup
(250 mL) jars to within 1/2 inch (12 mm) of top. Remove air
bubbles and adjust headspace if necessary. Wipe rims. Place
hot metal lids on jars and screw on metal bands fingertip
tight. Do not over-tighten. Process in boiling water bath
for 15 minutes (see Note). Remove jars. Let stand at room
temperature until cool. Store in refrigerator for up to 1 month
after opening. Makes about 5 1/4 cups (1.3 L).

*1 tbsp. (15 mL): 21 Calories; 0.1 g Total Fat (0.1 g Mono, trace Poly,
trace Sat); 0 mg Cholesterol; 5 g Carbohydrate; trace Fibre;
trace Protein; 8 mg Sodium*

Pictured at left.

NOTE: Processing time is for elevations 1001 to 3000 feet
(306 to 915 m) above sea level. Adjust the processing time
for elevation in your area if necessary.

*Left: Spiced Plum Jam, above
Right: Rhubarb Ginger Chutney, above*

FREEZER SOUTHWEST SALSA

Another way to use your garden's abundance of zucchini and tomatoes at the end of the season! This recipe makes enough to freeze several containers of spicy salsa, perfect to have on hand for unexpected guests. This recipe is part of a suggested menu on page 166.

Diced zucchini (with peel)	4 cups	1 L
Chopped onion	1 1/3 cups	325 mL
Diced green pepper	1 cup	250 mL
Diced red pepper	1 cup	250 mL
Coarse (pickling) salt	2 tbsp.	30 mL
Chopped tomato	4 cups	1 L
Can of black beans, rinsed and drained	19 oz.	540 mL
Frozen kernel corn	1 cup	250 mL
Can of tomato paste	5 1/2 oz.	156 mL
Apple cider vinegar	2/3 cup	150 mL
Brown sugar, packed	1/3 cup	75 mL
Finely chopped pickled pepper rings	3 tbsp.	50 mL
Prepared mustard	2 tbsp.	30 mL
Ground cumin	1/2 tsp.	2 mL
Ground nutmeg	1/4 tsp.	1 mL
Salt	1/2 tsp.	2 mL
Pepper	1/4 tsp.	1 mL

Combine first 5 ingredients in large glass or stainless steel bowl. Let stand, covered, at room temperature for 6 hours or overnight. Drain. Rinse with cold water. Drain well. Transfer to Dutch oven.

Add remaining 12 ingredients. Stir well. Bring to a boil on medium, stirring often. Reduce heat to medium-low. Simmer for 30 minutes, stirring often. Carefully fill clean plastic containers to within 1/2 inch (12 mm) of top (see Note). Let stand at room temperature until cool. Cover with tight-fitting lids. Store in refrigerator for up to 2 weeks or in the freezer for up to 6 months. Makes about 8 cups (2 L).

1/4 cup (60 mL): 41 Calories; 0.3 g Total Fat (trace Mono, 0.2 g Poly, trace Sat); 0 mg Cholesterol; 8 g Carbohydrate; 2 g Fibre; 2 g Protein; 210 mg Sodium

Pictured below.

NOTE: Use plastic containers without any cracks or leaks. There are plastic freezer jars designed to store food in the freezer available at grocery stores.

Freezer Southwest Salsa, above

Spiced Beet and Onion Pickles, below

SPICED BEET AND ONION PICKLES

Using the strained cooking liquid provides even more beet sweetness and rich colour in these nicely spiced pickles. Choose beets that are 2 to 3 inches (5 to 7.5 cm) in diameter for uniform slices.

Fresh beets, scrubbed clean and trimmed (see Note 1)	3 lbs.	1.4 kg
Water	6 cups	1.5 L
Thinly sliced onion	2 cups	500 mL
Apple cider vinegar	1 1/2 cups	375 mL
Granulated sugar	1 cup	250 mL
Coarse (pickling) salt	1 tbsp.	15 mL
Mustard seed	1 tbsp.	15 mL
Garlic cloves, thinly sliced	2	2
Whole allspice	1 tsp.	5 mL
Whole cloves	1 tsp.	5 mL
Cinnamon sticks (4 inches, 10 cm, each), broken up	3	3

Combine beets and water in Dutch oven. Bring to a boil. Reduce heat to medium. Boil gently, covered, for about 25 minutes until tender. Drain beets, reserving cooking water. Rinse beets with cold water. Peel (see Tip, page 154). Cut crosswise into 1/2 inch (12 mm) slices. Strain 4 cups (1 L) reserved cooking water through coffee filter into same pot.

Add remaining 9 ingredients. Stir. Bring to a boil. Reduce heat to medium. Boil gently, covered, for about 8 minutes until onion is softened. Add beets. Heat and stir for about 8 minutes until boiling. Remove from heat. Transfer beet and onion with slotted spoon to 5 hot sterile 2 cup (500 mL) jars to within 1 inch (2.5 cm) of top. Add cooking liquid to within 1/2 inch (12 mm) of top. Discard remaining cooking liquid and solids. Remove air bubbles and adjust headspace if necessary. Wipe rims. Place hot metal lids on jars and screw on metal bands fingertip tight. Do not over-tighten. Process in boiling water bath for 35 minutes (see Note 2). Remove jars. Let stand at room temperature until cool. Store in refrigerator for up to 1 month after opening. Makes about 10 cups (2.5 L).

1/4 cup (60 mL): 19 Calories; 0.1 g Total Fat (0.1 g Mono, trace Poly, trace Sat); 0 mg Cholesterol; 4 g Carbohydrate; 1 g Fibre; 1 g Protein; 44 mg Sodium

Pictured above.

NOTE 1: To prepare beets for use, leave root and 2 inches (5 cm) of stem intact to prevent bleeding.

NOTE 2: Processing time is for elevations 1001 to 3000 feet (306 to 915 m) above sea level. Make adjustment for elevation in your area if necessary.

FALL & WINTER MENUS

BACK-TO-SCHOOL CELEBRATION:

Creamy Cheese Tomato Tarts (page 28)

Sun-Dried Tomato Pretzel Twists (page 109)

Cheesy Garden Macaroni (page 81)

Meatball Veggie Soup (page 34)

Sweet Potato Brownies (page 139)

Butterscotch Hot Chocolate (page 16)

GREY CUP / SUPER BOWL PARTY:

Cranberry Bison Meatballs (page 24)

Chicago-Style Popcorn (page 149)

Nacho Potato Skins (page 27)

Freezer Southwest Salsa (page 164)

Harvest Chicken Chili (page 77)

THANKSGIVING:

Spiced Roast Turkey (page 76)

Stuffed Acorn Squash (page 85)

Slow-Roasted Salmon (page 56)

French Onion Bread Pudding (page 101)

Maple Sprouts (page 94)

Parsnip Slaw (page 42)

Apple Onion Bread Ring (page 121)

Apple Rhubarb Crisp Pie (page 124)

HALLOWEEN PARTY:

Pumpkin Pizza Wedges (page 23)

Candy Apple Cocktail (contains alcohol) (page 15)

Classic Chicken Pot Pie (page 73)

Caramel Apple Cookies (page 141)

Chocolate Orange BOO Cakes (page 133)

SUNDAY DINNER:

Autumn Aromas Roast Chicken (page 75)

Potato Kohlrabi Scallop (page 87)

Nutty Lentils and Wheat (page 91)

Herb Stuffing Buns (page 119)

Apple Cheddar Walnut Salad (page 42)

Butterscotch Maple Tapioca (page 132)

DINNER PARTY:

Eggplant Antipasto Rolls (page 28)

Bavarian Stuffed Pork Roast (page 61)

Rhubarb Ginger Chutney (page 163)

Roasted Fennel Gratin (page 105)

Sweet Potato Knots (page 114)

Plum Hazelnut Trifle (page 134)

AFTER-DINNER FIRESIDE GATHERING:

Jalapeño Cheese Fondue (page 27)

Triple Gingerbread With Pear (page 132)

Autumn Vegetable Samosas (page 21)

Spiced Apple Cider (page 17)

Vanilla Honey Sipper (page 18)

Fall Fruit Snack Mix (page 149)

MEASUREMENT TABLES

Throughout this book, measurements are given in Conventional and Metric measure. To compensate for differences between the two measurements due to rounding, a full metric measure is not always used. The cup used is the standard 8 fluid ounce. Temperature is given in degrees Fahrenheit and Celsius. Baking pan measurements are in inches and centimetres as well as quarts and litres. An exact metric conversion is given on this page as well as the working equivalent (Metric Standard Measure).

OVEN TEMPERATURES

Fahrenheit (°F)	Celsius (°C)	Fahrenheit (°F)	Celsius (°C)
175°	80°	350°	175°
200°	95°	375°	190°
225°	110°	400°	205°
250°	120°	425°	220°
275°	140°	450°	230°
300°	150°	475°	240°
325°	160°	500°	260°

SPOONS

Conventional Measure	Metric Exact Conversion Millilitre (mL)	Metric Standard Measure Millilitre (mL)
1/8 teaspoon (tsp.)	0.6 mL	0.5 mL
1/4 teaspoon (tsp.)	1.2 mL	1 mL
1/2 teaspoon (tsp.)	2.4 mL	2 mL
1 teaspoon (tsp.)	4.7 mL	5 mL
2 teaspoons (tsp.)	9.4 mL	10 mL
1 tablespoon (tbsp.)	14.2 mL	15 mL

CUPS

1/4 cup (4 tbsp.)	56.8 mL	60 mL
1/3 cup (5 1/3 tbsp.)	75.6 mL	75 mL
1/2 cup (8 tbsp.)	113.7 mL	125 mL
2/3 cup (10 2/3 tbsp.)	151.2 mL	150 mL
3/4 cup (12 tbsp.)	170.5 mL	175 mL
1 cup (16 tbsp.)	227.3 mL	250 mL
4 1/2 cups	1022.9 mL	1000 mL (1 L)

DRY MEASUREMENTS

Conventional Measure Ounces (oz.)	Metric Exact Conversion Grams (g)	Metric Standard Measure Grams (g)
1 oz.	28.3 g	28 g
2 oz.	56.7 g	57 g
3 oz.	85.0 g	85 g
4 oz.	113.4 g	125 g
5 oz.	141.7 g	140 g
6 oz.	170.1 g	170 g
7 oz.	198.4 g	200 g
8 oz.	226.8 g	250 g
16 oz.	453.6 g	500 g
32 oz.	907.2 g	1000 g (1 kg)

PANS

Conventional Inches	Metric Centimetres
8 x 8 inch	20 x 20 cm
9 x 9 inch	22 x 22 cm
9 x 13 inch	22 x 33 cm
10 x 15 inch	25 x 38 cm
11 x 17 inch	28 x 43 cm
8 x 2 inch round	20 x 5 cm
9 x 2 inch round	22 x 5 cm
10 x 4 1/2 inch tube	25 x 11 cm
8 x 4 x 3 inch loaf	20 x 10 x 7.5 cm
9 x 5 x 3 inch loaf	22 x 12.5 x 7.5 cm

CASSEROLES

Canada & Britain		United States	
Standard Size Casserole	Exact Metric Measure	Standard Size Casserole	Exact Metric Measure
1 qt. (5 cups)	1.13 L	1 qt. (4 cups)	900 mL
1 1/2 qts. (7 1/2 cups)	1.69 L	1 1/2 qts. (6 cups)	1.35 L
2 qts. (10 cups)	2.25 L	2 qts. (8 cups)	1.8 L
2 1/2 qts. (12 1/2 cups)	2.81 L	2 1/2 qts. (10 cups)	2.25 L
3 qts. (15 cups)	3.38 L	3 qts. (12 cups)	2.7 L
4 qts. (20 cups)	4.5 L	4 qts. (16 cups)	3.6 L
5 qts. (25 cups)	5.63 L	5 qts. (20 cups)	4.5 L